To M.J.L.

Salmon Fisher of the Year 1982..!

Wishing You a Merry Christmas

A SALMON FISHER'S ODYSSEY
Rivers and Reflections

Salmon at the Falls. A painting by Raoul Millais.

JOHN ASHLEY-COOPER

A
Salmon Fisher's
Odyssey

Rivers and Reflections

ILLUSTRATED WITH 7 COLOUR PLATES
AND 65 TEXT PHOTOGRAPHS

H. F. & G. WITHERBY LTD.

First published in 1982 by
H. F. & G. WITHERBY LTD.
5 Plantain Place, Crosby Row,
London, SE1 1YN

Filmset in Monophoto 13pt Apollo
and printed in Great Britain by
BAS Printers Limited,
Over Wallop, Hampshire

The author with Michael and David Wills after a successful weekend's fishing on the Wye at Erwood in April 1935, referred to on page 82. Major M. D. H. Wills, M.C. was killed in action in Libya in 1943. Major Sir David Wills, C.B.E., has fished the Spey for many years.

Preface

Salmon fishing has been one of my main pursuits for over 50 years since I caught my first fish at Abergeldie on the Aberdeenshire Dee in 1931. Since then I have been fortunate to have been able to fish for salmon in many different rivers in many different countries.

It is as a consequence of this that I offer this volume, as a book written by a fisherman primarily for fishermen. It describes my recollections and experiences of the rivers I have fished in Great Britain, Ireland, Norway and Iceland, and sets down a record of the conclusions I have drawn from these experiences. I hope this may prove of possible interest. I have endeavoured to give practical advice on fishing methods when discussing individual rivers and the fishing on them.

The first part of the book deals principally with my own philosophy of salmon fishing together with some ideas about the history of the sport and some suggestions and guidelines on how to get the best from it. There is a chapter on the behaviour of salmon and another on flies.

The second part of the book is a description of the rivers on which I have spent so much of my life. I have fished most of them over a substantial number of years, and not for just odd days, so all the information I give is as reliable as my memory and records allow. The fishing diary I have kept over so many years has proved invaluable; memory plays strange tricks with lapse of time, and recollections become blurred. Some of the rivers I have not fished recently, and there are others of which my experience has not been as great as I could wish. There are, of course, a large number of still other rivers which I have never fished at all; and I would like to make it clear that I have not included descriptions of these in this book. The maps have been purposely kept very simple, just indicating where those rivers are to which I have referred.

There will be those who disagree with some of my theories and conclusions, and so it should be. Life would be very dull if we all held identical views about fishing, or anything else. I shall be satisfied if I have at least provided something of interest to ponder upon.

My generation of fishermen may well be lucky to have enjoyed such good fishing as has been our lot, and we should congratulate ourselves upon our good fortune rather than bemoan the deterioration that has befallen salmon fishing of late. Time will tell, but perhaps our heirs will regard our fishing as halcyon days in much the same way as we envy our predecessors in the early years of this century.

Finally my thanks go to my many fishing friends and companions, whose experiences have made such a valuable contribution towards my knowledge of the various rivers described, and without whose company the whole delight and inspiration derived from a lifetime of salmon fishing would have been lacking.

Wimborne St. Giles   J.A-C.
May, 1982

Contents

SCOTLAND (*Continued*)

Rivers of the North Coast

The Dee at Lower Invercauld. The opposite bank belongs to Abergeldie.

Colour Plates

Acknowledgements

My grateful thanks for help in the preparation of this book are due first and foremost to my publishers, whose encouragement and advice have been invaluable. To Captain Raoul Millais I am indebted for the superb picture included as the frontispiece and to my wife Julian for the lovely water colour of the Trees Pool, Aboyne water, on the river Dee. Others whose assistance has been most welcome are as follows: Colonel R. Bradford, The Hon. Mrs. Jean Bruce, Mr. Jeremy Clay, Lt. Cdr. Crampton-Thomas R.N., the Earl of Dalhousie, the Hon. Hew Dalrymple, Cdr. Walter Drax R.N., Lord Dulverton, Major Derick Foster, Colonel Arthur Gemmell, Captain Peter Gibbs, Mr. R. N. Graham-Campbell, Captain Peter Green, Captain Patrick Hazlehurst, Mr. V. W. Huntington, the Marquess of Lansdowne, the Hon. J. Leslie, The Earl of Leven and Melville, Colonel A. M. Lyle, Major C. D. Mackenzie, Major A. Mann, Major John Mills, Colonel G. Kidston-Montgomerie, Major D. A. C. Rasch, Colonel the Earl of Stair, Major Anthony Tabor, Mr. Andrew Tennant, the Lord Trenchard, the Lord Tryon, the Hon. Aylmer Tryon, and Major Sir David Wills. I am grateful to them all; also to Mrs. Georgina Rose and the editor of the *Field* for the stimulating article quoted on page 30. The poem 'Spring Salmon' by Patrick Chalmers is from *Green Days and Blue Days* published by Methuen.

I wish to thank Mrs. Barbara Burnett-Stuart for her considerable help in locating photographs of some of the Scottish rivers, also to Mrs. Anne Voss Bark for assistance with the Tamar photographs and Mr. David Henriques for those for the Wye. I am indebted to the following for permission to include photographs of rivers as follows: the Awe, Mr. Kenneth Keane; the Deveron, Mr. A. J. G. Bodie; the Findhorn, Pamla Toler; the Ness, page 107, Mrs. Barbara Hargreaves, and page 111, Mr. William Marchington; the Oykel, the owners Oykel Fishing; the South Esk, Mr. Kenneth M. Hay by courtesy of the

Earl of Southesk; the Tamar, Mr. Ray Bishop; the Test, Miss Hilly Hoar by courtesy of Broadlands Estate; the Thurso, Mr. M. Luciani by courtesy of Lord Thurso, and the Wye, page 85, Miss Catherine Humphreys and pages 81 and 90 Mr. Peter Keyser. I would also like to thank Mr. J. Stansfeld for allowing me to photograph the North Esk.

For Plate 2 I am indebted to Mr. Alan Parker who photographed my Spey flies, and Royal Studios at Wimborne for the photograph of my fishing diary. The remaining photographs in the book are my own. The maps were kindly prepared by Mr. Alan Witherby.

J.A-C.

SPRING SALMON

It's oh, but I'm dreaming
  Of grey water streaming,
Great rivers that go gleaming
  Where brown the heather blows,
Ere May's southern graces
  Rub out the last white traces
From high and mountain places
  Of stubborn, storm-packed snows!

The chill wind that searches
  The low-lying birches,
The old red grouse that perches
  And swaggers in the sun;
I'm fain for its blowing,
  I'm restless for his crowing,
And its I that would be going
  Where the spring salmon run!

Patrick R. Chalmers.

General Reflections

In many fishing books there is, it frequently seems, one misleading aspect which has been overlooked. This relates to topography. Authors are inclined to give general advice on fishing tactics, tackle, patterns and sizes of fly and bait, season and patterns of salmon and grilse runs, and so on. What they fail to make clear is the vital point that their remarks, far from being general, apply to one particular river or locality which is their favourite hunting ground.

For instance, an author's experience or preference might lie in the north east of Scotland on the Findhorn, Spey or Deveron, or in the east on the Dee or North or South Esk, or indeed in Wales on the Wye or Usk or in the south of England on the various rivers of Hampshire, Dorset or Devonshire. These are only a few examples, but they bear out the point that the fishing in all these areas has many different features and so have the habits and the runs of the fish. The process of fishing must be varied accordingly. It should be made absolutely clear when generalizing whether remarks and advice are of universal application or whether they refer to one particular river or area. What applies in one place may very well not do so in another. By failing to reveal this difference, an author may mislead an inexperienced fisherman which can lead to disappointment on the bank. Even old hands, while usually able to read between the lines, can sometimes be led astray.

In this book I have therefore tried to differentiate clearly between the various rivers and localities in which I have fished and to outline their different characteristics together with the varied habits of their fish, and their runs, and the different methods and equipment best suited for them. I have generalized only about such matters as are applicable anywhere, from the Arctic to as far south as Atlantic salmon are found, and in particular about what is common to all salmon fishing in the British Isles.

Fishermen, perhaps above all other men, hold individual and incontrovertible views against which they cannot easily be persuaded. One such instance is the vexed question of whether to use fly or bait, a matter which everyone must work out for himself, subject, naturally, to any local fishery rules. There are fly-only men and bait-only men, and those who use either fly or bait as the spirit moves them. Men of each category are apt to argue determinedly for their choice in this matter and tempers may rise. I no longer allow myself to be drawn into such discussions if I can possibly help it. For a long time I was as keen on bait fishing as I was on fly. Indeed, having caught over two thousand fish on bait in my time I feel qualified to write about the subject. However, as time went on I found myself drawn more and more towards the use of fly which I felt brought greater satisfaction and interest. About fifteen years ago I gave up bait fishing altogether and since have relied entirely on fly in all types of water. I have never regretted this choice as for one reason it makes matters very simple. How often has one seen fishermen dithering over a choice between bait and fly, trying first one, then the other, often failing with both? The fly-only man is liable to no such uncertainty. Admittedly he will have to make his mind up about size and type of fly and whether to fish deep of shallow; but these questions may be quickly decided and the answer is often obvious.

It is wonderful what success necessity brings—for instance, if after a couple of hours fruitless fly fishing there is no question of dropping the fly rod and turning to minnow, spoon, prawn or worm, the fly fisherman who perseveres will find that by degrees his skill with the fly improves beyond all recognition. He will find himself taking fish at times and in places where he would formerly have reckoned his chances as zero without resorting to bait of some kind. There is nothing to equal the satisfaction of casting a fly well and the feel of the tightening fly line as the fish takes hold, or of the sight of the rise and the breathtaking moment of uncertainty whether the fish is hooked or not.

To throw a long line with a bait is certainly gratifying as is a long drive on the golf course; and great accuracy with bait on a small river is also satisfying. However, modern bait reels make casting easy, and the whole process of bait fishing cannot compare with fly fishing as to artistry.

Whether bait or fly fishing is the better suited to catching more fish is quite another question. That more fish are taken on bait is beyond dispute in most rivers where bait is permitted; but that is largely because bait fishing is a much easier method and more quickly learned. It is true, too, that the number of bait fishers often far exceeds that of fly fishermen, especially of skilful ones! So the number of fish on the bank is not necessarily a fair criterion. More relevant factors surely concern the type of water and the time of year involved. For example, fishing water like the Lower Wye or Hampshire Avon in February or March, one's chances with bait would be far superior than with fly. On the other hand, in rivers such as the Naver, Helmsdale or Aberdeenshire Dee, fly will give you all the fish you want once the fish are there. If you are a shooting man, would you prefer a limited number of driven pheasants, high, fast and curling, or a large number of low birds, no fun to kill and aggravating to miss? It seems to me that this is not an inapt comparison. These days with so much talk of 'conservation' it would probably do no harm if more of our rivers were restricted to fly-only (anyhow after mid-April), and not only the rivers of the far north. Owners need have no fear that as a result the demand for their fishing would decline. On the contrary, if what happens on rivers north of Inverness is any guide, it would probably increase.

Such are my views on fly and bait fishing which I have developed over a long trial of both methods. I give them merely for what they are worth and feel sure that a large proportion of present day salmon fishermen will probably disagree with them. If I was to hear a note of pride in the voice of any of my bait fishing friends remarking 'I got him on a fly', and I felt this was in any way due to my influence, I should feel adequately rewarded.

Aspects of fishing about which fishermen are apt to hold perhaps less decided views are many. For example, is it preferable to concentrate on one particular river, or even a single beat, or to diversify one's effort over many different rivers in many different places? One has often seen owners of a good beat who prefer to dedicate all their activities to it, and seldom, if ever, fish elsewhere. It is easy to understand this attitude, though few of us are fortunate enough to be in a position to adopt it, even if we wished to. It means that an exceptionally detailed knowledge is acquired of the beat in question and the best methods of fishing it. However, one might feel that fishermen who are prejudiced in this way are missing a great deal. Is not variety the spice of life? It is not engendered by tying oneself to one particular water. There is something to be gained from a change of scene, though at intervals each season one may hark back to the old familiar haunts one loves. As one travels from river to river, old friendships with fellow fishermen and ghillies are renewed and new ones are made. How enjoyable all this can be. So, too, is the change of landscape, almost all delightful, that different rivers provide; varying from the lush green meadows of the south of England, through a kaleidoscope of changing patterns as one journeys northwards, to the snow-capped mountains and foaming torrents of arctic Norway. In addition one encounters and perhaps becomes involved in the local fishery problems of different rivers, both fascinating and provoking. One meets people of so many different types and nationalities, all with different backgrounds and characteristics. Apart from the difference in surroundings and companions, no two rivers are quite the same and fishing methods and the habits of salmon differ too.

Doesn't all this contribute something which the salmon fisherman can ill afford to miss? In fact, there is no reason why he should not have the best of both worlds. Unless he is unlucky enough to have only strictly limited fishing time during the season, can he not have his own favourite bit of river and still fish elsewhere when it's out of season? There are few beats which can provide good fishing for more than a maximum of four months during the season, so there are other months during which good fishing can be enjoyed in other places.

Another matter about which divergent views may be held concerns the preference for big rivers or small rivers. One has often heard remarks like 'Oh, him? The Spey (or Tay or Tweed) wouldn't do for him. He's a confirmed small river man;' or 'Catch a salmon in that trickle? I'd sooner kill a pig in a ditch!' Such attitudes seem to me to be overdone. Of course fishing in big rivers and small rivers is in each case quite different. And there is too a difference in fishing medium rivers, and between fast mountain torrents and slow lowland waterways.

Small rivers have all the charm of constant variety between pools without the need, normally, for a fisherman to dwell long in any one place. Such rivers require more delicacy for successful fishing, lighter tackle, more care in keeping out of sight, less wading. In fact, their fishing entails greater finesse and less hard work. On the other hand, big rivers usually offer bigger fish with the chance of an outstanding one. They offer the opportunity for some spectacular long-distance casting, great excitement, and sometimes the chance of greater numbers in the bag. So there is a great deal to be said for both. Why, then, is there a need to disagree too strongly over the differences? Why not enjoy both and learn to fish skilfully on both to the fullest possible extent? After all, it can well be said that there are no 'bad' salmon fisheries (except through the fault of man), but simply that some are better than others! Personally, I love all salmon rivers which have not been spoiled by pollution, water abstraction, over-fishing and the like, and whether they are big, small or medium, I lose no chance of making the most of them all. As they each have their particular merits I would not care to be bound permanently to any one type.

Whether loch fishing or river fishing is the more fun is a question which does not, I feel, arouse quite the same dissension. Though there are many keen loch fishermen, both trollers and fly fishers, surely nineteen out of twenty salmon fishermen would opt for river fishing if given the choice? I cannot say that loch fishing requires no skill, but I think the skill lies largely with the boatman's knowledge of the best fishing grounds in relation to the wind and weather conditions.

Fly fishing from a boat on a loch, or even off the bank, can be great fun at times; the sight of a salmon rising to a fly in the still water gives a momentary thrill as great as any experienced on a river. Nevertheless, loch fishing can be desperately dull when fish are scarce or not taking. It can be argued that this applies to river fishing too, but at least on a river there are changes of pool, changes of scenery and changes in the manner of fishing. That 'last resort' of loch fishing—trolling—must surely be the dullest of all forms of salmon fishing. Although I must admit to have fished little on lochs, except on the Grimersta lochs in Lewis, and I realize that such fishing requires a smaller financial outlay than river fishing, for my own part I have no hesitation in echoing the words of Eric Taverner in the Lonsdale Library: 'It is rarely worth while fishing for salmon in these large sheets of water if a river is available.'

I know that I am contradicted in this by that outstanding authority 'Jock Scott' who has written so many excellent salmon fishing books. In *Salmon and Trout Fishing Up To Date* he has a very informative and interesting chapter on 'Salmon Fishing in Lochs' which ends: 'Salmon fishing in lochs can be great fun' . . . 'Loch fishing should not be dismissed as boring.' The late Ian Wood too was a great protagonist of loch fishing, especially on Loch Lomond.

While I accept without reservation the advice of such acknowledged authorities on almost all fishing matters, it will take more than that to persuade me to forsake rivers for lochs, especially in view of my own experience and what I have heard from others. I may be wrong, and perhaps if I lived at Altnaharra or Luss I might feel differently about this. But I doubt it.

The Helmsdale at Kildonan.

Considerations on Salmon Fishing

The non-fishing world is apt to regard devotion to fishing as a form of eccentricity or madness. Do you remember the *Punch* cartoon of the lunatic inviting the unsuccessful fisherman to 'come inside'? On a freezing March afternoon with fingers blue from cold in a north-easterly blizzard, and feet numb from all-day wading in an apparently fishless river, you may have to remind yourself sharply that you are doing it strictly for fun. Nevertheless, the fascination remains; and how great is the reward when, in spite of every other impediment, the moment of triumph arrives, as sooner or later it must.

Fishing for sport certainly dates back to 1400 BC or earlier. Mr. C. Chevenix-Trench, in his *History of Angling* (1974) has reproduced for us the picture of an ancient Egyptian nobleman of that date angling with a rod, line and hook in a perspectiveless pond, full of queer looking ancient Egyptian fish; and it is apparently possible that in the far east, China for example, fishing for sport goes back to a still earlier date. So anglers have good precedents for their particular form of madness, and in any case, there are reputed to be three million of them in Britain alone. Let such a dedicated weight of numbers speak for itself. Salmon fishermen may form a comparatively small proportion of this total, but all the same, it does seem that the sport is becoming over-subscribed. The number of fishermen has increased threefold at least on most rivers in the last thirty years, but the number of salmon has not increased. Large numbers of net-caught fish do not necessarily indicate a big escapement of fish up the rivers. In 1980, for instance, we were told that there was a glut of spring fish in the Tweed nets, but rod catches further up the river were poor. Nor has the extent of fishing increased, rather the opposite. It seems likely that some sort of restriction will eventually have to be imposed. There are a variety of possibilities—'Fly Only' from mid-April onwards, prohibition of the sale of rod-caught fish, curtailment of the rod fishing season, curtailment of netting, a limit on the number of rods. Any or all of these might be applicable. There would be opposition to all of them, but many people would support them too.

One thing is certain; to be happy in his own mind, a salmon fisherman should be clear whether he is fishing for the fun of it, that is for the sport, or for another purpose. The complication arises nowadays that fishing is so expensive, both for owners and tenants, and fish are so valuable in the market, that some proportion of the catch is inevitably sold to recoup at least part of the big outlay involved. I have heard of cases where a substantial profit has been made through sales of rod-caught fish. It is an easy step from this for the less scrupulous fisherman, even, sad to say, on some of the better private beats, to fish with the main object of catching fish by any means, fair or foul, in order to sell them in the market for the high price they will obtain. Now without doubt anyone who allows such considerations to become dominant in his mind will not only earn himself a bad name in the fishing world (which is a remarkably small one), but he will inevitably in due course spoil his own enjoyment of this wonderful sport. Financial considerations in any fisherman's mind should as far as possible be kept in the background, rent and other expenses being paid with a good grace, and not begrudged if the fishing fails to come up to expectation. On a good water, good seasons and bad seasons are apt to balance out over a period of time, so one should be philosophical over a bad season and look upon the rent paid partly as a premium towards the next good one. If on the other hand the rent and expenses are more than one can comfortably afford in the first place, one is unwise to take the fishing relying on the sale of fish to make up the difference. If it turns out badly one will be distracted in mind and thus fail to enjoy it; and sooner or later one will be let down badly, and feel like a race-course punter who has tried to get out on a heavily odds-on favourite that finishes well down the course.

With it once clearly established that sport and fun are the prime objectives, coupled with the company of good friends, the fisherman can move to further considerations. Assuming that he is not the owner of a beat to which he wants to give primary attention, also that he cannot fish on and off throughout the season (or even if he can, lucky fellow!), when and where he is going to fish are two essentially important considerations. If he wants to fish early in the year from February to early April, his best bet will be on an east coast river in Scotland, and unless he is a dedicated and skilful fly fisherman, he will probably have to spin if he wants to catch much. Fly fishing at this time of the year is very difficult, if it is to be successful. Spring in the north-east of Scotland comes late, some six weeks later than in the south of England, and by mid-April the water temperature has seldom risen above 44°F. The west coast of Scotland and the Solway coast are much warmer, but few rivers there have any sort of spring run, and it is more often late June before any significant number of fish comes in. One used to hear stories of the Awe, Orchy, Lochy, Spean, and Grimersta, to give a few examples, having a plentiful run of spring fish between March and May, but alas, no longer! Make no mistake about this. The spring fishing on the west coast, in present times sad to say, is a dead duck. You would be ill-advised to touch it. An east or north east coast river should provide the best chance at that time of year. In fact nowadays this area seems to be the only one worth considering early on. Rivers elsewhere, in addition to those mentioned on the west coast of Scotland, seem to have fallen right away. Where is good spring fishing to be found in England now? Eden, Wye, Usk, Avon, and Devonshire rivers seem to have lapsed lamentably. Or in Ireland, what has happened to the Boyne, Slaney, Blackwater, and Suir? And the Shannon, Erne and Lee have gone long ago.

In addition to choosing a river in a good area and which is likely to be productive, make sure you have the type of river you like. For instance, if you don't care for boat fishing don't go to the Lower Tweed or the Lower Tay, particularly in spring. Or, if you don't like deep wading, don't go to the Dee or Spey; you must be satisfied with one of the smaller rivers, of which there are plenty. It is important also to go to the right part of the right river if that can be arranged. For instance it gives you a very poor chance if you go to an upper beat such as Castle

Grant or Tulchan on the Spey in February or March. Mid-April or later is soon enough there, even though the lower river may be prolific in the earlier months. Equally the Dee above Aboyne is only occasionally likely to be of much use before April, or the Tweed above Kelso before mid-March. Be careful therefore that you do not take on any beat, however famous its reputation, when it is out of its good fishing period, i.e. too early, or for that matter too late; or if you do take it on, that you realize you are gambling on an outside chance.

I say 'too late' as well as 'too early', because if for example you want to fish during July or August, it will be of little use your going to a river like the lower or middle Dee, where all you can reasonably hope for then, without exceptional luck in the way of weather, will be an odd red fish, one or two grilse, and some sea-trout. At that time of year you should fish on a river where fresh salmon and grilse are continuing to come in, the lower Spey might be your choice, or one of the good beats on the Tay, or the Ness, or the Beauly, or Helmsdale, Thurso, or Naver, or almost any of the west coast rivers. Now too there is a substantial grilse run building up in the south of England rivers, quite a new development, and the summer months there are rapidly becoming the most prolific. In fact there is now a wide choice for anyone who wants to fish at this time of year, quite a contrast to what was the case thirty or forty years ago, when spring fishing was the *dernier cri* and summer fishing of little consequence.

For October or November there is little alternative to the Tweed, which still possesses a first class run of the old type of autumn fish, so renowned in our grandfathers' day.

I haven't elaborated on what used to be the cream of the season in most places, namely mid-April to early June. Apart from those of the west coast of Scotland, most rivers still fish reasonably at this time, though nothing like as well as they used to. Many reasons are given for this deterioration which are largely misleading, such as pools being gravelled, fish running through, water too low or too cold, and so on; but the bare fact is that there are many more fishermen now, and only around one spring fish in the rivers now for every ten that there used to be! What in turn is the reason for that is another and many-sided matter; but make no mistake, it is general shortage of spring fish in the rivers which is the essential trouble.

What size of river do you prefer? Big, medium, or small? Or don't you mind? They are all different and need different tactics. If you have a decided preference you must take this into account when making your plans. If small rivers of the west coast type are your firm choice, spate rivers that you can cover with a trout rod and in thigh waders, you will feel lost and disillusioned with a beat on a river such as the Tay or Spey. Or if you are a confirmed Norwegian fisherman, you will probably regard small rivers as utterly trivial. You may well devote some prior thought to this though, as outlined above, the best answer is perhaps to be as catholic minded as possible and endeavour to get the best out of everything. It makes matters easier!

All the above may seem obvious, not to say platitudinous, to any experienced fisherman, but it is amazing the number of people one meets from year to year who are disappointed simply because they have not investigated beforehand the water they propose to rent.

Surroundings also play a noteworthy part in the enjoyment of fishing. Fortunately nearly all salmon rivers lie amid lovely peaceful countryside of one sort or another. How much is the enjoyment of fishing the Spey for instance inspired by the wonderful clear air of Banffshire or Morayshire, the sight of the heather-covered slopes of Ben Rinnes, or the Cromdale Hills, or the Cairngorms in the background, and of the mighty Spey tumbling seawards through foaming rapid and pool? Or one might visit the Blackwater in County Cork in the last days of April, when the greenery and lushness of the surrounding hillsides and meadow land is unbelievable in its luxuriance; or by contrast sit and admire the almost incredible colours of the arctic sunset in northern Iceland, reflected on lake and snow-capped mountainside which borders a crystal-clear, briskly flowing river, generous in its harvest of fish.

The large part which surroundings play in enhancing the enjoyment of fishing is often overlooked until one has to fish in a setting less pleasant, alongside a main road for instance, or on the outskirts of a sizeable town, or close to a popular holiday caravan camp. In fact, in these days of jet planes, cars and buses, it is impossible to find any fishing ground too remote. Even in far away spots like Labrador and Newfoundland one is told that anywhere now, where an automobile or sea-plane can penetrate, rapidly becomes over-rodded. One has heard some gruesome stories, such as how the Grand Falls pool on the Humber is fished by up to forty canoes at a time, which make no effort to get out of each other's way when a fish is hooked. Ah well! All this, and the black fly too!

Sir Edward Grey wrote that one of the main attractions of salmon fishing is 'the tremendous uncertainty'. This is without doubt true, and it is the fascination of the unknown which is half the fun. Anticipation indeed is often better than reality, though not always so, and what a pleasant surprise it is when the opposite occurs! Take the uncertainty away for more than a few days, and what happens? Little short of boredom. There is the story of the two trout fishermen who found a virgin lake in the Rocky Mountains, full of trout averaging 2 to 3 lb. They found these fish ready takers, so that it made no difference what strength of leader they used, nor what pattern of fly, large or small. With every cast up came a fish which seized the fly, and was either lost or landed, irrespective of whether a good cast gently let fall the fly like thistle-down or whether a bad one slammed it down in a tangled cat's cradle of monofilament. After twenty minutes of this, these men thought they had arrived in Paradise, but after an hour or two they packed up, bored stiff.

Similarly there was a certain small river in Iceland which I knew well and used often to fish. It was small enough to cover wading knee-deep with a trout rod. The water was held at a good fishing level every day by a hydro further upstream where it ran out of a lake. Grilse and small salmon were prolific in this river and such steady takers that, if one did not catch double figures in a day to one's own rod, one was doing poorly. Most of the fish were between 4–7 lb, and though occasionally one got a monster of around 18 lb anything over 10 lb was a large one. Although it was a delight to return to this river every year, the curious thing was that one did not want more than a few days on it. The truth was that in spite of most things that one could possibly want, the wildness, the remoteness, the wonderful scenery, the birds, and the sparkling stream with its falls, rapids, and pools full of fish, there was one thing lacking—uncertainty. One knew the river was going to be in good fishing order, that the fish would be there, and that one would catch a lot. The only uncertainty was how many. There was no chance of a really big one, and there was the awful problem of getting the fish back a mile or more to one's Landrover at the end of the day. There were no ghillies, and pack ponies invariably ran away. What a world of good a three-foot spate and a blank day from time to time would have done one! But they never happened. As it was one would hardly dare to say that one got bored, but blasé undoubtedly, and very very tired.

River Dee at Cambus O'May.

Behaviour of Fishermen

Most salmon fishers are a mutually friendly crowd, ready to exchange news and views and to give helpful assistance in any way they can, in fact good sportsmen. This is as it should be, and long may it last. Just occasionally however one meets an exception to the rule, who either through intent or more often ignorance, brings an unpleasant atmosphere into the proceedings.

There should be an accepted code of behaviour in fishing, just as there is in shooting or in motoring, where any transgressor is pulled up sharply. In present days with the increasingly large numbers of fishermen, it is as well that this should be brought strongly to the attention of beginners and even the more experienced sometimes benefit by being reminded of it. The code of conduct left to us by our fathers and grandfathers was on the whole a good one, and we should do our best to pass it on. Good sportsmanship and good manners involving due consideration for the welfare of others go hand in hand. They are the oils which lubricate the whole machinery of fishing and make it the fun it should be.

Trouble is liable to arise when opposite banks are in different hands. This can so easily lead to a spirit of rivalry, which in the end, if it goes too far, can spoil the fun for everyone. Jealousy is a bad background for anything, therefore one should do one's level best to keep on the best possible terms with one's opposite neighbours, as well as those on one's own bank, easy enough when they are already one's good friends, but not so easy perhaps if they are strangers. If possible it is always a wise move from the very start to make some working arrangement as to how pools shall be fished, so as to cause the least possible mutual interference to all concerned. And once such an arrangement has been made it need hardly be said that it should never be infringed in the slightest degree, or all confidence is likely to be lost. Any re-adjustment should be made only after full consultation with and consent by all who are involved.

It is silly to start racing for pools, in order to be on them first, at the start of the day or at any other time. It is ludicrous, undignified, and does no good in the end. If in high summer one is going to get out of bed at dawn to fish the pools before the sun gets on them, a perfectly justifiable procedure, it is as well to let one's opposite neighbour know about it, so that he can do the same if he likes and not feel left out of the running. When one arrives on a pool and finds an authorized fisherman already fishing it, whether on one's own bank or opposite, one should give him a good run for his money. It is absolutely inexcusable at all times to go in in front of him; and one should not push on too closely behind him, so as to make him uncomfortable and keep him looking over his shoulder. In a big river one is perfectly justified in fishing down behind an opposite neighbour, provided one gives him plenty of room. But if he hooks a fish one should at once stop fishing until he lands it. This again is a hard and fast rule, and it is as much a question of expediency as of politeness. Just consider what is going to happen if you continue fishing and hook an active fish while your neighbour is still playing his. If the two fish become intertangled, one or both will certainly be lost, and there will be no thanks for such impatience; but how often one sees this rule broken! If one is oneself the leading rod, with someone else fishing behind, one should naturally keep moving on down the pool at a fair rate and not linger too long on the best places.

It is particularly infuriating, when one has hooked a fish in a certain place and landed it some little way downstream, to return and find that someone else, whether on one's own bank or opposite, is fishing the lie where one hooked it. This too is a notable breach of conduct, which occurs only too often nowadays. It usually arises as a result of too many rods on the water, but in any case this sort of thing is pure bad manners, and as already said one should give one's opposite neighbour a fair run for his money, and in return expect to be given one by him.

If you are a bait fisherman it is productive of good feeling to offer a
fly fisherman first chance down a pool. In days gone by this was a
normal civility; but now it seems rare. If in fact I was myself the fly
fisherman in question I would never take advantage of such an offer;
but nevertheless I would be grateful for it. Such considerations all
help to lighten the atmosphere. Equally a friendly wave of the hand
across the river first thing in the morning or at any other time is a
small gesture, but it can do a lot of good and should not be
overlooked.

Fishing marches can be a source of trouble, particularly when they
are sited in an awkward position, midway down a pool. Some
fishermen like to stand on a march and cast as far as they possibly can
downstream into a neighbour's water (with a bait rod this may be for
60 yards or more). Such an action is patently both unfair and illegal,
besides being maddening for the downstream owner. A far better
system would be for the whole pool to be fished on alternate days, or
alternate weeks, by both parties concerned, or else for the march post
by agreement to be moved upstream so that casts from it would
hardly intrude, if at all, into the lower beat.

It goes without saying that every fisherman should be scrupulous
in obeying his host's instructions as to when and where to fish, or
about any other points. Cheerful willingness should be the rule,
under all circumstances. And never, never, should the guest or tenant
stop to have 'just an odd cast' somewhere on the way to but outside of
his allotted beat. Supposing he is found attached to even a small fish,
let alone a 30 pounder, on someone else's water, just how is he going to
explain it away?

There may be local rules on the beat you are fishing as to whether
or not bait is allowed as well as fly, and if so what type of bait
(prawns, plugs, and worms are often barred). There may also be rules
about the type of fly; treble hooks are sometimes forbidden, or more
than two flies on the cast. If such rules exist it can be assumed that
there has been good cause in the past for their existence, so they
should be punctiliously obeyed. It is surprising how many Mepps
spoons or discarded shrimp mounts or worm hooks one is apt to find
left on the banks of rivers sacred to 'fly only'. Too many people

appear to have little conscience about breaking rules of this sort when they think they can get away with it. This again is unpardonable and selfish.

Boats, oars, rod boxes, and hut doors should always be chained and/or locked up at the end of the day. All these seem to have a curious fascination for wandering youths or other types not entitled to touch them. An unlocked boat is asking for trouble; young mischief makers just can't leave it alone, until finally the bottom is stove in or else it disappears at full drift down the river. Open hut doors too are simply an invitation to all and sundry to enter. Other precautions are already familiar to those who love the countryside. Gates should be closed and fastened to keep in cattle or sheep, growing hayfields should not be trampled down indiscriminately and foot paths should be kept to; fires should not be lit in dry weather without particular care being taken to see they are properly extinguished, and cigarette ends should not be thrown into dry grass or undergrowth. (Anyone who was on Speyside in July 1976 may remember the disastrous fires that took place near Carr Bridge and Craigellachie, and the hundreds of acres of forestry destroyed.) Nylon monofilament should not be discarded in long lengths on the bank, but cut up into short pieces of two or three inches—being semi-invisible and almost imperishable, it forms a death trap for birds if they become entangled in it.

Incidentally, if you find a piece of lost equipment such as a fly or bait box, or a telescopic gaff, or a 'priest', or anything else, it is worth taking a good deal of trouble to restore it to its rightful owner. You will earn a disproportionate amount of goodwill by doing so. And while on the subject of goodwill, be careful not to be drawn without good reason into ghillies' feuds. Most ghillies are tolerant and affable, but quarrels between opposite numbers are not unknown, their roots buried in the mists of the past. It is a great mistake for the fisherman to allow himself to be drawn into such conflicts, without direct and immediate reason. Unjustified hostility can be spread from ghillies to rods—and on the contrary it is far better to try in every way to smooth down any latent ill-feeling and as far as possible to make everyone happy.

Here, to conclude this chapter, is part of a delightful article by Mrs. Georgina Rose in the *Field* of a little while back.

The Opposition, some awful truths.
A lady salmon fisher reflects on an eternal matter of contention, and some sequels.

People who believe that fishing is a blameless, patient, and contemplative sport (it has been called all four) will believe anything. On the contrary it produces more passionate feelings than any other. This is due to the behaviour of other anglers rather than to that of the fish.

Single bank salmon beats are among the most inflammatory factors, and the characters who loom all too large across the river are not known as the Opposition merely because of their situation. One-upmanship over them can become as important as catching fish. There are tales of total warfare breaking out, of ghillies brawling, and anglers throwing baits at one another, but I hope these stories are apocryphal.

All Oppositions, whatever the river or conditions, seem to have some things in common. One of these is an illusion that all the fish are lying under the other bank. Of course one knows well that the best taking places are on their side of the current; why else would one be treading water whilst throwing a perilously long line?

One tries to help them by example; as for instance coming up behind a very slow body and fishing a little faster and then removing oneself from the water, ostentatiously gesticulating to the ghillie before the lines entangle. Surely the Opposition must have the message that the fish are bored by seeing the same fly more than five times.

Sometimes, by constrast, one finds a speed merchant on one's tail. The tactics are to fish carefully and show him how every inch should be covered. Again, if one has a ghillie one shouts and points out to him any rises real or imaginary.

When the other fisherman is reasonably close the proper drill is to wave him through with a gracious gesture (good manners always pay), thereafter remaining in the river, or close at hand. Perhaps he may become unsettled by one's unblinking stare. Like being allowed through at golf, it can be unnerving and result in a mistimed cast which produces a bird's nest, or a tuft of the bank, or a fly caught on the top of the rod. Such moments make any Opposition temporarily tolerable.

I believe firmly in telepathy. Why else does one always find the Opposition making a move towards the same pool as oneself? It is undignified and difficult to run in waders in full view of the other side. When the path is fringed with bushes one can break into a trot, but this plays havoc with the breakfast kipper.

People fishing the fly opposite may have annoying habits, but bait slingers arouse the strongest emotions. Unless there is a specific agreement to the contrary, they have a perfect right to spin whatever the height of the water. There is, however, something infuriating about having a piece of shining metal thrown at one.

When the water is low, one feels that even should they fail to catch a fish they will have succeeded in shifting every inhabitant of the pool. That confiding head-and-tailer one had met first time down will by now be several miles away.

This is not to say there is no skill in spinning, but fish can be caught on a bait with a minimum of practice, so it is customary for all Oppositions to arm the non-fishing lady of the party, if such be present, with a spinning rod, dropping the spinner at varying but insignificant distances from her feet.

One puts to the back of one's mind the hope that she might throw herself in (she generally looks a little unsteady) and prays instead that no unsuspecting fish will lay hold. The chances are she will soon get bored and go in search of tweeds or ruined castles, but should she catch anything you can be sure she will remain planted morning, noon, and night henceforth.

Looks and mannerisms are magnified across a river. As one smiles, primly if not inwardly, at the antics of a stout man skipping unhappily from rock to rock, it is as well to remember one is also being viewed through an equally distorted lens. Perhaps there is something to be said for wearing waders in this age when everyday clothes leave nothing to the imagination.

Once, at a dinner party, I was talking to my next door neighbour when we were interrupted by a bellow from the man opposite who had overheard our conversation, 'So you are the pretty poppet!' As far as I knew I had never met him, so I looked startled. So did his wife and my husband. It transpired he had fished opposite me the previous year, and this was the nickname I had been given. There can be worse, especially from the Opposition.

Behaviour of Salmon

A lifetime of fishing is simply not long enough to learn all there is to know about salmon fishing. There is always more to learn about methods of fishing and about the fish themselves. When a fisherman has caught some 500 salmon he is apt to think he knows the long and the short of the whole business. With 1500 fish to his rod he begins to be less certain, and by the time he has landed several thousand he has realized he will never get to the bottom of the matter.

Fishing is in many ways like chess. Although there are set rules governing how the pieces move, there is no end to the subtleties of play or limit to the gambits involved. One is always learning. This is what makes fishing (like chess) the fascinating problem it is. Major Richard Waddington in his admirable book *Salmon Fishing—A new Philosophy* (1947) has made the point that Disco Troop, the skipper in Kipling's '*Captain Courageous*' was the most successful fisherman on the Grand Banks of Newfoundland 'because he could think like a cod.' And the best salmon fisherman, Major Waddington says, emerges from the rut of his fellows because he can think most like a salmon. How absolutely true this is and every moment while he is on the river the expert fisherman will be using his eyes to watch for every movement of fish which will give him a clue as to where they are lying or if they are moving, whether there are some in a taking mood, and what their reaction is to his fly or bait. This in turn should give him an indication how to shape his tactics so as to induce them to take. It may be argued that it is difficult enough, especially for a novice, to achieve this when on most rivers in the U.K., at any rate on the larger ones, all that can be seen of the salmon is when they head and tail, or jump. This is true, but many a fish has lost his life through

31

the indiscreet advertisement of his presence and his lie by a conspicuous jump. Exactly why salmon jump no one knows, nor why when a good stock of salmon is present so many of them are apt to start and stop jumping at the same time. They jump much more often than any other fish in the river; only when the water or the air is cold do they remain quiescent. Be the reason what it may, the fisherman has much cause to be grateful for this brand of activity.

In this connection it is important to be able to distinguish between the jump of a running fish and a resting fish. A fish that jumps sideways and falls back sideways with a pronounced splash on his side, or else leaps high and does a belly flop or falls back tail first, making what might be described as a lazy jump, is almost certainly a resting fish. This becomes a certainty if he jumps three or four times at intervals in the same place. By contrast a fish that makes a purposeful porpoise-like jump, in a distinct arc upstream, and clear of the water, is without doubt a runner. So is the fish that shows two or three times in quick succession, each jump or splash being progressively further upstream (the inexperienced angler sometimes imagines that two or more different fish have shown in this case). A fish that jumps in unusually shallow water, whether close to the bank or in mid-river, is also most probably a runner, as is the fish showing in the middle of a rapid or in the middle of a fast-running streamy pool when the water is cold (an unlikely resting place in either case). It is certainly useful to be able to differentiate between the jump of a fresh fish and a kelt, to avoid being misled by the latter in spring. The kelt's jump makes a much less substantial splash, and is an altogether less impressive activity. Also the body of the kelt, while in the air, is apt to look thin.

Pools under bridges or below falls or rocky outcrops where one can station oneself without frightening the fish, are good places, with clear water, to watch the behaviour of salmon at any time, and particularly when they are being fished over. If there is any way in which one can approach to 'thinking like a salmon' there is no better one than this. There are a number of places in Scotland and elsewhere where this can be done, but Iceland above all gives wonderful opportunities for it. Most of the rivers there are small and have a number of pools of the rocky 'pot-hole' type, in which it is easy to spot fish. The water is as clear as a swimming bath, and there are frequent falls below which fish collect. The result is that the fish are often in full view while one is fishing over them, which gives one a wonderful opportunity to study their reactions. One never fails to learn something from this; and what a help it is! both at the actual moment, and at other times and places elsewhere, when in the normal way of things one is fishing over fish that one cannot see in the water.

Fortunately for us fishermen salmon are very much creatures of habit. It is fascinating how one sees adult fish, salmon or grilse, on entering a river for the first time, making haste to take up precisely the same lies as their predecessors, almost as though they had known from previous experience exactly where to go. This gives the angler a certain indication of where he should fish.

A lot of ink has been spilt over the question of whether it is running fish or resting fish that take the anglers lure, and many theories have evolved about this. It would seem in fact that not enough thought has been given to exactly what a fish is doing when he takes. If he is in the actual physical process of swimming upstream against the current, a fish would surely be unlikely to take, as his mind (such as he has) would be concentrated on his progress. This can be proved in real life if you can spot a running fish in a small river, perhaps when he jumps on entering the tail of a pool, and then jumps again a few yards upstream; or if you can actually see him moving upstream in the water. In ninety nine cases out of a hundred he will swim past your lure with aloofness. (In the hundredth case he may do something different, as no rules in fishing are inviolate.) The same thing can happen if, as on rare occasions is possible, you can see in the water a shoal of running fish actually making their way up stream through your pool. Cast over them, and you will find them utterly unresponsive as they move on. But, here is the crucial point! Let one of those fish stop and rest, even for a few seconds, and without any doubt he may well snap up your lure. Here then is an example of the so called 'running' fish that takes. But is he really running? This surely is a mere splitting of hairs and is not worth argument.

Resting fish on the other hand as is generally known will often take, particularly when they are newly arrived in their chosen lie;

though the longer they remain in it, ignoring the procession of flies or baits fished over them, the more recalcitrant they become. However, this will not prevent their taking freely when they first install themselves in a fresh lie.

So it follows that it is a sound principle for the fisherman, except on rare occasions, to confine his main activities to the well-known pools or lies where, if there are any fish in the neighbourhood, they are most likely to be found. On almost every beat, even amongst a number of good pools, there are certain outstandingly good 'taking places'; and when fish are on the move it is worth fishing such places several times during the day, to see what has pulled up there. Such places are often at the very neck of a pool, where fish are apt to pause before proceeding further upstream, or else right at the tail of a pool where again they like to pause on their first arrival there from below, though they may be elsewhere too.

Sometimes, however, certain lies are notoriously bad taking places. 'I can never catch that fish' says a boatman, as a fish jumps in some deep hole with a slanting sideways current or a back eddy. One has often heard such remarks, not of course meant literally, but meaning that all fish lying in that place for some reason, probably to do with the depth and set of the stream, seldom if ever take. Such places are better left alone, unless the fisherman has time to kill.

The position of good lies varies with different heights and conditions of water. There are low, medium, and high water lies, also cold and warm water lies, and occasionally lies that operate well under all different circumstances. The successful fisherman will usually be able to recognize all these different types of lie, even when unaided on a strange river, 'reading' the river as the Americans call it. This may well need time and experience, so good local advice is always an effective and welcome short-cut.

At this stage it is worth considering what constitutes the nature of a good lie. One can make a fair estimate of this, though without being a salmon one cannot specify exactly! To begin with, the salmon in fresh water has got to live for weeks and months without food, and finally go through the exertions of spawning; so it is obvious that he needs to expend the minimum amount of energy in the meantime. Fortunately for him his shape is beautifully streamlined, which makes this easier; but he definitely needs to find shelter from any strong stream in a place where he can rest for long periods without effort. Therefore he favours a broken bottom rather than a flat gravelly or silty one, and where the irregularity of rock outcrops or boulders breaks the force of the low-level current. As a rule resting fish prefer to lie on or very close to the bottom. Occasionally however a restless fish will hover in mid-stream, like a trout, or will cruise around in mid-water. This occurs particularly in deep pools, where the current is slack. Sometimes too a fish will find a lie on an underwater ledge, half way up a rock face which descends steeply into the depths. So though one is apt to assume that fish are always to be found on or close to the bottom, this is not invariably the case. Boils on the water surface are usually a sign of obstructions, and often indicate lies, not only downstream and to one side, but often immediately upstream of the obstruction. Falls and weirs are also the unmistakable cause of fish stopping and taking up their position in well-established lies, which again are likely to be upstream as well as downstream of such obstacles. The nature of this upstream shelter can be appreciated by anyone who stands close on the windward side of a high wall during a gale. The amount of check to the windstream is surprising.

As well as shelter, however, the fish does look for a slight stream in order to help him pass water through his gills, and so to breathe. The simple opening of his mouth and gills, when he is lying head towards the current, will achieve this with least effort; while if he is in dead stagnant water he will either have to move forward with his mouth open, or make a deliberate swallowing motion, to obtain the same result. He also needs reasonable depth of water for security, and prefers around five feet to eight feet of water in which to lie, with if possible a deeper hole immediately downstream into which he can retire if alarmed. He needs also to lie where the oxygen content of the water is nearest to his requirements for comfort i.e. he prefers slack deep pools when the water is very cold, as the oxygen content there is less excessive; but later, when the water is warmer and its oxygen content therefore diminished, he likes shallower and streamier water which is more oxygenated.

One type of background, on which the salmon seems to prefer above all to lie, is smooth shelving rock with indentations here and there. If there are rock outcrops from or on the bottom of a pool, where current and depth are suitable, you may be sure that salmon will congregate there, choosing these before other likely lies in the pool. In a pool in the Straumfjardara river in Iceland, where one could see the bottom everywhere, I once saw thirteen salmon and grilse lying like sardines on a single flattish rock two yards square in the middle of the pool, which was otherwise fishless for its forty yards length. It was a remarkable and revealing sight.

In flood time, when the current in mid-river becomes uncomfortably strong, salmon will look for easier water nearer and nearer to the bank as the river rises; and in full flood they will often lie tight under the bank as close to it as they can get, provided the water there is deep enough. Even under flood conditions they still have their favourite places where they like to lie, and one of the most fascinating moments in fishing is waiting for a high water catch to come into order as a river rises, and preparing to fish it as soon as the water steadies. Anticipation then rises high, and fish that have just moved in under these conditions are usually ready takers.

What has been said about salmon lies so far applies particularly to North Country and Scottish rivers, with their faster stream. These are mostly similar to each other in character, hill rivers, fast running, with a rocky or gravelly bottom, a strongish current, and well defined rapids and pools. They are quick to rise and fall, and may rise many feet after a really heavy rain or snow melt. Their water is usually clear or very clear, except after rain when it is apt to be discoloured by peat or other forms of fouling.

Welsh and West Country rivers tend to be similar in character, though sometimes with considerably slower stream (e.g. in the lower Wye) and with more discolouration. In these rivers salmon on the whole follow the Scottish pattern as concerns their lies, and are to be found where a Scottish angler would expect them to be.

English South Country salmon rivers in the chalk stream area, e.g. the Itchen, Test, Avon, and Frome are of totally different character. They are slow running, with a deep and solid flow and a copious weed growth in summer. No North Country fisherman would at first sight of them have any clue as to where salmon would be likely to lie, indeed he would probably refuse to believe they were salmon rivers at all, so unlikely looking would they appear to him. Nevertheless all these rivers, except the Itchen which is the least productive of the four, produce several hundred salmon and grilse to the rod every year, and the Avon in addition has a similar sized net catch. The water in these rivers is nowadays only moderately clear, and they have a gravel bottom where it is not covered by silt. There are no large boulders, but weed growth gives shelter which salmon like. There are no clearly defined pools and few shallows, but there are deep holes from place to place. So discovery of lies is difficult, unless helped by local advice. But the interesting fact is that, although in such water it might be thought that salmon would lie anywhere, in fact this is not the case; salmon here are just as choosy as elsewhere, and have their own preferred lies in the same places year after year, as regularly as clockwork. Usually these are at the lip or the tail of some deep hole, or near where some outcrop on the bed of the river causes a boil to appear on the surface. Weed also is an attraction, provided it is not too thick. Salmon like to lie alongside it, or below or above weed clumps. If there are weedless stretches of river, scoured out by exceptional winter floods, salmon will desert these in favour of more weedy ones.

Irish rivers are of two main types, the streamy and rocky west coast ones, much like those of the west coast of Scotland, and the deeper slower flowing rivers of the south and east coast. The latter are reminiscent of the lower Wye, or the lower Tweed, or even the Hampshire Avon. Salmon lies in these Irish rivers conform to type, in similar places to those elsewhere in British rivers, and there is little difficulty in finding them if one knows what to expect.

Scandinavian rivers, such as those of Norway and Iceland, in many respects resemble Scottish rivers; but their water is clearer, and in Norway the current is usually much stronger. Salmon lies as a rule are to be found here more or less where they would be expected, on the Scottish pattern, but there are some differences. In Norway salmon appear to dislike the strong streams, probably for the simple reason that they are so very strong, and they prefer the side currents or pot holes at the side of the main stream. Also it comes as a surprise in Norway to find falls that become impassable to fish when the water is too high rather than too low as is more normal in Scotland. The strength of the current is responsible for this. The falls on the Sand River and at Aarnehol on the Rauma are examples. Beware if your beat is upstream of such falls in a high water year, when the fish remain congregated below them, unable to pass.

In Iceland the Scottish pattern of lies generally applies, except that again salmon are apt to shun the strong streams and prefer quieter and deeper water. Perhaps this is because the water is very pure and very highly oxygenated. Sometimes a pool, that in Scotland one would have picked on as certain holding water, for some reason never contains fish. Perhaps the bottom is too smooth or the current the wrong speed, or there is a total absence of shelter. One cannot tell. One has to learn by trial and error in such cases; but generally speaking the Scottish fisherman will find himself at home in Iceland as regards likely lies.

Of lies in other countries where Atlantic salmon are found e.g. Canada, France, and Spain, I have no first hand knowledge and so make no comment about them. I suspect that they follow normal patterns, except perhaps in Canada where the water during the fishing season is normally much warmer than in Britain, or so one is told. In this case one would expect the salmon to favour the streamy water where oxygen is more easily available.

Returning to home waters, there is one factor which should never be forgotten, which is that river beds and consequently salmon lies can sometimes change. This applies particularly to the fast running rivers of the north, above all to those which hold massive quantities of loose gravel and which are subject to high floods. The Spey, especially in its lower reaches, is a typical example, and to a lesser extent the Tay, Dee, and Lochy amongst others. How often has one heard of certain good pools being 'gravelled' or 'washed out', and ceasing consequently to hold fish. The converse can also be true and good pools be 'ungravelled' or 'reformed' again. Presumably this process has been going on since the last ice-age, and it is amazing where all this gravel still comes from; but it does mean that lies can come and lies can go, so if you are thinking of renting or buying a beat in a particularly gravelly stretch of river, with few solid banks, it is worth bearing this in mind.

The author bringing in a fish to land it in his boat.

Flies and Fly Making

Salmon flies have undergone great changes lately in basic pattern and design. The hair wing is now all the current fashion, and rightly so, since it looks much more lifelike in the water than the old fashioned feather wing; but hair wing flies need to be properly tied, and above all to be not too bushy or too bristly, thus allowing every hair to be seen to vibrate in the stream in a fashion reminiscent of the legs of a living creature. This superiority of hair winged flies applies particularly to the large flies used in spring and autumn, two to four inches long. Instead of Jock Scott, Silver Doctor, or Durham Ranger on big single hooks, we now use the Tosh, Garry Dog, or some other long hair winged pattern, usually tied on a tube with a treble hook at the tail; or later, with the approach of summer, the Hairy Mary, Stoat's Tail, or Munro's Killer in smaller sizes. As to the type of hook mount, the fisherman can make his own choice, as a result of experiment; and it is very important for him to have confidence in what he is using. There seems to be little difference in hooking and holding qualities between double hooks and treble hooks, until one gets down to the very small sizes, no. 9 or smaller, when trebles are better. At the opposite end of the scale, the sizeable treble hook is preferable to the large single, both for hooking and holding. The big double hook is too clumsy and performs badly above size 4.

Incidentally, for the smaller sizes of fly generally in use for warm water fishing, I have for a long time mistrusted the long-shanked single hooks invented and made popular by Mr. A. H. E. Wood of Cairnton. It seems to me that these hooks frequently fail to take a firm enough hold, and that far too large a proportion of the fish hooked on them get away during the course of play. This applies particularly in big rivers such as the Spey and Tay, where hooked fish often run out a long line in a strong stream and the strain on the hook-hold is greater. For a long time past I have therefore given up using this type of hook, and prefer the double or the treble. The fine wire French trebles now on the market are excellent hookers, and hold well. But one has to watch them carefully, as the wire is not strong. They should be discarded the minute that one of the hooks starts to bend, and they would never do for holding large fish in a strong stream as in Norway. Mounted on a tube fly for normal salmon fishing however, and for grilse, they are first class.

In size, hooks should normally be in proportion to the size of the fish one expects to catch. For grilse and small salmon one needs small hooks and fine wire (the only likely exception being in early spring or autumn when one is fishing with big flies). In proportion, as the size of fish and the strength of the current increases, one's hooks should increase both in size and strength together with the overall size of fly; until if one is hoping for 30 or 40 pounders in a foaming Norwegian torrent one's single hooks should be as large as 6/0 to 8/0, and one's trebles proportionately large and strong. At all times hooks should be made of the best metal obtainable and correctly tempered, not so excessively as to be brittle or so insufficiently as to be pliable. They should be kept at all times needle sharp, with some form of sharpener. Once bent or damaged they should be ruthlessly discarded, and never bent back into their original shape which invariably weakens them. My friend, Mr. David Shaw, once showed me some hooks which Robert Pashley, the great Wye fisherman, had specially made to his own design. They were unbelievably sharp, and though the wire was fine it was very strong. The idea was said to be that these hooks should enter the fish's mouth like a sharp hypodermic needle, which no doubt they did.

For floating line fishing small double-hooked or treble-hooked flies are best, smaller in size for the Dee for example, than those which would be used in a corresponding height of water in the Spey or Tay or Tweed. Pattern of fly matters little, provided the dressing is scanty. For larger flies a hair-winged dressing is best, with the hair wing thin and sparse. Such a wing is best for clear water anywhere;

only in coloured water is a thicker wing more advisable. Colour of wing seems to make little difference, though if I was to be confined to a single colour I know I would choose black, for all sizes of fly. Large flies should be tied on a tube (with a treble hook), or else on a single hook of not too coarse metal and with its point kept really sharp. I do not like the heavy brass tubes. They are the most awkward things to cast well; and if it was necessary to fish deep I would far prefer a heavier sinking line together with a lighter tube.

Any salmon fisherman who takes the trouble to learn to make his own flies or baits adds a new dimension to the scope of his fishing. Arthur Ransome sums it up very fairly in his book *Mainly About Fishing* (1959). He writes: 'A fish caught on a home-made fly is a greater satisfaction to the fisherman than one which has been tricked by a fly bought in a shop. Why? Because it better satisfies the fisherman's instinctive desire to recreate conditions in which he depends on himself alone in his voluntary contest with nature.'

Fly tying is not difficult, contrary to most people's ideas. A few lessons from a professional or a competent amateur, and the subsequent guidance of a good book on the subject will enable any fisherman, reasonably gifted with his fingers, to acquire all the necessary basic ability. With further practice it will not take him long to tie any type of fly he wants. Not everyone needs to tie like a Crosfield or a Pryce-Tannatt, and for strictly fishing purposes it is quite unnecessary to be able to tie the old fashioned and elaborate built wing patterns. Admittedly flies of this type are works of art when well tied, and represent the highest products of the tyer's skill. I have many of these which bear this out. But, unfortunately perhaps, it has now been firmly established that the salmon's taste in what is attractive differs from ours. To him plain black or light brown or yellow hair apparently means more than the feathers of Indian Crow, Jungle Cock, Golden Pheasant, or dyed Swan that look so delightful to us. Therefore for the strictly utilitarian purpose of taking fish, a variety of hair-wing flies, large or small as needed, are not only more deadly, but are easy to tie, each one taking only a few minutes. The plainer feather winged patterns are also good killers, such as the Blue Charm, Logie, Thunder and Lightning, March Brown, Black Heron, and others. They are not much more difficult to tie, and the brown mallard wing seems an attractive feature. It is only when we get to the elaborate built wing, multi-hackled and jointed body flies, beloved of Victorian fishermen, that real difficulty in tying begins. These sort of flies will of course kill fish; no doubt hundreds of thousands of salmon have been caught on them in Britain, Norway, and Canada and elsewhere. Nevertheless they are rapidly going the way of the dodo.

If any fisherman feels inclined towards taking up fly-tying, let him not therefore be put off by the idea that it will either be too skilled or too laborious, which is simply not true. Not only is the tying an absorbing hobby in itself, very useful for the long winter evenings, but it gives the fisherman an unlimited field for experiment; he can produce any pattern of fly that he likes, whether standard or of his own devising, with any variation to his own taste in size, material, detail, or hook. Moreover he will have the fun of trying the effect of his product on the fish, when he is next on the river. It has also been said in the past that the tying of flies does not lead to any saving in cash, when the equipment and materials have been paid for; but nowadays this is not true either. The cost of material for simple hair winged flies is negligible, in fact if the tyer is a shooting man he can probably collect almost all he needs at no cost at all. But the price of shop tied flies, as we all know, is considerable. Over the period of years the fisherman fly-tyer can save a considerable sum. In addition he has the means of constructing useful presents for his angling relatives or friends who do not themselves tie. The satisfaction of hearing from them how they have caught fish on his productions is worth a lot of trouble. Listen, finally, how T. E. Pryce-Tannatt one of the greatest fly-tyers of all time sums up the whole subject in his *Meditations of a Middle Aged Angler* (1932):

> There will develop the ability to experiment with materials and methods in the devising of new or improved patterns. This is, without doubt, the most interesting aspect of fly dressing. . . . It may be going too far to say that no fly-fisherman can hope to be of really first class grade unless he can dress flies—but it is certainly true that no fly-fisherman can know the full extent of the pleasure of fly-fishing unless he does, or is at least able to, dress the flies he uses.

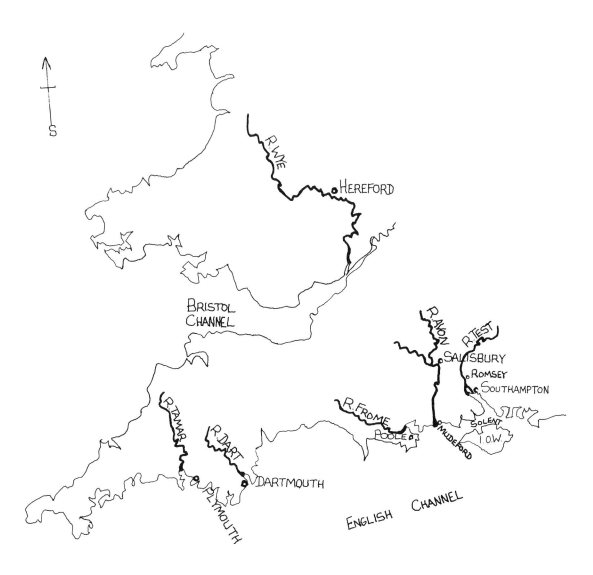

R.WYE

HEREFORD

BRISTOL
CHANNEL

R.AVON

R.TEST

SALISBURY

ROMSEY

SOUTHAMPTON

R.FROME

SOLENT

POOLE

MUDEFORD

I.O.W.

R.TAMAR

R.DART

DARTMOUTH

PLYMOUTH

ENGLISH CHANNEL

0   60
MILES

S

44

ENGLAND AND WALES

Rivers of the South and West

Test—Avon—Frome—Dart—Tamar—Wye

Since I was born and bred in Dorset and so did a great deal of my early fishing in the south of England, for this reason and no other I have started this account with such rivers as I have fished in this particular area, continuing with two rivers in Devonshire, also the Wye.

The Hampshire and Dorset rivers are mainly chalk streams in origin. Their waters are consequently alkali; they are also generally slow-running, but nevertheless hold a fair stock of salmon, grilse, and sea trout.

The Test, Avon, and Frome are the three principal rivers in this category. They all produce enjoyable fishing, though of a completely divergent character from that of the north country.

Devonshire rivers are of a totally different type. Their headwaters usually spring from high ground such as Dartmoor or Exmoor, their water is acid, and their current normally much faster. Their stock of fish is extensive, though heavily netted.

The Wye is a magnificent river, in a class of its own. It is the most prolific salmon river in England and Wales, with an annual rod catch of 4,000/5,000 fish. In the past the Wye's best fishing period was in the spring during March and April. Now this is less certain, and more fish are caught later in the year.

The Test

Broadlands: Looking up the Rookery and Lord Louis.

The fame of the Test as a trout river is world wide, but it is not generally known that its lowest 6 miles between Romsey and Southampton Water is the most prolific piece of salmon rod fishing, in proportion to its length, in the whole of England and Wales. It also produces a good number of sea-trout, including some large ones.

This river is a true chalk stream, and rises near Overton, 8 miles west of Basingstoke. Its 45 mile course lies slightly west of due south, via Whitchurch, Stockbridge, and Romsey, to enter the head of Southampton Water in two separate channels at Redbridge, close to Totton. It is a smaller river than the Avon, little more than half its size, but bigger than the Frome. All the principal salmon fisheries, Broadlands, Nursling, and Testwood, lie downstream of Romsey, where there is a formidable obstacle to the passage of fish in the shape of the hatches at Saddlers Mill. Not many salmon are caught above this point; and there used to be an unwritten agreement amongst all Test fishery owners that upstream of Romsey trout fishing took precedence, and salmon were regarded as interlopers. To the best of my knowledge this still holds good; except that a lot of salmon pass through Saddlers Mill in the autumn to spawn above Romsey, though some remain to spawn below.

The main reason for the Test's big rod catch, it should be explained at once, is that it is nowhere netted and that it has been totally free of nets since the turn of the century. What other salmon river can say the same? In addition there is reasonably good spawning ground, both in the main river and its side streams. The feed for the fry and parr, as in other south country rivers, is superlative, although there is plenty of competition from brown trout and coarse fish.

Pollution is negligible, except in one area—Southampton Water. The tidal estuary there gives considerable cause for anxiety. How can it be otherwise when a shipping centre as big as Southampton is concerned, together with the many industrial installations sited on the estuary?

The water in the lower Test is not of the totally clear quality that one is led to expect in chalk rivers. As in the Avon and Frome there seems nearly always to be a cloudiness marring the true transparency. The cause of this is not firmly established, but it does seem that nowadays one has to go near to the headwaters of rivers of this type before perfect clarity is obtained. Salmon fishing however suffers little if at all thereby.

My own experience on the Test took place during the years 1948–1956, when I fished it every season at intervals, both at Broadlands and Nursling, and I had had odd days at Broadlands before the 1939 war. I found it a good fly river; and looking at my fishing diary I find that, of the 301 Test fish that I caught during those

years, 186 were on fly. It was then far easier to catch fish on fly in the
Test that it ever has been before or since on the Avon or Frome, the
other main south country salmon rivers. This was because the Test was
shallower, streamier, and had a much more concentrated stock of fish. I
imagine the same applies nowadays, though I do not know how much
fly is still used. It was seldom necessary to cast a long line on the
Test, a fairly small river. Accuracy was more important, and in many
places one had to pitch the fly within inches of the opposite bank. Fly
fishing on the Test had a special fascination in that one almost always
saw the rise of the fish. Although the current in most places was quite
strong, the surface was usually glassy, and the fish made a clearly per-
ceptible V in the water as they rose at the fly. There was a moment of
tantalising uncertainty as to whether the fish had taken it or not. It was
fatal to tighten too quickly, many an over-eager performer got caught
out on this one! One had to wait until the line began to draw—then one
could breathe a sigh of relief, and draw back. He had got it! Often in
contrast he rose at it, but did not take, and one could enter into a
campaign of varying tactics in order to induce him to do so. There was
much one could do in the way of changing the pattern and size of fly
and of fishing it faster or slower, but without doubt the best plan was to
abandon an interested fish for an interval of time, perhaps half an hour
more or less, and then return to fish him again, taking particular care to
keep out of his sight when walking along the bank. If necessary a
staggered approach of this sort could be repeated more than once, until
the fish was pulled or hooked, or had lost interest.

Most Test fishermen, as usual on south country rivers, used bait—
devons or plugs in the Spring and later prawns or shrimps. It was
easier to catch fish with these. It was also easier to keep a bait line
clear of the floating cut weed which was apt to come down the river,
in spite of the two weed nets which were operated at the top of the
Broadlands water. These last were an outstanding boon for the
Broadlands, Nursling, and Testwood fishing downstream. They
stopped 90% of the odd bits of cut weed that came down at any
time—and they were lifted at night to allow fish to pass upstream.
Only during the recognised weed cutting periods for the whole river
did they fail to operate. I have often wondered whether the Nursling

and Testwood fishermen realised how much they owed to these nets. As a result of their operation floating cut weed was far less of an annoyance on the Test than it always has been on the Avon and Frome, which have no such nets. Nevertheless even on the Test it could at times be very tiresome.

There were three main hatch pools on the Test below Broadlands. These were at Nursling Mill on the 'Big River', at the 'Drawing Room' pool on the 'Little River' (the Test at Nursling divides into two separate branches which have separate entries into Southampton Water), and at the big tidal pool at Testwood on the Big River. Fishing in these hatch pools was intriguing; the best lie for the fish was not in the main current, but in the back wash on either side close under the bank, where the stream swung back towards the hatch, to be caught up anew in the downstream rush.

Apart from these hatch pools, Broadlands, Nursling, and Testwood all had extensive fishing on both banks along the main river, and in the case of Nursling along the 'Little River' also.

Broadlands had about $3\frac{1}{2}$ miles of fishing, divided into 5 beats, with up to 2 rods on each beat. Nursling had around 1 mile of 'Big River' and $1\frac{1}{2}$ miles of 'Little River' below where these two channels divided, and Testwood about $\frac{3}{4}$ mile above the main Testwood pool. The 'Big River' below Nursling Mill, which belonged half to Testwood and half to Nursling was pretty well ruined by misguided dredging for agricultural purposes in 1945–46. I don't know how far by now it has recovered, but the 'Little River' always held plenty of fish (so did Testwood pool, though to my regret I never fished the latter; new fish came into it on every tide).

The salmon rod fishing season on the Test opens early, on January 17th, and closes on October 2nd. A few fish could always be caught early in the season at Nursling and Testwood, but the main run of small summer salmon does not start to come in till towards the end of April. June has always been the most prolific month until lately, when the numbers of grilse in July and August have considerably increased. Towards the end of August and in September both grilse and salmon become red, and very few fresh ones still enter the river so late in the season.

Broadlands used to fish a maximum of 10 rods, Nursling 4, and Testwood 2. So the river was not over-fished. There was also an occasional rod fishing above Romsey. I imagine these numbers are still adhered to; there is really no room for more.

Sometimes when you hooked a fish on the Test, he weeded you— not deliberately, as hooked trout do—but if he ran hard up or down stream it was odds on that he would become entangled with a clump of weed sooner or later. Usually he would come free without difficulty, if you got well downstream and pulled from below. But if he was badly entangled the best course was to hand line him from downstream, gently at first, but with increasing pressure after a few moments. This seldom failed, and it was very rare to lose a fish through being weeded; not more than one in forty of the fish one hooked escaped in this way. Weed in fact was in many ways a blessing as well as a menace. If winter floods scoured a stretch of river bare of weed, fish would not lie there during the following season. They preferred the weedy stretches, and above all liked gravel channels between clumps of ranunculus. No doubt the weed gave them shelter and shade as well as oxygenating the water. It also provided shelter and food for parr.

The present rod catch in the Test is 400–700 fish, many of them grilse averaging 7 lb, and the remainder small summer fish of two sea-winters averaging 11 lb. In the 1950s it was sometimes over the 1000 mark. The big springers of former days, averaging 16–18 lb, as in the Avon and the Frome, have now become very scarce. The record Test salmon weighed $47\frac{1}{2}$ lb and was caught at Nursling in the 1920s. I do not know the weight of the record sea-trout, but double figure weights were not rare. I caught two myself of over 10 lb. One of these was on a Canadian fly called 'The Patent', the wing of which consisted of hair from a grey squirrel's tail. I could see the fish lying on a bare patch of gravel, and cast several times to him, allowing the fly to pass by him, sunk, in nymph fashion. He seemed to take no interest in it, but then suddenly changed his mind, whipped round, chased after the fly and seized it. It was very exciting, as one could watch the whole process. I had thought he was a salmon, but he turned out to be a sea-trout of 11 lb. This fly was given me by the late Sir Richard

Fairey, who was a keen Nursling fisherman. I wonder if it is still used on the Test? There was an ardent vogue for it at one time in Canada. It was used in quite large sizes, up to 2 inches long, and always fished in nymph fashion, cast upstream. I still have one or two of these flies in my fly-box, but have hardly ever tried them elsewhere. I wonder if any of my readers have knowledge of them?

The Patent

An unfortunate accident occurred at Nursling shortly after the end of the 1939–45 War, when Mr. L. Douglas, the popular American ambassador to Britain, was invited to fish there one day in March. He arrived, armed in the usual American fashion with a short single-handed fly rod of 9 feet or less, and with a longer than usual nylon monofilament leader at the end of his line. The question then arose as to what sort of fly should be used; and the keepers quite correctly told him that the best size was a 4/0 pattern such as a Jock Scott or Mar Lodge, in view of the high and cold spring water. Mr. Douglas' short rod was however quite unsuited to control such a large and heavy fly on a long leader in the high March wind. It was not long before the big hook, by sad misfortune, became embedded in the pupil of one of his eyes. He was led off in great pain to hospital, where not unexpectedly he lost the sight of that eye . . . a grim lesson to all of us that it is unwise to fish with unbalanced tackle.

The record Test brown trout weighed 18 lb and was caught by Brigadier T. Hickman on June 9th 1922, in the pool below the road bridge at Romsey. The Brigadier was using not a fly but what was discreetly described as 'Local Lure' It is perhaps better left at that!

The Romsey slaughter-house was not far upstream. Another huge brown trout of 16 lb was caught in the same place in 1904. Elsewhere on the lower Test big trout in the 4 or 5 lb class were to be found occasionally. They rose to the grannom and mayfly, but to little else. An unusual visitor one summer in the 1950s was a dolphin. This enormous creature weighing several hundred pounds made its way from Southampton Water up the 'Little River' at Nursling, until it reached the 'Drawing Room' hatch pool, where it could penetrate no further. The problem was how to dispose of it. Eventually the river keeper despatched it with several shots from a rifle. What happened to the carcass is not related!

Nowadays, sad to say, the outskirts of Southampton have spread, and a motorway has been built across the river at the top of the Nursling water. Some of the old peace and quiet of the neighbourhood must inevitably have been destroyed.

Nursling was always the most attractive of the Test salmon fisheries but both it and Testwood are perilously close to the suburbs of Southampton. One can only hope that they will not be engulfed in the foreseeable future.

The Avon

Colonel Kidston-Montgomerie playing a fish on the Somerley water.

The Hampshire (or Wiltshire) Avon rises in the Vale of Pewsey, and has a southward course of approximately 60 miles via Amesbury, Salisbury, Downton, Fordingbridge, and Ringwood, to enter the English Channel at Mudeford, close to Christchurch.

The Avon itself is not a true chalk river, but its main tributaries the Wylye, Nadder, Bourne, and Ebble, which join it at or near Salisbury, are largely so. It is the biggest of the south of England rivers, and holds a wealth of fish of many sorts besides salmon, e.g. sea-trout,

54

brown trout, grayling, pike, barbel, chub, and other species of coarse fish, so much so that it is a wonder that its salmon survive to the extent which they do. During their young life in the river they must have a wholetime struggle for existence. In any of these chalk rivers, Avon, Frome, Test, or Itchen alike, if you watch a spawning hen salmon she will be surrounded by an array of brown trout, grayling, or other fish, and every time she shivers herself to shed some eggs there will be a concerted dive by these unwelcome attendants to grab the eggs before they sink into gravel crevices in the redd. It reminds one of fish being fed in a stew pond. The cock salmon hovering in the neighbourhood will do his best to chase intruders away, but his efforts will be little better than those of an elderly schoolmaster trying to keep a crowd of unruly boys out of a sweetshop! And the struggle only starts at this stage.

Like other south country rivers the Avon is comparatively slow running, with a deep and solid flow, lacking rapids and well defined pools, varying little in height, and not subject to sudden rises and falls. It has a copious weed growth, and a bottom sometimes of gravel but often of silt. It is similar in character to the Test and Frome; but slower running than the former and less serpentine than the latter, while bigger than both.

The quality of its water is good. There is little pollution, certainly not enough to do any damage to salmon stocks. On the other hand the water seldom runs fully clear, except in the headwaters. Below Salisbury even in midsummer there is a certain cloudiness in it, which is hard to explain, but so far as one can tell this does no harm to the fishing.

In high water the Avon runs reasonably fast, at about $4\frac{1}{2}$ knots, but in medium or low water at perhaps half that speed or less. Its height depends mainly on the previous winter's rainfall, which feeds the springs during the spring months and thereafter. This is a delayed action process, and the water height does not fluctuate markedly or suddenly, as in hill-fed north country rivers. In fact a north country fisherman would be hard put to it, at first sight of the Avon, to recognise it as a salmon river at all, so unlike it is to the normal conception of one. Nor would he have any idea of where the salmon would be likely to lie, since all the river looks very similar, without distinct features in the way of rapids and pools, shallows and rocks. Experience would be the only sure teacher of this, apart from some local expert, if one could be enlisted to help.

The best fishing is from Longford Castle, just below Salisbury, downstream to Christchurch, over about 30 miles of water; only odd fish are caught further upstream. The best beats on this main part of the river are at Somerley, just above Ringwood, and the Royalty at Christchurch. There is also a good hatch pool at Bickton, a mile below Fordingbridge, which can produce 80 or more salmon in a good season.

Thanks to the kindness of many friends, I have fished the Avon on odd days or weeks at intervals ever since 1935, so have witnessed the trend of its fishing over a long period. I think that the general catch has certainly increased over these past thirty or so years, both by nets and rods. But at the same time so has the extent of the good fishing water. From Bickton upstream to the Salisbury area, fish are now killed in fair numbers, where formerly the catch was nil; and this is now an established occurrence, so that the pattern of Avon rod fishing is undoubtedly changing. But on the lower part of the river from around Ringwood downstream, the chances of the individual rod seem to have sharply deteriorated. The stock of resident fish in this part of the river has become decidedly less over a prolonged period, while the number of rods has patently increased, with the inevitable unsatisfactory results.

Quite apart from the actual fishing, however, there is great delight to be experienced in other ways alongside a river during spring or summer in an English south country water meadow. If one looks for quiet tranquility, here indeed it is to be found in abundant measure, as the river glides quietly by, bordered by luxuriant hay crops or scattered osier beds, with animals birds and wild flowers all contributing to the harmony of the scene. Such rare visitors as otters, ospreys, grebes, bitterns, and kingfishers, amongst others, all disclose their presence to the south country fisherman from time to time. Their company adds immeasurably to his enjoyment of the day's sport.

The Avon is an indifferent fly river. It lacks adequate current, and the fish often lie tight under the bank in deep water, where a fly cannot swing over them. It can only hang, which often is not attractive enough. Floating cut weed is also a great handicap to fly fishermen, more so than to bait fishermen. It is much easier to dodge such weed with a bait line than with a fly line. The net result is that few Avon fishermen use fly, and thirteen out of fourteen Avon fish (or thereabouts) are caught on baits of various sorts, devons, spoons, prawns, or plugs. This floating cut weed is a permanent hazard to fishermen in south country rivers. Weed has inevitably to be cut, it blocks the water channel and causes flooding otherwise, and two cuts during the fishing season are normally necessary. The difficulty is to synchronise the cutting all up and down the whole length of the main river and tributaries, so that the minimum of disturbance is caused to fishermen. Though the Water Authority and the various fishery owners concerned have made considerable efforts to achieve this, the results so far leave much room for improvement. It takes the best part of a week for cut weed from say the upper Avon, Wylye, or Nadder to reach the sea at Mudeford, and if such weed is held up by any form of obstruction on the way it may take longer. Also a rise in the water after rain will at any time fill the river with pieces of cut weed that have temporarily been lodged along the banks. To arrive on the river for a long-awaited day's fishing, only to find it full of floating weed, if completely unexpected is nothing short of infuriating. No one as yet seems to have found a satisfactory answer as to how in a sizeable river like the Avon this annually recurrent nuisance is to be avoided.

The rod fishing season lasts from February 1st to September 30th. The best fishing period is normally from May to mid-June. Little fishing is done after July.

A study of the Avon fish reveals a remarkable change in recent time in counterpart to what has happened on the Test and the Frome. Up to about thirty years ago the Avon salmon were almost without exception three or even four sea-winter spring fish, averaging around 20 lb in weight. 30 pounders were common, and several 40 pounders were killed most seasons. The record rod-caught fish weighed $49\frac{1}{2}$ lb. It was killed on February 27th 1952 by Mr. G. M. Howard in the Green Banks pool above the railway bridge on the Royalty water.

This huge fish took a silver sprat. Mr. Howard also killed two other fish of $41\frac{3}{4}$ lb and 41 lb on the Royalty, both in 1951. Higher upstream a 48 lb fish was taken at Bisterne by Mrs. Shawe in April 1936, and a yet larger one of $48\frac{1}{2}$ lb by Mr. Gladstone near Ringwood that same year. Other 40 pounders at that time, and indeed up to the 1950s were not rare. The average size on the Bisterne water in 1935 was recorded as 22.40 lb (for 135 fish), in 1936 26.35 lb (for 82 fish), and in 1937 26.40 lb (for 40 fish, including four of over 40 lb before April 11th). Other beats on the Avon no doubt had a similar average at that time. It would seem doubtful whether such a high average weight has ever been exceeded on any other British river, though many of them have of course produced larger individual weights as well as much more numerous catches.

Up to thirty years ago in the Avon two sea-winter fish of 10 lb to 14 lb were a rarity, and grilse unknown. But in the 1950s a change started. The big springers gradually began to become scarcer, and the smaller 10 to 14 pounders increased. Of late years the former have largely disappeared, while the latter form the principal salmon stock. The main salmon run does not now start to enter the river before late April, with only odd fish earlier. And in addition to this, an entirely new factor has emerged in the form of an extensive grilse run in July and August. It is extraordinary that these fish, judging by the net returns, are now more numerous than the salmon, and seem to increase in numbers every year. This is a somewhat bitter pill for the older generation of Avon fishermen, who remember with nostalgia the former 20 lb average.

How is this recent proliferation of grilse to be explained? Is it that the bigger fish have been eliminated by the high seas and drift net fishing, in conjunction with our own estuary netting and increased rod fishing? Or is it due to a natural change in the habits of the salmon that so many of them now return after only one winter in the sea, as opposed to two winters, or even three or four winters? Or is it due to some other cause? Who can say? At least the trouble is not U.D.N., as the Avon like the other chalk rivers has been free of this; and at any rate it may be reckoned preferable to have a good run of grilse in July and August rather than nothing at all (the salmon run being virtually over by then). But would it be better if the grilse stayed longer in the sea, and came back as salmon one or two seasons later? There would be fewer of them, many having perished in the meantime; but from the rod fishing point of view the answer might be in the affirmative, while the nets might prefer a bird in the hand.

Be this as it may, the Avon salmon, except at the start of the season when there are a few bigger ones, now average 12 to 13 lb and there are few of over 20 lb. The biggest rod-caught fish in 1980 was only 28 lb. It is true that in 1981 there has been some increase in the numbers of bigger fish, several of over 30 lb having been killed. All the same the stock of such fish is nothing to what it was in pre-War days; and it remains to be seen whether the 1981 increase, welcome as it is, is to be permanent or merely temporary. As an illustration of what used to be the case, I would quote my own experience in 1936, when I was but 20 years old, and a very inexperienced though keen fisherman. The late Lord Normanton kindly gave me permission to fish at Somerley, which was hardly ever then let, as the fish-pass at Ringwood had only recently been improved and the Somerley salmon fishing was previously held to be hardly worth consideration. Between April 14th and April 23rd in five days fishing I caught 5 fish (admittedly all on bait) averaging 27 lb, the two biggest being 33 lb apiece. Now a single rod could not do anything like this in a whole season on that water, although fish of that size were quite common in the lower Avon in those days.

Another factor about the Avon which must be noted is the presence of hatches and hatch pools. Like other south country rivers, the Avon in the past has been used to further the irrigation of water meadows to help the growth of grass. Hatches were built to create an upstream head of water for this purpose, and the water meadow system was introduced from Holland as long ago as the mid-17th century. It is likely too that even before that date obstructions of sorts were introduced into the river, creating a head of water to provide power for mills. Now hatches of any sort can easily form an obstruction for salmon, particularly if they are lowered to a substantial extent in order to create an upstream head of water. For many years the hatches at Ringwood, for example, were reckoned to be a formidable obstacle, few fish getting through them until an improved ladder was built in the 1930s. Now an entirely new set of modern hatches has been installed at this point, together with a thoroughly efficient salmon ladder, which enables fish to ascend freely. There are also two sets of hatches at the Royalty near Christchurch, which in the past have been the cause of controversy. Again new ladders have recently been constructed here, making it much easier for salmon to ascend. Hatches at Winkton and Somerley present no obstacle to fish. They are permanently wide open. Bickton, 5 miles upstream from Ringwood, has two sets of hatches which have been reckoned something of an obstruction in the past, but two improved ladders, recently completed, should allow fish in future to pass freely. There are also hatches near Breamore, Downton, and Britford, as well as further upstream. At these too the Wessex Water Authority plans to improve the passage for fish, wherever needed. The result should improve the access to good spawning grounds, with a consequent future increase in stock.

At the moment the main spawning area in the Avon lies between Downton and Wilton, both in the main river and its tributaries, such as the Ebble, Wylye, and Nadder. There is good spawning ground upstream of this area, and it seems likely that their upstream passage being made easier fish will spread yet further upriver to spawn. General experience and observation of spawning shows that, other things being equal, the wider the distribution of good spawning grounds in a river the greater the stock which the river can carry. So the prospects for the future Avon stocks seem promising.

The recent yearly rod catch in the Avon averages around 500 fish. The net catch is usually about one-third higher than that of the rods. This combined net and rod catch puts the Avon well ahead of the Itchen, Test, and Frome, the other south country salmon rivers, as a producer of salmon and grilse—though the Test is not netted, and the Frome by one net only in Poole Harbour. As elsewhere the number of rods on the Avon has increased beyond all anticipation since 1945. It is now safe to say that there is a minimum of 35 rods per day fishing at any good period in the season, and there may well be more. Before the War the number might have been 12, if as many. The story elsewhere is much the same, and it is an old one, perhaps older than generally realised if Thomas Bastard's verse, written as long ago as 1598, is taken into account:

> 'And now the sport is marred, and wot ye why?
> Fishes decrease and fishers multiply.'

It is to be hoped in the future, however, that a more plentiful stock of fish will serve to counterbalance favourably the increased number of rods.

The Frome

Everywhere along its banks are fertile water-meadows.

Dorset, rather surprisingly, has three salmon rivers, the Frome, Piddle and Stour. In present times the Stour salmon, owing to pollution and dredging more than anything else, have become virtually extinct. The Piddle, a small chalk stream which runs into Poole Harbour at Wareham, seldom produces more than 20–35 rod-caught fish in a season. Only the Frome is in a reasonably thriving state.

This slow running, meandering, chalk river rises near Evershot, 4 miles north of Maiden Newton in west Dorset, and has a course of around 40 miles as the river runs, through Dorchester and Wool, to enter Poole Harbour near Wareham.

Only the bottom 14 miles of the Frome, from Moreton down to the tidal reaches just above Wareham, are of any account for salmon fishing, and this stretch holds sea-trout as well, together with coarse fish of various kinds. Higher upstream, in the Dorchester area and above, the Frome has a high reputation as a dry fly river for brown trout.

In character the Frome closely resembles the Hampshire Avon, though it is less than half its size. Nowhere does it run fast (in fact it is slower running than both its sister rivers, the Avon and the Test) and it has a bottom composed alternately of gravel and silt, the latter predominating in its lower reaches. Its course from Wool downstream is nothing short of serpentine in character, twisting and turning back on itself to an amazing degree. In several places two fishermen can be casting back to back within 25 yards of each other, and yet one be fishing 300 yards downstream of the other. In late spring and summer there is a prolific weed growth which tends to block the channel, and at least two weed cuts each season are normally necessary. Everywhere along its banks are fertile water-meadows, intersected by ditches and carriers, with cattle grazing at frequent intervals. To the south is the soft green swell of the nearby Purbeck hills, and the whole setting is one of lushness and peacefulness, typical of the southern English countryside at its best, yet hardly reminiscent of the more rugged surroundings normally associated with the presence of salmon and sea-trout.

But salmon and sea-trout there are, however unlikely looking a salmon river the Frome may be. In Victorian times and in the early years of this century the Frome salmon were netted almost to extinction, but things are much better now and have long been so. In fact the Wessex Water Authority, the present owner of the nets, very wisely and in the interests of fish conservation does not now exercise its netting rights at all, and only one outside net operates in Poole Harbour.

The Frome like the Avon varies little in height, and is not subject to sudden rises and falls. There are hatches at East Stoke and at Bindon, as well as higher upstream, but all are kept wide open and form no obstacle to the passage of fish at any time. Pollution is relatively absent, and does not harm salmon. Some years ago there was an unfortunate case of this near Bovington, where all fish of all kinds between Wool and Poole Harbour appeared to have been killed, but the ill-effects of this have worn off now.

As in the Avon, however, the water in the lower Frome is hardly ever completely clear, and possesses a certain degree of cloudiness. It is not to be supposed that this does any harm to the fishing.

Frome salmon are very similar in type to those of the Avon. In years gone by the big three and even four sea-winter springers were typical of this river. There were few small summer fish, and they were not much sought after. The springers used to average 20 lb, 30 pounders were common, and one or two 40 pounders were killed every season.

W. Earl Hodgson in his *Salmon Fishing* (1927) writes: 'The average weight of fish killed in the Frome has always been remarkably good. The five fish caught by myself in 1905 were no exception to the rule. The average was just under thirty pounds. The largest, a fine salmon, weighed 41 lbs; the smallest 22 lbs. All were taken on fly.' Is this not enough to make one's mouth water?

The record Frome salmon weighed 49 lb and was killed in the 1930s. Some unkind critic likened the catching of these big Frome fish to 'killing a pig in a ditch' (the Frome averages only 10 yards in width), but such disparagement was not justified! In any case these big fish have almost completely disappeared now.

The salmon stocks in the Frome rose to an all-time high in the early 1960s. The two sea-winter summer fish by then had proliferated, though the big springers were becoming increasingly scarce. Since that time, however, there has been a sad decline all round and the catch now is made up by many fewer small summer fish running from April onwards and averaging 12 lb. Grilse also are now appearing in July and August, in the same way as in the Avon and Test, and in fact outnumber the summer salmon, a new and strange state of affairs for this river too. These fish average 7–8 lb. It is true that 1981 showed some improvement both in size and numbers of fish, but as in the Avon it remains to be seen whether this improvement is to be sustained or whether it was merely a flash in the pan. Only time will show.

A few sea-trout enter this river, and they are sometimes large. They can be seen at times rising to the mayfly. The record Frome sea-trout weighed no less than $22\frac{1}{2}$ lb and was caught above the hatches at Bindon by S. R. Dwight in May 1946. Another huge fish of 21 lb was caught by R. C. Hardy-Corfe in 1918. The captors of these fish were both salmon fishing at the time, so their achievement was less spectacular than it sounds since they were using strong salmon tackle.

In May 1981 two more huge sea-trout were caught at Bindon by the Hon. Aylmer Tryon and by Mr. C. R. Rothwell respectively. They weighed $15\frac{1}{2}$ and 15 lb, but again they were both caught on salmon tackle. Perhaps the best achievement in this line took place on the neighbouring Piddle, when on September 25th 1979 Lt. Commander D. Crampton-Thomas caught a 14 lb sea-trout. This great fish was taken on an orange bodied nymph, size 10, fished on a $3\frac{3}{4}$ lb B.S. nylon leader, with an 8 ft. rod. The fight lasted for an hour before it was landed.

Another good sea-trout was caught, in the Frome this time, by Lord Tryon. This notable episode took place in early July 1954, in the hatch pool at Bindon. Lord Tryon says that he was trying to catch a brown trout for supper, and he cast a small dry sedge to a neat little rise which he imagined to be that of a trout of perhaps 1 lb. The fish took the sedge and was hooked, and then the fireworks started. There followed a downstream rush of more than 100 yards, before a more gradual return upstream, giving place to a long drawn-out struggle which ended eventually with a beautiful sea-trout of 8 lb safely on the bank.

The record Frome brown trout weighed $12\frac{3}{4}$ lb. It was caught on a dry fly near Dorchester by the Rev. S. Filleul in 1907. A washing basket had to be borrowed to land this huge fish, all available landing nets being inadequate!

The Frome, like the Avon, is an indifferent fly river for salmon. It is deep, narrow and sluggish. Fish often lie close under the bank, and there is usually no room for a fly to swing over the lie. All the same, if a good fisherman perseveres with it, fish can not infrequently be caught on fly. For instance, my great friend Aylmer Tryon, an excellent Frome fisherman of long standing, caught six in one morning at Bindon some years ago, an unparalleled achievement showing that fly fishing is by no means unproductive, given an adequate stock of fish. But in present times it is safe to say that, as in the Avon, thirteen out of every fourteen Frome fish are caught on bait. Most Frome fishermen do not use fly at all, and prawns are a particularly favoured bait. It is pointing out the obvious that more fish would be caught on fly if it was more used. But many modern salmon fishermen do not know how to fish a fly at all, let alone how to fish it skilfully. It is a pity, as they lose the main joy in fishing through this omission. The Frome and Piddle Fishing Association has now asked its members to limit the use of prawn.

The number of rods normally fishing the Frome has greatly increased since the war, as on other rivers. When I first fished the Frome in my young days before 1939, there would not have been more than 10 rods fishing the whole river on any given day, if as many. Now the daily number is often more than 30 in the best part of the season, which is in May and June for salmon and July and August for grilse.

In 1979 the total Frome salmon and grilse rod catch amounted only to 177. This was below recent average, which is around 250. Maybe this is no great number in proportion to the number of rods which fish this river, and no great number compared with the catches from other more prolific rivers. All the same, Dorset may well reckon itself lucky to have a salmon river at all, especially one that is so little netted and which, like the other chalk rivers, has never suffered from U.D.N. One only wishes that the 30 and 40 pounders of days gone past were still with us, and that the stocks of smaller salmon would multiply to keep pace with the ever increasing number of rods.

The salmon spawning grounds in the Frome lie mainly between East Burton and Dorchester, i.e. towards the middle reaches of the river rather than in the headwaters, but there are odd redds to be found higher upstream as well as lower down. No doubt the immature fish suffer considerably from competition with brown trout and coarse fish as well as from depradations by pike, but the survivors must benefit inordinately from the luscious chalk river feed.

My own Frome experiences date back to as long ago as 1932 when during Easter holidays from school I caught my second salmon ever, at the Crab River bend on the East Stoke beat. It weighed 15 lb and took a Silver Grey size 3/0. Since then I have always had a soft spot for the Frome, and have fished many different stretches of it periodically, whenever I have had the chance. This river has a curious fascination, partly because it is such an unlikely looking salmon water. In the 1930s, at any rate, one had a fair chance of hooking a really big fish though I never did so myself. I remember rising an enormous one somewhere not far above the Swanage railway bridge. I was fishing with a large Green Highlander of about size 6/0, when this huge fish boiled up at it, showing the whole length of his back at hardly more than a rod length's distance. He appeared to be well over 40 lb. Of course in my youthful excitement I whipped the fly straight out of his mouth, whereas if I had done nothing it was just possible that I might have hooked him securely. One learns the hard way and I have never forgotten it! Later on I did catch one of 26 lb, which was then of only modest size for the Frome, though it is the biggest I have ever caught in that river.

My kind host of former days was R. C. Hardy-Corfe, or 'Corfie' to his many friends. He had a cottage at Holme Bridge, and on the walls of his sitting room were arrayed models of some seven 40 pounders, all killed by him on the Frome. The biggest weighed 48½ lb. Corfie was a great character and an outstanding all-round fisherman. He was a good fly fisherman, but better still with a bait, particularly with a prawn. All his 40 pounders as I remember clearly were killed on bait, except one of 41 lb which he used to describe as 'a very big fish for a fly.' He used to say that any duffer could kill a fish on a fly, while minnow fishing was considerably more skilful, and only the real expert could consistently catch them on a prawn. Of course he had Frome fishing primarily in mind, and in those days one's bait-fishing reel was either a Nottingham or a Silex, none too easy to handle. But although at that time I accepted as Gospel every pronouncement which Corfie made about fishing, in the light of my later experience I would put the order of skill in exactly the opposite direction. In the Frome above all it is particularly difficult to catch fish consistently on a fly, and I do not believe any Frome fisherman of present times would dispute this. Corfie was a most kind and generous person; I learnt a great deal from him about the elements of fishing, and will always be grateful. In fact for some years, following in his footsteps, I became a very keen bait fisherman, especially with prawn and shrimp, as well as a fly fisherman. It was not till I started fishing regularly in Scotland after 1947 that I arrived at eschewing the prawn and shrimp, and eventually all the other types of bait. In my early days on the Frome the shrimp once brought me five fish in a day, the biggest being 24 lb.

During these latter years I have often fished at Bindon, thanks to the unlimited kindness of my friend Aylmer Tryon, one of whose outstanding exploits I have mentioned above. Bindon is quite one of the pleasantest and most productive beats on the Frome, and it has the advantage of a hatch pool at Bindon Mill and of double bank fishing rights for part of its length. It is always a delight to fish there, whether one catches anything or not.

An outstanding feat on this water was performed in March 1963 when the present Lord Tryon was fishing on the right bank of the 'Bunny', above the Bindon hatches. He hooked a large fish on a 'Yellow Belly' devon. This fish ran upstream for about 100 yards, but Lord Tryon found it impossible to move from where he stood when he first hooked it, owing to obstructions on the bank. He therefore attempted to wade across the river to the unobstructed left bank. Now the Frome at this particular point runs full and fast in March. Lord Tryon soon found himself in the unconventional position of being out of his depth and treading water in thigh waders in a strong and cold current, with his rod held high aloft and a large salmon under what could only have been described at best as remote control. With some difficulty he gained terra firma on the opposite side; but by this time the fish had doubled back, and was now downstream of him. It had to be stopped from passing under the 'Bunny' bridge; but all went well, and after an hour it was gaffed. It weighed 35 lb and was fresh run. Anyone acquainted with this place will well realise the epic nature of this contest!

The Dart

Casting needs to be accurate, but seldom with any length of line.

My great friend the late General Tom Acton was responsible for introducing me to this lovely Devonshire river. I must say at once that to anyone used to the south country chalk streams, such as the Avon, Test, or Frome, the Dart comes as a complete surprise. It seems almost incredible that within 70 miles crow flight of the luscious water meadows of Dorset and Hampshire one can discover this tumbling hill stream, which in character of flow resembles nothing more closely than the Banffshire Avon, 600 miles away. At least that is what

69

immediately sprang to my mind at my first sight of the Dart above Holne Bridge, amazing though it may sound to those who do not know it.

The main Dart has two headstreams, the East Dart and West Dart, which rise high up on Dartmoor at a height of over 1500 feet. After a short course of some 10 miles apiece, these two hill streams unite at Dartmeet to form the main Dart, which runs in a south-easterly direction with one or two circuitous bends through a steep wooded valley to enter tidal water at Totnes, 16 miles downstream. Below Totnes there is a further 10 miles of tidal estuary leading to Start Bay and the English Channel.

The valley of the Dart is so well known for its beauty that it needs only a brief description here. The headwaters on Dartmoor run in an alternately rocky and gravelly channel, often deeply eroded, through peaty and sometimes boggy slopes covered with heather, bracken, or rough grass. The fall is steep, a descent of some 600 feet in the first 10 miles to Dartmeet. During the next 7 miles to Holne Bridge the fall is as steep or steeper, one of 800 feet as the river plunges off Dartmoor and winds its way through deep and heavily wooded combes, never slackening its swift current between abrupt rocky outcrops. Only below Holne Bridge does the descent at last ease, and the fall over the remainder of the Dart's course past Buckfast Abbey to Totnes amounts to a comparatively modest 150 feet. At Totnes there is a high weir, below which lies the tidal estuary, and the surroundings of this lower part of the river are of rolling or steeply sloping farmland, studded with frequent woods. There is also a high weir near Buckfast Abbey, which appears to form something of an obstacle to the passage of fish, though they surmount it easily enough in high water.

The water of the Dart is renowned for its clarity, and it is a simple matter to spot fish in its pools anywhere upstream of Holne Bridge, particularly with the help of polaroid glasses. Salmon have their exact lies according to the water height, seldom varied, while sea-trout, from June onwards, lie thick all over the various pools of their choice. An experienced Dart fisherman will thus have little difficulty in discovering whether or not there are fish in his beat, and if so in what quantity. Lower down below Buckfast Abbey the river is slightly bigger, and it is not quite so easy to spot fish, even in such a limpid stream. Yet the clarity of the river undergoes little change even after rain, when its level rises rapidly with flood water running down the steep slopes off Dartmoor. Even if it does colour to any degree, the Dart will quickly run clear again after an hour or two. It is remarkably pure.

The salmon rod fishing season lasts from February 1st to September 16th and the netting season from March 15th to August 16th. The sea-trout rod season is from March 15th to September 30th.

The Dart by nature is a prolific salmon river, but unfortunately during these last fourteen years it has been badly affected by U.D.N., a large proportion of the spring salmon run each year having died. It is curious that this disease has been so devastating in its effects on salmon and sea-trout in the Devonshire rivers, but has not in any way affected the chalk rivers, Frome, Avon, and Test, such a small distance salmon-wise to the east. It would seem that this disease flourishes only in acid water, such as flows off Exmoor and Dartmoor, and has no potency in the strongly alkali water of the chalk rivers.

Previous to the arrival of U.D.N. the salmon stock in the river was fair though not profuse. Totnes weir has been provided with an efficient salmon pass, and incoming fish can surmount it easily enough. The weir at Buckfast has been considerably more formidable; whether this has now been made easier for the ascent of fish I do not know; but when I last saw it I should have thought it might well have given cause for some concern to the upstream owners. Dartmoor however has an exceptionally high rainfall, so there are plenty of floods from time to time to help the fish over this weir. It is not generally known that at two points, Yes Tor and High Willhays, Dartmoor rises to over 2000 feet, a surprising altitude for the south of England, and there are several other tors or hills nearly as high. Inevitably such high ground draws the rain. Even so, a fish with sea-lice above Holne Bridge, only 9 miles from the head of the estuary, is a rarity.

The most prolific salmon stretches on the Dart are below the weir at Totnes, and below the weir at Buckfast Abbey; but in a high water year the river above Holne Bridge can also produce a good number of fish. From the end of March till mid-May is the best spring fishing period, though any time thereafter till the end of the season can be good, whenever there is rain and a rise in water. If the river on the other hand remains low for any length of time, fishing becomes very difficult and salmon are reluctant to take. By September fish are becoming red. Dart salmon average around 10 lb and anything of 20 lb or over is scarce. There is a grilse run late in June, and in July and August, which helps to increase the stock.

The whole river provides good fly water, with plenty of streams, and no great depth in pools. 'Fly Only' is the rule above Holne Bridge, though below that point bait is allowed. One's casting needs to be accurate, though seldom with any great length of line, the river in places being only a few yards wide and rarely more than twenty. There are many over-hanging trees, which have to be avoided; and there is much scrambling up and down steep rocky banks, which can become dangerously slippery in wet weather to those who are not well shod. Another unusual hazard is the presence along the banks of vast numbers of voracious ants, said to have been introduced many years ago as excellent supplementary pheasant food. Whether this is so or not, let no angler sit down on the bank for any length of time anywhere near one of their numerous habitations. He will bitterly regret it during the subsequent week if he does!

Fishing the Dart is not easy; during my experience of the fishing above Holne Bridge I never knew a single rod to catch more than three fish in one day, and that number only once. This must be a rare achievement on the upper part of the river, though it may have been accomplished more often further downstream at Buckfast or Totnes. On the other hand one seldom had a completely fruitless day without some encouragement at least in the form of a rise or pull. The water was not hard fished, in fact when the river was consistently low salmon fishing was often abandoned. I remember starting fishing once on a bright June morning, with the river low and one would have said in hopeless fishing order, when three casts in the neck of a narrow but deep pool were enough to produce a most unexpected return in the form of a fresh run 9 lb salmon. Tom Acton observed that this unlooked-for piece of good fortune was the result of the river having been left quiet for the previous few days. No doubt he was absolutely right. There could not be a more profitless procedure than the overfishing of small rivers, anywhere, with their water out of order. Yet it occurs distressingly often.

My friend Tom Acton, with a nice fish caught on a summer's day.

During past years I used frequently to drive down to Devonshire from my home in Dorset for a day or two's fishing on the Dart, usually for salmon, but occasionally we went out at night for sea-trout also. We always fished on the $2\frac{1}{2}$ mile stretch of water upstream of Holne Bridge, which was quite delightful. There were always some fish present in April, May, or June, though never in great numbers. We hardly ever had a total blank, though three salmon in one day was the most we ever caught, all on fly and the biggest 16 lb. This may not have amounted to a large kill, but as one is so often reminded the pleasure in fishing is not by any means governed by the size of the bag. In the case of the Dart, the delightful character alone of the river, coupled with the company and the charm of the surroundings more than made up for any shortcomings in the stock of fish. And there were always sea-trout to fall back on from June onwards.

Regarding tackle and methods of fishing, the usual type of outfit for small river fishing, either fly or bait, will be all that is needed. In February or March a fly of about $1\frac{1}{2}$ to 2 inches long will be best, and baits of equivalent size. Later in the season there should be a reduction in the size of both, except possibly in the strongest streams or at dusk. A line with a sinking tip, and later a floating line throughout, are all that one needs, together with a monofilament leader down to 10 lb B.S. as required. As the summer advances, morning and evening will, as usual everywhere, be found the best times for fishing; but it is noticeable that in many places on the Dart the river is so well shaded by trees, once the leaf is grown, that the sun seldom reaches the water.

As to wading, as might be expected in a small river, there is little of it. A lot of fishing is done directly off the bank, and elsewhere it is seldom necessary to wade more than knee-deep. Thigh waders are all that one wants, but see that their heels and soles are made as far as possible out of some 'non-slip' material. This is a wise precaution anywhere, but particulary so here, where there are so many smooth rock outcrops underfoot.

Not enough mention has so far been made of the Dart sea-trout and sea-trout fishing. I should say straight away that potentially the Dart is one of the best of the smaller sea-trout rivers in Britain, so much so that many of the local experts prize the sea-trout far higher than the salmon. Sea-trout are apt to run in large numbers at any time from the middle of June onwards, and they quickly permeate through the whole length of the river. They vary in weight from the herling size right up to double figures, and it used to be an enthralling sight to walk down to a good sea-trout pool on a low water summer day and see the bottom black with fish of all sizes, large and small. Some of the best pools held them by the hundred. In my limited experience it was a waste of time fishing for them in daylight, and merely caused panic. 10.30 p.m. was quite soon enough to start, and the darker the night the better. It was an eerie business waiting on the river bank until the light faded; then starting to fish with a single-handed trout rod, without being able to see the fall of the fly, but knowing one was surely covering fish with every cast. One drew a smallish fly slowly through the water, and tightened at the slightest pluck. Then the fireworks would start. Even a two pounder could behave as though mad, while the antics of a 6 or 8 pounder were unbelievable and all the more electrifying since they took place in the pitch darkness. No wonder that many of the local fishermen concentrated entirely on this night fishing for sea-trout to the exclusion of all else.

But sad to say there is a reverse side to this inspiring tale of both Dart salmon and sea-trout. During the past 14 years the scourge of U.D.N., as already said, has drastically affected the stocks of both kinds of fish, and the Dart seems to have been as hard hit by this foul disease as any river in Britain. For this reason recent rod catches have dramatically declined, and there would be little point in quoting them with the river suffering from an unnatural and to be hoped temporary plague. It cannot be overlooked that U.D.N. punishes the sea-trout just as cruelly if not worse than the salmon. One can only hope that by now there is some sign of improvement in the Dart, as there is in most rivers elsewhere, and that we shall live to see the day when the horrible U.D.N. is but a distant memory.

Net fishing is carried out on a large scale in the Dart estuary, the catch running into four figures. Netsmen both here and elsewhere are apt to argue that it is a waste to let fish run up a river if they are doomed in any case to die of disease. One must admit that there is some reason in this; but like some other arguments that have been put forward in the past by commercial fishermen it could set a dangerous precedent.

Of good hotels for the visiting angler there are plenty in the neighbourhood. Perhaps the handiest and pleasantest is the Holne Chase Hotel, 3 miles from Ashburton. This was once a private house, is close to the river, and is in a beautiful and peaceful setting, with a pleasant view down the river valley. It also has a mile of fishing for its guests. One could hardly ask for more.

The Tamar

Of all the salmon rivers in the south of England the Tamar is perhaps the most attractive, and with the exception of the lower Test the most prolific in fish. It is 40 miles long, and rises 7 miles to the north-east of Bude, in the high ground close to the coast of north Cornwall. For much of its subsequent southerly course, to fall into Plymouth Sound downstream of Gunnislake, the Tamar forms the boundary between Devon and Cornwall. It is a medium/small river, the upper course of which winds its way slowly through hills and meadows, while the middle and lower reaches, where the best fishing is to be found, have a good streamy flow over a rocky or gravelly bed. Its banks here are often abrupt, and in some places formed by cliffs or outcrops of rock. There are pools of many different types, interspersed with fast streamy runs, so for the fisherman there is no lack of variety. In general the lower Tamar pursues a rather circuitous course in deep valleys with high slopes on either side, which are apt to be thickly wooded. Thus the fisherman is often provided with shelter, both from troublesome winds and from over-bright sun, a not insignificant asset.

For nearly all its course this river provides good fly water. Its pools are seldom deep, and as already mentioned there is a fair streamy current, even when the water is low. One peculiarity should however be mentioned, and that is that its water seldom runs completely clear; nearly always there is colour in it, due one is told to its slow flow through the agricultural land on its upper reaches. Aesthetically this may be a drawback, and it is in pronounced contrast to the clear water of some other Devonshire rivers such as the Dart and Tavy. But in actual fact it seems to make little difference to fishing, as fish both run and take quite freely in spite of it.

I must admit that my experience of the Tamar has been limited. However, on my brief visits there I felt so much attracted by this delightful river that I could not forbear to refer to it in this book,

Greystone Bridge spans the middle Tamar in attractive
surroundings.

however circumscribed my knowledge of it may be. This again is a river on which I would be glad to fish more often.

The main fishing on the Tamar is at Endsleigh, near Milton Abbot, six miles north-west of Tavistock. This was the fishing lodge of the Dukes of Bedford, who formerly owned the bottom 14 miles of river, from Greystone Bridge to Gunnislake. An amusing anecdote about a former Duke of Bedford, whether true or not I do not know, is that before making a fishing visit to Endsleigh he would instruct his keepers to cast over the pools with hookless flies. They had to count the number of rises or pulls which they received, and note their exact location. This information was then passed to the Duke, who could direct his subsequent activities accordingly.

Endsleigh is now the headquarters of the Endsleigh Fishing Club, which controls absolutely the upper 7 miles of this stretch, also the lower 7 miles in partnership with the Lower Tamar Fishing Club. The former club was established at Endsleigh a few years after the death of the 12th Duke of Bedford in 1953.

Endsleigh House was built in 1811 by the then Duke, whose family used it as a holiday home. It is a large and most comfortable building, with a beautiful garden amid delightful surroundings, and it looks down on the river below. The banks of the Tamar here are plentifully endowed with azaleas and rhododendrons, planted by earlier Dukes of Bedford. They provide a riot of colour when in flower.

The members of the Fishing Club form a private syndicate which fishes both banks of the above stretch. Nevertheless rods are frequently let to the outside world at all periods of the season, which is from March 3rd to October 14th. Tenants are encouraged to stay in the House at Endsleigh, which as I know well from personal experience is a very pleasant *pied à terre*.

The Endsleigh water is undoubtedly the best stretch on the whole river. It is divided into 5 beats, with two rods on each one. Spinning is allowed up to the end of April, but after that on the bottom beat in some pools only. On all the other beats 'Fly Only' is the rule from May 1st to the end of the season. The average catch for the past seven years has been 234 salmon and grilse, though in 1980 309 were caught, nine out of ten of them on fly. Salmon do not run large, and average

9–10 lb. A 20 pounder is a big one. There is a fair run of grilse from late June onwards. Any time from the beginning of May can produce rewarding fishing, April and March being less prolific. Actually September and October produce more fish than any other period of the season, but as can be imagined most of them are becoming red by then.

Upstream of the Endsleigh water, the well-known Arundell Arms Hotel at Lifton has extensive fishing rights both on the main Tamar and tributaries. I have no personal experience of this fishing, but I am told it is some of the best hotel water in England for salmon, sea-trout, and brown trout, and it is certainly situated in lovely surroundings.

There are two main tributaries of the Tamar, amongst many smaller ones, and these are the Lyd and the Inny. The former joins the main river near Lifton, and holds salmon and sea-trout, though in limited numbers; while both of them produce quantities of small brown trout. There are also other smaller tributaries holding both sea-trout and brown trout. Sea-trout in the Tamar run at any time from late May onwards, the best months for them being June and July.

The usual outfit for a medium or small salmon river is all that the fisherman needs in the way of salmon tackle.

In the early part of the year he may choose to use a light bait outfit, or a sunk fly of 2 to 3 inches long. Later a rod of 12 feet or 13 feet will be adequate, and local fishermen prefer a line with a sinking tip even then.

It is not necessary to use flies smaller than size 6 owing to the previously mentioned and habitual colour in the water. A light portable salmon landing net is often useful. Gaffs are not allowed after August.

Wading presents little difficulty. The current is rarely strong, it is seldom necessary to wade more than knee-deep, and many pools can be fished off the bank or from croys. Thigh waders are usually adequate. Trouser waders may occasionally be wanted in one or two pools, and when the water is high. It is as well to include them in one's kit.

It was Lord Trenchard who kindly introduced me in the first place to the Tamar. The motor drive there from Dorset through the lovely

Devonshire countryside is in itself a worthwhile experience, particularly when one has left the main road at Tavistock and wanders through the leafy Devonshire lanes towards Milton Abbot. One's first sight of the river, a silver thread in the depths of a steep wooded valley, arouses a keen sense of anticipation, not blunted on one's arrival on its banks to perceive the attractive character of its streamy current and the variety and quick succession of the numerous pools. Most of these seem to hold fish by mid-June.

I have not so far mentioned netting in the Tamar. Unfortunately this river, like the Dart, has a long tidal estuary where extensive netting is practised, the season being from March 3rd to August 30th. The catch of salmon and sea-trout is large, though there does seem to be sufficient escapement up the river for the stock to be maintained.

I hope this brief description of a very lovely river has been adequate to make clear its many attractions. As I said at the start of this chapter, it is hard to think of another salmon river in the south of England which can surpass it.

Salmon netting below Cotehele.

The Wye

In the background there is always the magnificent sweep of the Welsh hills.

The Wye is the finest and most extensive salmon river in England and Wales. This splendid river is so well known, and so much has been written about it, that I do not feel qualified, from my limited experience of it, to attempt here any elaborate description or comment. Many books about this river are easily obtainable; but for those who want detailed and reliable information about Wye fishing, its history, and background, there could be no better reading than

H. A. Gilbert's *The Tale of a Wye Fisherman* (1929) and J. Arthur Hutton's *Wye Salmon and Other Fish* (1949). There is also a well-favoured Mecca for anglers in the form of Hatton's fishing tackle shop in Hereford, where much can be learnt.

Thanks to Mr. Peter Clay and Mr. Jeremy Clay I have had several excellent days on the middle Wye at Brockhampton. I have also several times been the guest of Captain Patrick Hazlehurst at Hampton Bishop and elsewhere, and of the Hon. V. P. Wills at Holme Lacy. I have also had odd days on other parts of the river, as at Erwood and at Kerne Bridge. But that is as far as my experience goes— I only wish it had been wider.

My first trip to the Wye was in mid-April 1935, when my great friends Michael and David Wills most kindly took me to fish at Erwood, not far below Builth. This was during our Oxford undergraduate days, so our experience of salmon fishing was still limited, though Mike and David were good performers even at that early age. Between us we caught seven big spring fish during two days fishing. Mike's biggest being 38 lb. I include a photograph of us with our catch on page five. Could one do this sort of thing now? I doubt it. One's first experience of the Upper Wye, with its magnificent rocky stream flowing through such a beautiful wooded valley, was certainly an eye-opener to a young tyro. And what splendid fish . . . !

Looking back on past experiences of the beats I have fished, listed above, I have preferred Hampton Bishop and Brockhampton. The former had the advantage of being above the Lugg's mouth and so less liable to discolouration, and the latter, further downstream, was also lovely water. Both these beats had good streamy fly pools and fishing rights on both banks, an incalculable advantage in present times. What tremendous fun it was to fish these magnificent stretches, always with the chance of a huge fish. The best pools were the Carrots Hole at Hampton Bishop, so beloved of J. Arthur Hutton, a big deep pool which fished better with bait than fly, and the Dean and Chapter and the Summer Ford at Brockhampton, both good fly pools, as good as any on the Wye.

The whole of the Wye's course lies in a delightful countryside, right from the source near Plynlimon (2460 feet) to the tidal reaches at Tintern, hard by the Forest of Dean. This is a district unspoilt by industrial development, nor is it tripper infested. In the background there is always the magnificent sweep of the Welsh hills or the Black Mountains, and in spring when the trees first come into leaf and the numerous apple orchards blossom the whole valley takes on the appearance of a veritable region of fairy land.

As to the river itself, what could be more attractive than its rocky tumbling upper reaches in Wales, as far as perhaps Glasbury, or lower down, its slower, deeper, and smoother course as it glides in wide bends between the high red banks or steep wooded slopes of Herefordshire and Monmouthshire? It has every type of water which the keen fisherman, whether he be a fly man or a bait man, could desire. There is bank fishing, wading, and even boat fishing for the devotees of each method. There is every sort of pool that the imagination can envisage, fast or slow, shallow or deep, gravelly or rocky—the variety is endless. What is more the Wye has a long fishing season from the last week of January to the end of September, or till October 25th in its headwaters. March, especially the second half of it, was always reputed to provide the cream of the spring fishing, though April was nearly as good, and May also. This still holds good in present times, though in the middle and especially the lower part of the river summer fishing is also good.

The great attraction of the Wye in the past has always been the presence of its outsized big spring fish, 'portmanteaux' as they were termed. This meant anything, broadly speaking, of 40 lb or over. Such fish were commoner than in any other British river. Did not Miss Doreen Davy, on March 12th 1923, catch in the Cowpond Pool at Winforton a $59\frac{1}{2}$ pounder, the biggest spring fish ever killed on rod in Britain? And the story can never be forgotten of the enormous fish lost by an unfortunate angler in May 1920 at Whitney, which was picked out of the river later in a decomposed state, with a devon minnow still in its mouth. When J. A. Hutton finally laid his hands on the decaying corpse, he wrote that 'it was in such a dreadful state that one had to keep well to the windward.' He gave its length as 57 inches, and scale examination showed an unheard of 5 years of sea life, with a potential weight of certainly over 60 lb, probably over 70 lb, and possibly over 80 lb.

During the 37 year period from 1910 to 1946 Hutton records 334 Wye salmon of 40 lb and over being rod-caught, including 11 of 50 lb and over. These were all spring fish, and no other British river could show such a record of this type of salmon. (The Tay might yield more 40 pounders, it is true, but they would mostly be autumn fish, rather than springers.) Wye 30 pounders were too common to excite much interest, and the average size of spring fish used to be 18 lb. The average annual catch between the years 1909 and 1943 according to Hutton was 2645 fish. 'No better than now,' is the immediate unthinking response, with numbers of fish only under consideration. But alas! this is painting a false picture. As in many rivers the number of rods has at least trebled since 1943, and the average size of fish has dropped by nearly half, so unfortunately as the observant reader will have noticed I have been using the past tense in most of my favourable comments to date. Unfortunately, as even the most devoted of Wye fishers will admit, things are no longer what they were.

H. A. Gilbert, rather arbitrarily, divides the Wye into two sections, the upper Wye as far as Lugg's mouth, $4\frac{1}{2}$ miles below Hereford, and the lower Wye from that point downstream. He was more interested in the former section of river than the latter, and describes it as being mainly of 'fly water', while lower down was predominantly 'bait water'. Broadly speaking this is true, as the upper reaches tend to be faster running, clearer, and shallower. Nevertheless there is plenty of good fly fishing well below Hereford, some of the best (in addition to Hampton Bishop) being at Brockhampton and on the Duke of Beaufort's water near Monmouth.

In one day in 1932 Robert Pashley caught 18 fish on the Vanstone, and 16 on another in 1935, all on fly. And is there not also a great deal of bait fishing, especially nowadays, carried on with good success above Hereford, right up to the headwaters, in spite of the presence there of many lovely fly streams? So it is perhaps as well not to be too categorical about divisions of this type.

Lower Wye: a view of the Rocks Pool just below Bigsweir Bridge.

One thing in particular should be realized about the Wye, or so it seems to me, and that is that by no means all its fishings are good. There are certain outstanding beats such as Whitney, Hampton Bishop, Brockhampton, Hill Court and Goodrich, and the Duke's water at Monmouth, to name but a few of these. There are also plenty of more moderate stretches; but in the 110 mile course of the river from Rhyader to the estuary there is also a good deal of water which from the fishing point of view is quite unproductive, except possibly for a few chance fish at odd moments. So the magic name 'Wye' does not by itself guarantee good fishing.

Every year one hears of vast sums of money being paid to purchase or rent very indifferent Wye fishing, producing only single figure yearly catches. What motive lies behind this is hard to visualize. It has rightly been said that there is much more to fishing than the mere catching of fish, nevertheless in many such cases bitter disappointment must be the result. 'Quem Deus perdere vult, prius dementat' so if you rent or buy a Wye fishing you would be well advised to make sure that it is a good one, also that (far preferably) it has exclusive rights on both banks. With fishing so easily accessible and in such demand as it is in these present times, this last has become an imperative need.

When on the Wye one hears much talk, and inevitably, of such tributaries as The Lugg, the Irfon, and the Ithon. The Lugg enters the main Wye from the north west, $4\frac{1}{2}$ miles below Hereford, at the bottom of the Hampton Bishop water. It is the largest tributary, and rises some 30 miles back, in Wales, amongst the hills of Radnor Forest. In its middle and lower reaches, through Leominster and on down, it is slow running and winding, gathering with it after rain a prodigious amount of the red Herefordshire soil. In wet weather it sometimes has the catastrophic effect as long as it is in flood of rendering the whole 46 miles of the Lower Wye from Lugg's mouth to Tintern completely unfishable. This is a perpetual hazard which has to be faced. A few salmon and grilse run up the Lugg to spawn, but it is of little account for angling purposes. Of the other two tributaries mentioned above, the Irfon runs in from the west at Builth Wells, and the Ithon from the north-east some 4 miles further upstream, just below Newbridge.

Both these tributaries, especially the Ithon, can dirty the main river, when they are in flood, for many miles downstream, as many Wye fishermen know to their cost. They are of little significance for angling, but do serve as useful spawning streams, and as a valuable contribution at normal heights to the general flow.

As to the present Wye stocks of fish and their weight, the story is depressing. The average weight has fallen sharply in recent years. It is now only around 12 lb for salmon in spring and less in summer. The big spring fish, for which the Wye was so justly renowned in the past, seem to be becoming ever scarcer. When I was fishing near Ross at the end of April this past year, (1980), I asked my ghillie if he had heard of any big fish being caught anywhere on the river during the season up to then. His answer was that he had heard of a 29 pounder from a beat above Hereford, but nothing bigger anywhere else—an answer enough to make Hutton turn in his grave! Numbers of fish, too, have fluctuated markedly during these past two or three years. One explanation given for scarcity of fish is the ill-effects on the then current stocks of parr and smolts of the drastically hot summer of 1976. The water that year ran at little short of lethal temperature for five months on end. There may well be some truth in this theory, as one only hopes may be the case, because if so nature should put matters right before long. Indeed the 1981 season showed an encouraging upturn in both numbers and size of fish.

But other unfavourable symptoms exist. For example it is said that nowadays the number of rod licences taken out during a season exceeds the number of fish killed—i.e. that the average catch on the whole river is less than one fish per rod. If this is true, it does seem that there is a case of substantial over-rodding. Another ill-sounding report is that the number of fish killed on worm now exceeds that killed on fly, and is approaching half the total bag for the whole river. One can only deplore that fishing should be thus debased on such a scale, and wonder how if so degraded it can survive as a sport in the future. The Welsh Water Authority has now introduced a ban on worm fishing for salmon and sea-trout in the Wye after September 30th. This is a step in the right direction, but it goes hardly far enough to have any appreciable effect. There is apparently considerable feeling amongst fishery owners that worm fishing should be banned altogether.

My Wye ghillie told me an ominous story this year. He is a keen fisherman and enjoys having a week's fishing holiday on the Spey every season. I asked him about a certain well-known junction pool on the beat he fished there, and he replied that it was no use trying to fish it when he was there, as a party of English (coarse) fishermen used to occupy it, sitting in a row on the bank, and fishing for salmon by trotting down worms and floats in coarse fishing style. To my mind this sort of thing should be firmly stopped. The writing is on the wall.

The rod season on the Wye lasts from January 27th to October 16th, except that in the headwaters above Llanwrthwl Bridge (11 miles upstream of Builth) it continues till October 24th. Now there never has been any proper autumn run on the Wye, according to Hutton, Gilbert, and other authorities. Why therefore is the season kept open for so long, particularly in the headwaters where many fish will be on the point of spawning? It is hard to understand.

There are other present day problems. One is the large scale water abstraction from the Elan water reservoirs for the Birmingham water supply. Water abstraction from any river seldom does good. This particular abstraction tends, naturally, to cause a permanently lower water level in the whole river downstream, to bring about a far quicker run-down of floods, and in summer to keep the upper Wye below a desirable fishing level. On the other hand low water in summer time, or for that matter at any time, benefits the lower Wye by inducing fish to remain down there instead of running on into the upper river. Possibly therefore this water abstraction, as long as it is not carried too far, is not without advantage to the fishings below Hereford, or more especially below Ross and Monmouth. There is no doubt that beats in this area fish best with lowish water, and that in the present is what they often get.

The Wye is a great coarse fish river. Myriads of various types of such fish inhabit the middle and lower reaches. From the point of view of parr and smolts, pike and chub are probably the worst menace. There is no shortage of either of these. The biggest Wye pike killed on rod and line was landed by Major W. H. Booth at Hay in

1910 and weighed 37 lb. Big chub run up to 6 or 7 lb; and there are plenty of brown trout in the upper river and headwaters which are rapacious devourers of ova parr and smolts, besides competing for the available food. But the presence of these fish is nothing new; it was always so, and any recent shortage of salmon cannot be attributed in any special degree to this particular cause.

Boating and canoeing in the summer can cause much trouble for anglers on certain stretches of the Wye, particularly on the lower half of the river. The public right of boating appears to have existed from time immemorial, and fishermen just have to take it as it comes. Indiscriminate boating can ruin any fishery, if it is practised repeatedly enough; and one hears stories of certain fishings on the lower Wye which in summer are rendered worthless through this cause. If you are considering renting or buying a fishing, it would therefore seem important to look into the situation re the public right and practice of boating on the stretch in question, before you take a final decision. Owners and anglers on the other rivers should also be warned of what can happen, as exemplified on the Wye, if indiscriminate boating becomes an established activity.

Finally a word about netting. It is satisfactory to be able to end this brief story of the Wye on a cheerful note. If there is any shortage of fish in the river at present, it can be asserted without hesitation that this is in no way due to over-netting by estuary or local coastal nets. What a contrast to the situation on the majority of rivers elsewhere, especially in England and Wales, and above all in Ireland!

The story of how excessive netting in Victorian times practically exterminated the Wye salmon, and of how since 1902 the Wye Fisheries Association and subsequently the Wye Board of Conservators both acquired and drastically reduced the netting, is an inspiring one. The full story is given by Hutton in *Wye Salmon and Other Fish* and by H. A. Gilbert in *The Tale of a Wye Fisherman* and this too deserves detailed study by owners and anglers on other rivers.

Since the start of this century netting on the Wye, though never totally abolished, has always been carried out on a modest scale and with careful discrimination to allow an extensive escapement of all classes of fish, but particularly the springers, up-river. The benefits have been paramount. All the magnificent Wye fishing from the Edwardian era onwards has been largely due to this beneficial action. Perhaps this is not fully realized by many of those anglers who have so greatly profited from it. If they care to examine the disastrous effects of a directly contrary policy, they only have to cast their eyes across St. George's Channel to the deplorable state of the potentially magnificent salmon rivers of Ireland.

One only hopes that the Welsh National Water Development Authority, which now controls the fortunes of the Wye, will be a worthy successor to its predecessor the Wye Board of Conservators, which over a long period has so effectively and advantageously discharged its heavy burden of office.

David Henriques fishing some streamy water on the upper Wye.

SCOTLAND

Rivers of the East Coast

Helmsdale—Oykel—Ness—Findhorn—Spey
—Deveron—Dee—North Esk—South Esk—
Tay—Tweed

The east coast of Scotland has rivers of all sizes from the Tay down to small streams like the Ythan or Nairn.

Their main distinctive characteristic is that they all, except the very smallest ones, possess a spring run of salmon, differing markedly in this respect from nearly all the west-coast rivers.

Many of them also have a prolific run of grilse between June and August, together with summer salmon.

The Tay and Tweed also have a fair autumn run, of both salmon and grilse, the Tweed being later than the Tay in this respect.

Most of the finest fishing in Scotland is to be found in the rivers of this area.

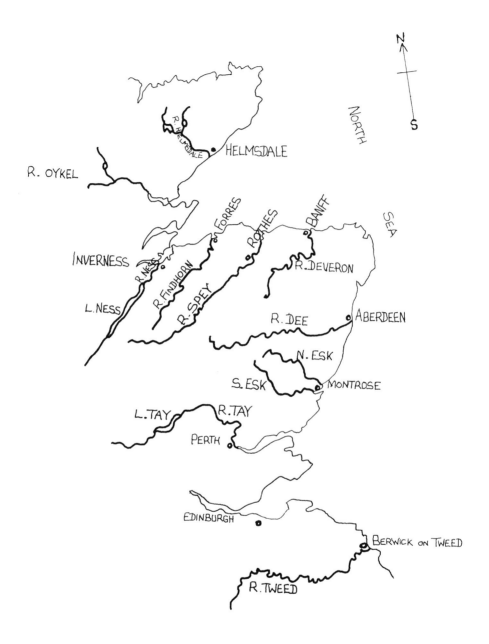

N

S

NORTH

SEA

R. HELMSDALE

HELMSDALE

R. OYKEL

FORRES

ROTHES

BANFF

INVERNESS

R. NESS

R. FINDHORN

R. SPEY

R. DEVERON

L. NESS

R. DEE

ABERDEEN

N. ESK

S. ESK

MONTROSE

L. TAY

R. TAY

PERTH

EDINBURGH

BERWICK ON TWEED

R. TWEED

0   60
      MILES

The Helmsdale

John McKay, a well-known ghillie on the Helmsdale. This small river provides superb fly water.

Without doubt the Helmsdale is outstanding and perhaps even the best amongst the smaller salmon rivers of Scotland. It rises in the interior of the county of Sutherland, at a height of 390 feet above sea level, in the wild hill country between Loch Naver and Loch Achnamoine, and descends south-eastwards through the Strath of Kildonan to fall into the North Sea after a course of 24 miles, with the village and small harbour of Helmsdale at its mouth.

In its upper reaches it is augmented by one sizeable tributary, flowing in from the north out of Loch an Ruathair and down Strath Beg, to join the main river two miles below Kinbrace. The whole valley is unspoilt and delightful, with heather covered hills on either side, rising to 2000 feet, a home for the grouse and red deer.

The only road up the Strath is a small one, not always close to the river-side, and only wide enough for one-way traffic except at intermittent passing places. Only the Inverness-Wick railway, which also follows the line of the Strath, otherwise serves to disturb the peace of these lovely surroundings, an example of east coast Highland scenery at its best.

Recently I was talking with my Helmsdale ghillie, John McKay, about the frequent presence of adders in the heather, both here and elsewhere in the Highlands. I had said that as far as I knew no wild creature preyed on adders, or kept their numbers down. John McKay replied that on the contrary red deer would often stamp on them and then proceed to eat them tail first. He said this with no hint of a smile, and I assume he was not pulling my leg!

John McKay produced a further profound observation, about fishing this time. He said that anyone can catch salmon when the fishing is easy; but when its difficult, that's when the good fisherman can catch fish and the others can't. . . . A simple statement but how true, particularly on a river like the Helmsdale, where fish are usually plentiful though not always co-operative.

Farms and crofts are scarce, ever since the evictions of the early 1800's. It was said that in 1810 the Strath of Kildonan could muster 4000 inhabitants, but those days are long gone. There is perhaps a hint of sadness in the sight of a glen once so thrivingly and now so meagrely populated, nevertheless from the angler's point of view no river nowadays can be too remote; seclusion is rare, and when one is lucky enough to have it in this modern world one cannot but be thankful.

The Helmsdale itself is enchanting. It is a perfect medium-small salmon river resembling a small sized Dee, with a most interesting variety of pools of every type, fast and rocky, narrow and tumbling, streamy and gravelly, slow and flat—they all occur in turn, and all are different in one way or another. The banks are mostly open and heather-covered, but sometimes the river forces its way through sheer rock barriers, and sometimes there are fir, alder or birch trees right down to the water's edge.

When fishing this river one changes one's beat every day, and so encounters all this diversity of background in quick succession. This in turn renders the whole process nothing short of fascinating.

In spite of its moderate size the Helmsdale is not a spate river. It has two lochs amongst its headwaters, Loch Achnamoine (5 miles long) which can be fished for salmon, and Loch Ruathair ($2\frac{1}{2}$ miles long). At the outlet from both these lochs there have for many years been hatches, controlled by the proprietors of the fishing, which have served to hold back a head of water, instead of letting it run away in excessive spates, thus being instrumental in keeping the river running at a good fishing height for long periods on end. This is in marked contrast to what so often happens elsewhere on Highland rivers of similar size. It would he hard to exaggerate the benefit to the Helmsdale fishing of this controlled inflow. How often on so many other rivers, both big and small, does one see violent spate water, owing largely to the present day increase in artificial drainage, hurtling sea-wards in one tempestuous rush, while in a matter almost of hours the river will have sunk to summer level once again. How one wishes in such cases that the flood water could somehow be restrained to keep the river running at a fair height, as one is told used to happen in olden days, for a much longer period. Well, on the Helmsdale the answer to this problem has to a large extent been found. This is not to say that the river level can never on occasion fall too low; for instance the drought spring of 1980 caused deplorably low water from April to July, to the great detriment of fishing. Excessive rain on the other hand can still cause immoderately high floods. Nevertheless the overall advantage derived from the controlled inflow is beyond all doubt, and there is far less uncertainty as to water level and conditions for a prospective visitor to the Helmsdale than in the case of other rivers of similar size.

Admittedly stored loch water is liable to be warmer and less oxygenated than fresh water off the hill, and no doubt it does not have the same invigorating effect on fish. Nevertheless make no mistake, it is a great deal better to have plenty of such stored water, even with its accompanying drawbacks, rather than to have a river at low summer level for long periods on end.

The fishing on the Helmsdale is better managed and controlled, through agreement between its owners, than on any other river I have come across, with the possible exception of the Naver. The greatest merit of all is that this river is not over-fished, unlike so many rivers nowadays when inflation and high taxation together press hard on proprietors. On the 24 miles of Helmsdale fishing, there are six beats, with a maximum of two rods on each beat. Moreover each beat is split into two sections, one above the falls at Kildonan (about midway up the river), and one below. So the two rods for the beat can fish either on the top section or the bottom section, or one on each, as they please. They therefore have extensive scope for their activities, as the two sections of their beat may be in widely separated parts of the river. If they want to fish after 8 p.m. in the evening they have then to change to their following day's beat, beats being changed daily in rotation.

This system works admirably, and it would be hard to devise a better one. It gives constant variety and change of scene, as well as plenty of elbow room, individual beats averaging $3\frac{1}{2}$ miles in length with both banks all the way. The only slight drawbacks are that it takes a long time for a newcomer to get to know the river well owing to the frequent changes of beat, also a great deal of motoring is involved. But these are minor inconveniences, far outweighed by the many accompanying advantages.

Although there are a number of small falls here and there on the Helmsdale, the only sizeable ones, forming any sort of obstruction to the passage of fish, are those at Kildonan about 11 miles upstream from the mouth. Though fish ascend these falls without difficulty in summer, in spring-time as long as the water is cold they prefer to remain below. The second week in April is soon enough for good fishing on the upper river above the falls; before then the lower river is best.

There is Association water at the bottom $1\frac{1}{2}$ miles of river down to its mouth at Helmsdale. This water is partly tidal, with some good pools, and local fishermen benefit from it with a fair catch of salmon, grilse, and sea-trout.

Everywhere on the Helmsdale fishing is limited to 'fly only', an excellent rule on a small river of this type, which provides superb fly water. No one who fishes there would wish it otherwise.

The rod fishing season opens on January 11th and closes on September 30th, but the cream of it undoubtedly is from mid-March to mid-May in the Spring and during July and early August in Summer. The stock of fish both salmon and grilse is excellent, and there is also a plentiful run of sea-trout in June and early July. Even in early August some fresh salmon or (mainly) grilse are still coming in; but after the middle of that month and during September there is no worthwhile run, and the fish in the river are becoming increasingly red.

As to big fish, the Helmsdale is a small river and the fisherman is lucky if he meets anything of over 20 lb. Spring fish average 9–10 lb and anything of 16 lb or over is nowadays a good one. The record rod caught fish weighed over 40 lb but was killed long ago. There have been odd fish of over 30 lb caught since 1945, but none lately.

There is a good grilse run from the end of June onwards, which lowers the average weight of fish caught, but noticeably increases the general stock. In fact by mid-July every year the Helmsdale seems full of fish almost everywhere, and the annual rod catch is around 2000–2500 fish, varying according to conditions favourable or otherwise.

The 1980 season was a difficult one. Spring fishing up to the end of March was good, but mid-April to mid-July saw unprecedented drought, with an ever-dwindling flow of water. Simultaneously there was a serious outbreak of U.D.N., the worst unfortunately for many years. All this was no help to fishing, which fell away badly. Then from mid-July onwards a series of outsize floods added further difficulties, so that the season was indifferent in terms of catch; nevertheless the stock of fish in the river was massive.

1981 was not so good. The water was extremely low during the spring owing first to lack of snow and subsequently of rain. And then when there was a rise of water later in the summer fish were not so plentiful as usual. Perhaps the excessive long-lining off the Faroes may have been partly responsible for this. Nevertheless by September the river was holding a fair stock of fish, and there should have been no shortage of spawners.

The Helmsdale is also net fished at its mouth, but not heavily; and the number of fish that succeed in entering the river is all that could be wanted for purposes both of sport and breeding. There is excellent spawning ground, widespread both in the main river and tributaries. The net fishing season starts on February 11th and ends on August 26th.

As to tackle, a rod of 12 ft to 14 ft is normally all that is wanted, except possibly in early spring with a big river running and high winds. All the usual patterns of fly do well, hair wings are perhaps best in big sizes up to $2\frac{1}{2}$ inches long early on when the water is still cold, down to size 7 or 8 in summer low water. Thigh waders are adequate, and it is usual to land fish by beaching them or with a landing net, as opposed to gaffing.

There is nothing peculiar or unduly difficult about the process of fishing this river, though expert knowledge of the water as usual counts for a great deal and is perhaps more than half the battle. A sunk line and big fly is best in early spring with cold water, and later on a floating line and small fly fished in the normal way when the water becomes warmer. It is seldom if ever necessary to throw more than 25 yards of line, and often little more than a rod's length is wanted.

How different is the process of fishing a small river like the Helmsdale to that of a big river like the Spey or Tay! The former is a much more delicate procedure with no need for long casting but every need for accuracy between rocks or up to the edge of high banks, no need for deep wading but every care wanted to keep out of the sight of the fish. One should know the river like the back of one's hand, all its various 'neuks' and odd taking places, quite apart from the main and obvious lies; also one should be able to 'dap' with two flies (see p. 99) where and when wanted. In a big river by contrast the main requirements are the ability to throw a very long line where and when needed in any sort of wind, proficiency in deep wading in a strong current whenever necessary, competence in playing large fish that may run out 100 yards or more of line and backing in a powerful stream, and if fishing alone in a boat a high degree of skilled watermanship—all of which is redundant in small rivers.

To return to the Helmsdale, at this point I should mention 'dapping' or 'dibbing', or by whatever name you like to call it. This is a favoured method of warm water summer fishing which involves the use of two flies at a time, a small one as tail fly and a larger one as dropper, the latter being 'dibbed' along the surface at the necks of pools or in fast streamy water, at the end of a short line. Fish will sometimes rise at a dropper fly fished thus when they will look at nothing else. In skilled hands this method can be deadly, but there is little new in fishing, and its protagonists, if they think that 'dapping' is an innovation of recent years, may be interested to turn to page 78 in the ordinary edition of Sir Herbert Maxwell's book *Salmon and Sea-Trout* (1898) where they will read the following:

'At Reedmouth, the junction of the Reed and North Tyne, there lived, in the days I speak of, a certain Doctor Begg, who rented the fishing of a couple of casts on the main river. When I first met him, early in October 1867, he had killed upwards of 150 salmon and grilse with the fly that season. And such flies! all of nearly the same pattern . . . fat fuzzy bodies, generally of grey rabbit or monkey wool, enormously over-winged on small single hooks . . . and nearly all of the same size, rather large, and tied on collars of undyed treble gut. He very seldom left his home before mid-day, when, if the water was in order, he would get into a pair of enormous wading trousers, button up his coat, clap on a cowboy hat, stuck all over with hairy salmon flies, take his spliced rod of the Castle Connel type off the rack, and stroll down to the river. Wading in almost to the armpits, he would begin on a fine stream which ran at the foot of his garden, ever since known as the Doctor's Stream, flinging his flies (he always used two of these monstrosities at once) across the current at right angles, and bringing them round to within a few yards of where he was standing. No low point and deep fly with him! On the contrary he gradually *raised* the point of his rod after delivering the cast, trailing the flies along the surface of the water, so that when he had finished the circuit his rod was quite erect. Any orthodox salmon fisherman who had seen for the first time Doctor Begg angling would have set him down as an incompetent bungler, yet as I have said he was remarkably effective'.

This takes the 'dapping' method back at least to 1867, but no doubt it was far older. Richard Franck in his *Northern Memoirs* published in 1658 referring to fly fishing in Scotland says: 'Dibble but lightly on the surface and you infallibly raise him.' In the days of long rods and plaited horse-hair lines this may have been one of the easiest methods of fishing, and so be one of the oldest.

The first time I was put wise to this method of fishing was some years ago, when my ghillie John McKay took me out one summer's day in July when the water was fairly low and the weather warm. I was the grateful guest of Mr. and Mrs. Jeremy Clay at the time, and it was my last morning's fishing as I had to leave in the afternoon. John McKay took me to a fast and not too shallow stream, which held plenty of boulders and deeper pot-holes, as well as a fair number of fish, some of them stale ones. Orthodox methods of fishing with a floating line downstream and flies of various different sizes had proved more or less abortive during the previous two days, and John told me that I ought to try dapping. He said that my dropper should be a double-hooked fly of about size 6, on a dropper point of about five inches (the length of his spectacle case). The tail fly was to be slightly smaller, double or treble hooked, with about 4 feet of 10 lb B.S. monofilament separating the two flies. But more important than the outfit used was the method of fishing. I was instructed to cast a short line straight across the current or slightly upstream, and to hold the rod well up so that the flies worked back across the current with the dropper dancing on the surface and the tail fly just submerged. To do this I started with little more than a rod's length of line out, but after some practice I managed to increase my length of line, until I was holding clear of the water as long a line as my rod would support with the flies working in this fashion, i.e. about seven yards. It did not take more than half a dozen casts before a fish made a dash across the current in pursuit of my dropper, seized it, and was firmly hooked. This caused no little surprise and excitement, as it was unexpected and at such short range that one witnessed clearly the whole episode. I duly landed this fish without trouble, it weighed only 8 lb, and carried on fishing. Within ten minutes a second fish had seized my tail fly and was also landed. It weighed 7 lb. Soon afterwards I hooked a much bigger fish of perhaps 18 lb, which I played for 10 minutes before for no apparent reason he came unhooked. This was quite enough to make me think hard, and I have employed this method of fishing at intervals and profitably ever since. Of course it needs streamy water, a light and longish rod, a light line, and appropriate flies, as well as being more easily practised in a smallish river. But it is a card well worth having up one's sleeve for use at the right moment.

In the strath of Kildonan, there are six lodges on the Helmsdale, owning the entire fishing on the river, apart from the Association water. These lodges are Kilphedir, Kildonan, Suisgil, Borobol, Achentoul and Badanloch. If you are lucky enough to stay at one of these, as I have done thanks to the kindness of Mr. and Mrs. Jeremy Clay and Captain Patrick Hazlehurst, it is an understatement to say that you will want for nothing in terms of outstanding hospitality. If you need hotel accommodation on the other hand, it is to be found in Helmsdale or its neighbourhood.

I cannot close my account of this river without once again laying emphasis on its charm. There are few places where I would rather fish, and the whole atmosphere is delightful.

The Oykel

Rock Run: the river has an excellent variety of pleasant streamy pools. The fishing is by fly only.

My impressions of the Oykel are but fleeting ones as I have never had the good fortune to fish for any length of time on this river, nor to have been on it when it was in good fishing order. My experience of it has been only when it was either much too high or much too low, a frustrating business on both occasions. So there are many fishermen who know much more about it than I do. But with this limitation accepted, I will do my best to do justice to such a lovely east coast stream out of my scant experience of it.

The Oykel rises far back towards the west coast of Sutherland and is formed by the junction of several small streams off the southern slopes of Ben More (3273 ft) in Assynt. For about 15 miles as far as Oykel Bridge the river runs in a south-easterly direction and is little more than a small highland stream running through wild hill country. At Oykel Bridge there are some sizeable falls, about 10 feet in height, which although passable for fish, do tend to check their ascent. It is said that it is normally mid-May before fish pass up them in numbers, though sooner no doubt in an early year. It would depend on the water temperature. Fishing on the upper Oykel above these falls can be quite good at times, given a fair amount of water, but July is soon enough to fish this upper part of the river with fair hope of success, by which time it can be as good or better than the fishing lower down. At Oykel Bridge is the excellent fishing hotel which is by far the best base for the visiting angler.

From this point down the river's course lies due east with minor changes in direction until after a further 7 miles it reaches the tidal water at Inveroykel leading to the Kyle of Sutherland and the Dornoch Firth.

600 yards below the falls at Oykel Bridge the river is joined on its right bank by its main tributary, the Einig. This stream is about two thirds the size of the upper Oykel and rises some 12 miles back to the south west. It is a very rocky and inaccessible small river, with a substantial fall about half a mile upstream of its junction with the Oykel. There are some spectacular rock formations at this point, as there are also on the main Oykel near its falls, and a lot of small pothole pools. Salmon seem to ascend the Einig quite freely, and like to rest in its Falls pool, which was great fun to fish. You clambered out onto a high rock formation above the fall, where you felt painfully conspicuous to the fish, and tried to make your presence as little obvious as possible by sitting or kneeling or sheltering behind a corner in the cliff face. You then cast with a short line into the white water at your feet in the neck of the pool, hoping that a fish would appear on one side or other of the torrent, and seize the fly. You manoeuvred your fly this way and that, as you thought best, and continued casting from the same vantage point, lengthening

gradually your line to the furthest possible extent. The tail of the pool was fished from a different stance lower down and on the bank, and you could often see the fish lying there as you cast over them. The whole process was full of interest and excitement, and strongly reminiscent of Iceland where there are so many similar small falls pools. But oh! for the free taking Icelandic fish!

As salmon can ascend the falls with no great difficulty, many do so to find a resting place in the remote upper river where they are left more or less in peace. There is but one lodge in this area. Quite good fishing however is to be found in the Einig, in the half mile between its falls and the Junction pool, where it enters the main Oykel and considerably augments its downstream flow; so this tributary is of all round value in providing both good fishing and extensive spawning grounds.

From the Falls Pool downstream is the best of the Oykel fishing, as far as Inveroykel. This section of the river known as the Lower Oykel is divided into 4 beats fished by up to 12 rods, with beats changed daily in rotation. The fishing is by fly only, and the river is most attractive, being of medium small size with an excellent variety of pleasant streamy pools. The lower Oykel is par excellence a spring river, with a fair run of fish averaging 9 lb from the middle of March onwards and with odd ones coming in earlier. There are no really big fish, $29\frac{1}{2}$ lbs being the record weight for this river, and not more than three or four 20 pounders are caught each year. April is invariably the best month of the season, though the last week of March can be good in an early year, and the first two weeks of May in a late one, given a reasonable height of water. After that the run seems to dwindle until July when, if there is rain and a rise in water, the grilse fishing can be excellent as long as the water lasts.

Both August and September can also produce a reasonable number of fish, given a fair amount of rain. At times during these months fishing can be first class, though at others it will be at a standstill. It all depends on the rainfall. By the last week of August fish are becoming coloured, and in September it is rare to get a fresh one.

It is frequently said by those who know the Oykel well that this river no longer holds its water level nearly as well as it used to. This may well be the case, as apparently there have been large scale drainage operations for the benefit chiefly of forestry in the upper reaches. The result is the usual one, the river rises more quickly after rain, and then drops away more quickly as soon as the rain ceases. To some extent such a rise and fall must always have been a characteristic of the Oykel, even if it has become more marked nowadays. And unlike the Helmsdale or Naver, the Oykel has no sizeable loch upon its course (only the insignificant Loch Ailsh), to help maintain its flow.

So anyone who fishes the Oykel in the latter part of the season must pray for rain. He may often get it and perhaps have an exceptional day's sport, but if he doesn't he may have to be content with casting practice or watching the birds! Up to the middle of May at any rate the water should remain at a reasonable height, unless the winter has been snowless or the Spring unusually dry.

The Oykel is a 'fly only' river, as has already been said, and the necessary tackle is what one would expect i.e. heavy fly tackle in spring up to mid-April or early May (according to water temperature), but light tackle after that. A 14 foot rod should be long enough, down to a 12 foot in summer conditions.

If anyone disputes the advisability of a rod as long as 14 ft or even 15 ft in small rivers such as the Oykel during the spring, he should remember that during this part of the season one often has to compete with fierce gales from the east or north east, which are absent later in the year. A shorter rod is of little use for this.

As to waders, in high or medium water long trouser waders are necessary in some places, and it is as well to have them. In low water however thigh waders are adequate everywhere.

The average annual rod catch for the Lower Oykel during the 14 years 1962–1975 amounted to 688 salmon and grilse. During the last 5 years this catch has increased but it must be remembered that there are 48 named pools, fished by 12 rods whenever the water is in good order during the 8 month season. They are supported by an excellent team of 4 ghillies.

The upper Oykel, above the falls at Oykel Bridge, is fished by an additional 8 rods; it produces a further substantial number of fish, although no ghillie is provided on it; and it is considerably smaller than the lower Oykel, lacking the influx of the Einig. Also, as mentioned above, it seldom holds a fair stock of fish before July. There are 59 named pools on the upper Oykel, though the river in its uppermost reaches becomes very small. The total catch seems a high one for a smallish river, but there are excellent and extensive spawning beds which do much to maintain the stock; also it must be remembered that the lower river is fished consistently during an eight month season, whenever there is water enough.

Netting in the Oykel is carried out in the tidal reaches near Bonar Bridge. The net catch is considerable, particularly in a low water year; but the majority of the netting rights are owned by one of the proprietors who has a considerable interest in the rod fishings. These nettings are exercised responsibly and many fewer nets are operated than was the case before the war. In fact several additional stations were purchased in the late 60's and these are not now used. It is also worth mentioning that there is a voluntary agreement which has been in force since 1948 to restrict the opening date for the net fishings to the 15th April. This does let the first of the spring fish into the river and, one hopes, allows a greater proportion of the spring fish to spawn than of the later summer runs.

The Oykel is a very delightful small east coast river. Those who fish it during the good periods of the season are indeed fortunate.

Stone Pool, low water.

The Ness

The fisherman needs plenty of backing on his reel in this wide river.

The Ness is a river of different character from all others in the neighbourhood. Its total length between Loch Ness at Dochfour and the tidal water at Inverness is only 6 miles, with a fall of 52 feet. It is a large river with a total catchment area of 700 square miles, and tends in most places to be wide and shallow, wider than the Spey for instance but with a current much less fierce, and its bed is shallower and more gravelly. The Ness is the lowest link in a river system which, in addition to Loch Ness, comprises the Moriston, the Oich and Loch Oich, the Garry and Loch Garry and headwaters. In this setting the Ness is comparable to the Lochy and the Awe, both of which are short but sizeable rivers, running out of large lochs, with headwaters such as the Arkaig, Spean, Roy, and Orchy, and secondary lochs higher upstream.

There are only three main beats on the Ness, apart from the Association water at Inverness which is partly tidal. The top one is Dochfour, about $2\frac{1}{2}$ miles long, and reputed the best on the river. There is a weir at its head where the river leaves Loch Dochfour, an appendage of Loch Ness, but there is a substantial gap in this weir which provides an easy upstream passage for fish. The next beat is Ness Castle, about one mile long with a broken down weir above its bottom pool, and the third is Ness-side, about three quarters of a mile long. All these three beats have the fishing on both banks. There is in fact a further short stretch of private water, between Ness-side and the Association Water, known as Holm Mills—but it only extends for a few hundred yards and is of minor account. Below this lies the Association Water of about $1\frac{1}{2}$ miles length, extending right into the burgh of Inverness, as far as the estuary into the Beauly Firth.

Fresh fish enter the Ness very early, as they are to be found in Loch Ness at the opening of the fishing season on January 15th. But in the spring they seldom stop in the Ness itself. A limited number of spring fish are killed on the Dochfour beat below the weir at the exit of the river from Loch Dochfour, but nowhere else on the river holds these fish. The great majority push on into Loch Ness and up the Moriston, or else up the Oich into Loch Oich, and up the Garry. In fact there is no spring fishing of any account in the Ness, and it is not till near the end of June that fish begin to stop in this river in any appreciable number. The best fishing period is normally between the second week of July and the second week of August. During this time fish are all fresh run, and average around 10–12 lb in weight. A certain number of them arrive after every tide, as there is no netting at the mouth.

Anyone who has watched netting operations in any river estuary will have noticed how the main runs of fish into the river occur soon after the high tide begins to ebb, when the fish near the mouth start to feel the draw of the river current. The Ness fish are apt to appear within an hour or two after high tide in any part of the river, as it takes them little time to travel the short distance involved. In fact there is a danger in any high water year of the majority of the summer fish travelling too quickly through into Loch Ness, in the same fashion as the spring fish. There are no obstructions worth mentioning to the passage of fish, and if they want to they can pass through the Ness in a matter of hours. Summer salmon and grilse however are usually inclined to stay in the river at least for several days and sometimes for much longer, which gives the Ness fishermen a fair chance to get at them. A further side-effect of the short distance from the sea is that fresh fish in the Ness are always untired and full of vigour when hooked. They have had no laborious journey upstream for thirty or forty miles, with numerous rapids to surmount en route, as have their cousins in rivers such as the upper Findhorn or Spey. The result is that their play is noticeably fast, hard, and far running; and the Ness fisherman needs plenty of backing on his reel in this wide and streamy river. It is unwise to use monofilament of less than 12 lb breaking strain for the fly cast. You will get broken before long if you do, and if you treat this as abnormal and persist in using such fine nylon you will get broken again. The author can vouch for this from bitter personal experience. A rod of 14 feet should be adequate to cover the water properly, or perhaps a light 15 foot or even 16 foot if you care to use one. It is an advantage in most places to throw a long line, if only for the reason that by doing so one covers more fish, and more fish too that have not already been covered by others who do not cast so far. This was one of the main arguments of Alexander Grant, the famous Ness fisherman of the early 1900s, in favour of a really long line. There must be a good deal in it. He invented the 'Grant Vibration' rods, and is recorded as having switch cast the amazing distance of 65 yards, without shooting any line, at a casting tournament in 1895.

The fishing season on the Ness continues until October 15th. September can be quite a good month in some years, still with a fair number of fresh fish coming in, though by the second half of it and during October the majority of fish are becoming red. It is surprising that more really big fish are not on record from a river system as large as that of the Ness and its feeders. Fish up to 30 lb have been common enough, but over that weight they are rare. I have not been able to discover any Ness 40 pounders, and the biggest I have read of weighed $37\frac{1}{2}$ lb. This is in striking contrast to many other sizeable Scottish rivers, such as the Lochy, Spey, Dee, Findhorn, Deveron, Awe, Tay, and Tweed amongst others; all of these have produced 40 pounders in numbers, and some of them 50 or even 60 pounders. There is no apparent reason for the lack of such big fish in the Ness. It is curious. The great majority of Ness salmon are in fact small or medium sized fish of between 8 and 16 lb but the 30 pounders and over are few and far between. There are also grilse and sea-trout, though in no vast number.

Thanks to the kindness of my friends Major J. Godman and Mr. W. J. Campbell of Ness-side, also of Mr. C. Shankland, I have fished the Ness-side beat and the Ness Castle beat on several occasions (though never, to my regret, the Dochfour beat). Both Ness-side and Ness Castle provide lovely fishing on attractive water, with a fair stream and fairly shallow pools, excellent for fly fishing though bait is allowed at times for those who want to use it. Most pools have a shallow and gravelly beach at their edge, so that those who like to land their fish by beaching them have usually little difficulty in doing so. This method of bringing fish ashore is particularly useful in the case of grilse (or for that matter of fish of any size).

The Black Stream and the Ladies Pool are the two best catches on Ness Castle, and the Green Shelter, the Gauge, and the Holm Pool on Ness-side, though this latter beat fishes pretty well continuously throughout its length. Boats are sometimes used for fishing on the Ness, particularly at Dochfour and Ness Castle, but as a whole wading is best, long trouser waders being essential, and the river bottom is normally not rough, nor is the current unduly strong. One needs to throw a long line in most places, the longer the better, and a 14 or 15 foot rod, whether of split cane, fibre glass, or carbon graphite is none too short. It is seldom if ever necessary to use large flies; any size between 5 and 8, according to river conditions, is appropriate. Only towards the end of the season may a bigger size be wanted. All the best fishing in the Ness can basically be classed as 'summer' fishing, and is all the pleasanter for that.

Barbara Burnett-Stuart fishing a Blue Charm on the Holm Pool on the Ness-side beat, two miles from Inverness.

The Ness water is always clear, coming as it does from a 24 mile long loch which acts as a thoroughly efficient filter; and it is not naturally subject to violent fluctuations in height. But unfortunately this river has recently been hydro-ed. How little or how much harm this will do to the fishing has still to be seen, and the Hydro personnel are cooperative. But the working of the Hydro does appear to cause unpredictable variations in water height; and even if such variations are mostly minor ones, they must tend to keep fish moving on upstream. This in turn can do little good to the Ness fishing, with the course of the river so short. Another drawback is that after a long dry period, with a rise in the river urgently wanted, when the longed-for rain eventually does come the Hydro is apt to pen all the increased flow of water back in Loch Ness until a satisfactory head of water for its purposes has been accumulated. So the Ness may get little or no rise in water level at such a time, when other neighbouring rivers are in full spate.

The biggest fish I have myself been lucky enough to catch on the Ness weighed 25 lb. This was on August 19th 1978, from the Black Stream at Ness Castle. I was wading at the neck of the pool from the right bank, and using a Stoat's Tail with a floating line and a 12 lb breaking strain leader. I saw the fish rise at the fly, it just broke the surface as it took, but I had no idea at first that it was such a good one. It turned out to be a beautifully shaped fish covered with sea lice, and the water being low at the time it ran all over the pool when hooked, jumping as it went and getting in the way of everyone else fishing there at that moment, so I was not popular, but I could not hold it on light fly tackle. Eventually it came ashore alright, and I beached it— not that this was in any way an outstanding fish for the Ness, but it happens to be the biggest I have seen caught in this river. No doubt the reader can well imagine how surprised and pleased I was at this unexpected gift of the Goddess Fortune.

The normal annual catch for the whole Ness in present times varies between 600 fish in a poor year to 1100 in a good one.

Plenty of fish are caught in Loch Ness by trolling, also in the Moriston, Oich, Loch Oich, and the Garry. This latter river until twenty five years ago was reputed to be one of the best spring rivers in Scotland, but since then it has suffered the fate of being hydro-ed and denuded of its natural flow of water. Thus another fine river has, sad to say, been lost for good fishing. The Moriston has also been hydro-ed, though with less drastic effects.

The Findhorn

A pretty river. There is lovely wild scenery all around.

Further east along the Moray Firth is the Findhorn, which rises in the forest of Coignafearn in the Monadliath mountains, at a height of 2800 feet above sea level. This river has then a north-easterly course of some 65 miles, past Tomatin, Drynachan, Glenferness, Relugas, and Darnaway, to enter the sea at Findhorn Bay, near Forres, half way between Nairn and Lossiemouth. It is a medium sized river and has a very pretty course indeed, through hilly and heathery country, draining some 346 square miles. To my regret I have myself had no great amount of fishing on it, only odd days or weeks owing to the kindness of Major Colin Mackenzie of Farr, Lord Cawdor, and Sir William Gordon-Cumming. So I do not feel qualified to write at any length about it, though at the same time I cannot fail to make mention of such a beautiful and famous river.

In its upper reaches the Findhorn is a typical highland stream, fast running, with rapids and pools quickly alternating, and with fairly open banks and heather covered slopes on either side. There is lovely wild scenery all round, and some of the best grouse moors in Scotland lie in this neighbourhood (though at present excess of tick has unfortunately put them under a cloud). There are no main roads or railways anywhere near, except where the Perth-Inverness main road and railway line cross the river at Tomatin.

About 30 miles from its mouth the river is spanned by the handsome Dulsie Bridge with a single arch, coupled with a smaller arch on the north bank. It originally carried the military road from the south to Fort George. Near the bridge the Findhorn enters a spectacular gorge, narrow and steep, with thick woodlands on either side. The cliffs on both banks rise in places to 150 feet or more, and one looks down on the deep black pools of the river below, as it winds through this defile, sometimes only a few feet in width. At Randolph's Leap near Relugas the gorge narrows to a width of only 10 feet. This outstanding feature of the Findhorn continues for nearly 16 miles to a point near Darnaway, where the banks open out again and the river pursues a normal course as far as its entry into tidal water at Findhorn Bay. This latter is a kind of sea-loch, $2\frac{1}{2}$ miles long by 2 miles wide at high tide, with a narrow outlet at its northern end into the Moray Firth. In the gorge there are numerous small falls, all of which are easily passable for salmon with the one exception of the main fall near Relugas between Glenferness and Darnaway, which fish seldom ascend before early April (depending on the water temperature). Most of the pools in the gorge are very deep, as can be imagined, and fishing them demands a somewhat goat-like activity on the part of the angler, with a good deal of rock climbing. Sudden spates on this river are not frequent, as the rainfall in this part of the Highlands is not as a rule heavy, but when they do arrive such spates are apt to be sensational, with the water confined as it is in the narrow gut of the gorge. To quote St. John in the *Wild Sports of the Highlands* on 'The Findhorn in Spate':

> Calm and peaceful as it looks when at the ordinary height, the angler, on a bright summer's evening, is sometimes startled by a sound like the rushing of a coming wind, yet wind there is none and he continues his sport. Presently he is surprised to see the water near which he has been standing suddenly sweep against his feet, he looks up the stream and sees the river coming down in a perpendicular wall of water, or like a wave of the sea, with a roaring noise, and carrying with it trees with their branches and roots entire, large lumps of broken bank, and every kind of mountain debris. Some mountain storm of rain has suddenly filled its bed. Sometimes on the occasion of these rapid spates I have had to gather up my tackle and run for my life, which was in no small risk until I gained some bank or rock above the height of the flood. When this rush of water comes down between the rocks where the river has not room to spread, the danger is doubly great owing to the irresistible force acquired by the pent-up water. The flood, when occasioned by a summer storm, soon subsides, and the next day no trace is left of it excepting the dark coffee-coloured hue of the water.

So much for St. John on Findhorn spates, and Sir T. Dick Lauder in his book on the Great Moray Floods of August 1829 describes the Findhorn on that occasion as rising to no less than 50 feet in places above its normal level. This was in the narrow confines of the gorge.

A humorous touch in connection with the 1829 flood is given by George Bain in his detailed book *The River Findhorn* (1911) who records that that 'the Relugas gardener actually captured with his umbrella a fine salmon at an elevation of 50 feet above the normal level of the Findhorn. A stone marks the highest point reached by the flood.' A fishing record in more ways than one, one would guess!

As to the quality of its water, the Findhorn is normally clear enough, with the river level steady for any length of time, and there is virtually no pollution. When the water rises after rain, however, and in time of spate, a lot of peat comes down as is only to be expected from the heathery and peat-covered surrounding hills, and the river is apt to run brown for several days. Low water spates are always slower to clear than high water ones, which is as noticeable on this river as on most others. Presumably high water brings greater dilution, and quicker clearance owing to its faster flow.

The Findhorn is a prolific river and has good runs of fish. The spring run between February and May is the main one, mid-April to mid-May being the best fishing period on the lower and middle reaches, and late May or June on the upper reaches.

Grilse and sea-trout arrive in numbers from June onwards, the latter seldom permeating as far as the upper river. There is no autumn run of salmon worth mentioning—just an odd fresh fish in the lower river during September. By mid-July most of the fish in the middle and upper reaches are beginning to be coloured, and by August and September as might be expected they are pretty far gone. There is a good deal of net fishing in the Findhorn Bay area, and the netting season lasts from February 11th to August 26th.

Most of the Findhorn provides first class rod fishing, for fly from April onwards and for bait earlier. Fishing can be difficult in the deep and swirly pools of the gorge, and accurate casting is necessary. The neck and tail of the gorge pools are usually the best taking places. Playing a fish in the gorge can be awkward, as the fisherman may not be able to move more than a few yards up or downstream and thus will be compelled to play and land his fish in a narrowly constricted area. If he cannot keep it there he may say goodbye.

Of the various beats there is little doubt that Darnaway, belonging to the Earl of Moray, is the best; but fishing is also good at Relugas, Logie, and Glenferness, also on Lord Cawdor's water higher upstream. Spring fish average 10–11 lb in size, but there are occasional big ones. An enormous cock fish of 42 lb was caught in July 1962 by Mrs. Anne Wise. This fish was taken from the White Stream on Lord Leven and Melville's lovely Glenferness water near the head of the gorge. It took a small single-hooked fly on a 9 lb B.S. cast, and was played for a long time on a light rod before being gaffed by the keeper Alick Robb. This fish was red, and would no doubt have weighed over 50 lb if it had been fresh run and in better condition. But what a notable capture, all the same! One can well imagine the shock which Mrs. Wise must have experienced on finding herself attached on light tackle to a monster like this, instead of to the grilse or nine pound salmon normally to be expected in July.

There are many good salmon pools on the Findhorn, the best known and most prolific is Sluie near the top of the Darnaway water, about 10 miles up from the sea. This fine pool normally holds fish in numbers, and has a great and well deserved reputation.

As to appropriate tackle, in spring a rod of 14 feet should be adequate or even a light 15 footer on windy days. In summer 13 feet or even 12 feet should be enough, if a shorter length is preferred. All the usual flies work well, with hair wings for choice here as elsewhere, from 3 inches long in the cold water of early spring to size 9 in low water summer.

When wading, in the lowest part of the river below the gorge it is best to have long trouser waders in the higher water of spring, though later on as the water level drops, thigh waders become adequate. In the gorge itself, wherever one can get down to the river, thigh waders are long enough, as it is hardly ever possible, or necessary, to wade to any depth, if at all. In the upper river above the gorge long trouser waders will only be wanted in time of high water or in certain particular pools where deep wading may be necessary. At other times and places, thigh waders will be enough.

To digress from fishing for a moment, it may be of interest to anglers on the Findhorn to know that there is a story of the last wolf in Scotland being killed nearby its banks in 1743. This feat was achieved by a great hunter called MacQueen of Pall-a-chrocain in the 'Tarnaway Forest of Morayland.' The story is told in the *Lays of the Deer Forest* by Messrs. Stuart.

One winter's day MacQueen received a message from the Laird of Mackintosh that a large 'black beast' supposed to be a wolf had appeared in the glens and the day before killed two children who with their mother were crossing the hills from Calder; in consequence of which a 'Tainchel,' or gathering to drive the country, was called to meet at a tryst above Fi-Giuthas, where MacQueen was invited to attend with his dogs. Pall-a-chrocain informed himself of the place where the children had been killed, the last tracks of the wolf, and the conjectures of his haunts, and promised his assistance.

In the morning the 'Tainchel' had long assembled, and Mackintosh waited with impatience, but MacQueen did not arrive; his dogs and himself were, however, auxiliaries too important to be left behind, and they continued to wait until the best of a hunter's morning was gone, when at last he appeared and Mackintosh received him with an irritable expression of disappointment.

'What was the hurry?' said Pall-a-chrocain.

Mackintosh gave an indignant retort, and all present made some impatient reply.

MacQueen lifted his plaid, and drew back the bloody head of the wolf from under his arm.

'There it is for you!' said he, and tossed it on the grass in the midst of the surprised circle.

Mackintosh expressed great joy and admiration, and gave him the land called Sean-achan for meat to his dogs'.

The Spey

The Big Pouch at Knockando. A good spey caster performing. The line is in the air on the forward throw, but the fly has not yet left the water.

The Spey is perhaps the most magnificent of Scottish rivers. It is not the largest, yielding place to both the Tay and the Tweed in this respect, but it is certainly the strongest and fastest, as anyone who has seen it in high spate will confirm. It flows through a wonderful countryside of unforgettable surroundings, and provides fishing for both salmon and sea-trout which is second to none.

From the fishing point of view there is little to choose between any part of the Spey from Ballindalloch downstream, (provided one is on one's chosen beat at the right time in the season.) Above that the fishing is not now so good as formerly. It has been estimated that about one fish in three ascends the Avon, (a main tributary which enters the Spey at Ballindalloch), instead of continuing further up the main river, so that the upper Spey loses a fair number of fish in this way. But all the Spey beats from Castle Grant down produce good catches, the lowest part of the river from Craigellachie downstream being without doubt the most productive. The question of appropriate time of year comes greatly into it. In the lowest reaches, Orton and the Brae water, February, March and early April are the best spring months. July, August, and sometimes September are the best summer months, while May and June are comparatively poor. From Delfur to Ballindalloch mid-April to the end of May is best in spring, and mid-July to mid-August in summer; while higher upstream mid-April to mid-June is best. Needless to say these dates are not hard and fast, owing to variations in climate every year, as any fisherman will understand, but they represent a fair average assessment. It will be noticed that they take into account only the bottom 50 miles of the Spey's 100 mile course, i.e. that part of the river below Grantown. It is this section which produces by far the best fishing, as higher upstream the fall in the river is much less steep, and there are few places where salmon congregate in any number. Around Boat of Garten is perhaps the best area in the upper river.

The Spey is snow-fed to a much greater extent than any other Scottish river, apart from the Dee. In the deep corries of the Cairngorms, let alone on the high upland slopes of these hills, frozen snow will sometimes last as late as June, and keep the Spey running at a fair height all through the spring, irrespective of whether or not there is rain. This can be a significant help towards getting a good stock of fish into the river, past the nets which operate near the mouth, below Fochabers.

I first fished the Spey in May and June 1948 on the Rothes beat, since when I have fished it every season at various different times and on every beat between Tulchan and the Brae water. Two things immediately strike one about this river, so it seems to me, the first being the sheer size and strength of its flow, and the second the speed

Colonel Pardoe boat fishing at Craig Neish.

with which the spring fish run through – here today and gone, not tomorrow, but sometimes within a matter literally of minutes—but more of this later.

It must be admitted that at first sight the Spey seems vast, up to one hundred yards wide in places from bank to bank in the lower river, and its strong current only serves to enhance its size. With further acquaintance however one finds that from a fishing point of view this great width of the river is of less significance than might at first be supposed. In medium and low water one can often wade up to half way across, in order to cover fish that are lying well over—or else they may be lying within a fairly short distance of one's own bank, in which case they may be covered by wading only a little distance, or even by fishing off the bank itself. If the pool has a strong central current, resting fish are most likely to lie on either side of the stream, rather than in the middle of it, and they can be covered from either side. In high water they are apt to approach closer and closer to either bank, provided the depth of water is adequate for them, to seek shelter from the main central rush; and they can easily be covered by bank fishing from one side or the other. The upshot of all this is that the Spey pools seldom hold fish all across their entire width. The lie is usually on one side or the other, or else near a comparatively narrow channel in the middle. Thus the impressive width of the river, so striking in the first place, from a fishing point of view can, to a considerable extent, be discounted.

The speed of the current is another matter. In low water it is strong, and in high spate little short of torrential, and much has been said and written about it. The Spey drops approximately 600 feet in its bottom 50 miles between Grantown and Spey Bay, an average of 12 feet per mile. Other rivers, the Dee and the Ness amongst others, have a similar rate of fall over part or all of their length, why is it then that the Spey current is so much stronger? I must confess that I do not know the answer to this, and must leave it to the hydrologists; but stronger it is without doubt, particularly in spate, as anyone who knows it well will confirm. It has been said that the Spey is the only river in Scotland which can be compared to a Norwegian river for speed of flow, a not unfair parallel. The other Scottish river which used so to be described was the Awe, before it was hydro-ed and its flow attenuated.

Big spates on the Spey can be very formidable, taking a sizeable toll in the way of drowned sheep and cattle, also of fishing huts, rod boxes, and boats washed away, and of banks eroded and pools 'gravelled.' The biggest spate of all was in 1829, when according to the book *The Great Moray Floods*, written by Sir T. Dick Lauder, $4\frac{1}{2}$ inches of rain fell in one night during early August over most of the Spey catchment area. The entire river valley below Aviemore was inundated, the water rising to over 25 feet above its normal level. In the burgh of Rothes, for example, the water poured through the streets, rising to the level of the first floor windows, and fifteen well-built houses were demolished. At Fochabers sight-seers on the bridge (before it collapsed) looking southwards perceived a vast undulating expanse of water, two miles broad in some places, stretching for twelve miles to the foot of Ben Aigan. Floating wreckage and drowned animals of all sorts were tossed on its surface. Every bridge across the

Spey was washed away, with the one exception of the bridge at Craigellachie, which still stands to this day and spans the whole width of the river with a single arch.

An amusing story of this flood of 1829 concerns the loss of a valuable violin, a Stradivarius or its equivalent, owned by a widow lady at the Mill of Tommore, near Ballindalloch, on the lower reaches of the Avon. This treasured instrument to the distress of its owner was somehow allowed to fall victim to the rising torrent, and was carried away on the crest of its wave towards the downrush of the prodigiously swollen Spey. A finally 'lost chord' one might have thought; but not at all—to the delight of its owner this violin was found intact some days later when the flood had subsided, washed up on the haughs of Dandaleith some fifteen miles downriver. History does not relate if its timbre was improved!

This great flood of 1829 is still a topic of interest on Speyside accompanied by stories of the vast damage caused in the way of multitudes of livestock drowned and widespread acres of agricultural land covered with gravel. Many of the small tributary burns were said to be swollen so high as to resemble the main Spey itself when at a normal height; this feature more than any other perhaps gives those who know the neighbourhood the most vivid impression of the disaster.

When fishing the Spey, as pointed out above, one often has to wade deep in a strong stream. This is an absolute essential in fishing a river of this type. One usually needs to throw a long line, the longer the better in most places, so here is where a long rod is wanted. 12 and 13 footers are of little use in this river, except in very low water summer conditions—14 feet is a better length, though none too long, and 15, 16 and 17 feet are what one needs in spring time. There is now little or no objection to rods of this length on the grounds of weight owing to the lightness of fibre glass and carbon graphite as rod material. It should never be forgotten that in spring one frequently has to fish against strong upstream gales blowing hard from the north and east, or from other directions, and short rods are quite useless for this purpose, as one would soon discover.

It is true that a long line is not invariably necessary. Sometimes the

Major David Rasch using a double Spey cast in a strong downstream wind.

neck of a pool can be covered with little more than a rod's length of line, and in high water fish can often be found close under the bank. But generally speaking, in big rivers such as the Spey, Tay, or Tweed a long line is an unmixed advantage, provided it is thrown clean and straight. 30 yards is none too long in many places, and 35 yards is often better. I would never attempt to throw such a line with the overhead cast, by the way—as I know my back cast would be much too clumsy, and my fly would be sure to get caught up in some obstruction, or to hit stones behind, or the bank. The Spey cast is infinitely more effective for such a purpose, and involves far less effort. I would use nothing else. It may take years to learn how to perform this cast really well, but once the ability is acquired the rewards are great. To cast such a length of line in a small river is totally unnecessary, and even in a medium sized one such as the Dee it is seldom wanted, but in a big river like the Tay, Spey, Tweed, or Ness it can make all the difference. It gives one the feel of really being able to 'command' the water, for want of a better term, instead of being impotent to cope with its great extent. In this connection, both as regards casting and length of line and rod, I feel I cannot do better than refer the reader to 'Jock Scott's' excellent book *Fine and Far Off*, also to the same author's *Salmon and Trout Fishing Up to Date*, (chapter twelve), where the whole matter is so succinctly discussed.

It is essential to be ambidextrous and to be able to Spey cast over the left shoulder as well as the right, in accordance with which bank of the river one is fishing from. Also one must be able to do the Double Spey, for use in a strong downstream wind. Many fishers find this latter cast easier than the Single Spey. Both these casts are better learnt right at the start of one's fishing career when one is still young.

Another consideration following from the large size of the Spey is that one needs plenty of strong backing always in readiness on one's reel. Those who normally fish in small rivers may only see their backing called into play at rare intervals, perhaps once in a year. If they fish the Spey, however, or any other big river, they will quickly find things taking a different turn. Any sizeable fish when hooked will run them on to their backing as often as not, and they would be well advised to make sure that it is long enough (120 yards is none too much), besides being strong (about 18 lb. breaking strain minimum), and ready to run freely off the reel. A quiet word of additional advice—this precaution should be taken *before* starting to fish, and not after some dreadful disaster has brought it, too late, into mind! The fisherman should not need to be reminded that when one wants one's backing, one's need is apt to be both sudden and overwhelming. There is no time then to see about snarls or over-riding or weak places. And care should be taken to ensure that the backing is firmly spliced to the thicker dressed line. I have seen a whole dressed line carried away by a Spey fish, because the owner had omitted to test this join before starting to fish—an infuriating thing to happen. He recovered the line next day but not the fish.

There is no river more than the Spey, with its width and strong current, where one is as more likely to be 'drowned' by a hooked fish, particularly by a big one. 'Creichie' on the Rothes beat was a terrible pool for this, if any of my readers know it. If one came out on the bank as soon as a fish was hooked, as one so often reads in books is the right procedure, one was almost certain to get badly drowned and probably broken. The best plan was to stay well out in the river in the early stages of the fight, and by holding the rod high make every effort to keep the line well clear of the central current if the fish ran upstream on the Aikenway side, as he nearly always did. By doing this and by wading upstream one could usually, though not always, avoid being 'drowned'. Only after the fish was half played out could one safely come out on to the bank. A different method, if there is a high bank behind one, is to climb straight to the top of it when a fish is hooked, and play him from a high vantage point. This too is usually successful in preventing one's line being drowned.

Another very noticeable feature of the Spey, not always appreciated, is the speed with which its spring fish are apt to run through. Up to the middle of June fresh fish are continually passing through all parts of the lower Spey below Grantown, day after day, and they seldom stop anywhere for any length of time. Certain good holding pools, such as Cairnty at Orton, Two Stones and Holly Bush at Delfur, Back of the Bog at Arndilly, the Boat Pool and Dailuaine at Wester Elchies, Dalmunich at Laggan, the March Pool at Tulchan/ Ballindalloch, and Polwick at Castle Grant amongst others, may hold them for a short time, until the next rise in water, of which there are many caused by melting snow on the Cairngorms, carries them on again. One continually hears it queried where all the running fish get to; it might be expected that beats higher up the river would be packed full of them; but in fact this does not happen. There is unlimited room for dispersal in the upper reaches, and while it is common knowledge that fish caught near Grantown, 50 miles up-river, often carry sea-lice, it may come as a surprise to readers to learn that sea-lice fish are also caught at Boat of Garten higher up still, and that fresh ones can be caught in Loch Insh near Kingussie as early as March. They also as a rule reach the Avon and the Feshie in April. Undoubtedly they have free access to a vast amount of potential holding water. Perhaps in some ways this is a drawback from the fishing point of view, as it makes necessary the presence of a huge number of fish if the whole river is to be stocked satisfactorily.

Nowadays in spring this seldom seems to happen, as spring fish, sad to say, have fallen away greatly in numbers over the past sixteen or so years. One can only count on finding them in the best holding pools, and then not always, while the more indifferent pools often go bare. This constant and rapid passage of early fish in the Spey has a decided effect on the appropriate method of spring fishing. On this river more than any other it does pay to persevere. Fish may arrive at any time. A pool may be empty at one moment, and at the next be full of jumping fish, while a further ten minutes may see all quiet again, with the shoal moved on. A fisherman on the spot at the right moment may quickly take a couple of fish from those which pause for a minute in their passage, and perhaps fish blank for the rest of the day. To the inexperienced it may seem as though for a short time and for some unaccountable reason the fish in the pool all 'woke up', and thus some of them took. This is usually a mistaken view. The truth is that a shoal is apt to arrive at one moment and be gone the next, or so it is in nine cases out of ten.

During July and August, however, more and more salmon become stationary in pools everywhere on the lower river, right down to Fochabers, and many remain to spawn there, either in the main river or its many tributaries. Far more fish remain to spawn in the lower reaches of the Spey than do in the lower Dee or Tweed for example, or in most other rivers. Such fish are virtually all summer-run. There is also a prolific grilse run from late June onwards, July being the best month for these fish, some of which penetrate far upstream both in the Spey and Avon. Sea-trout also arrive in huge numbers; but, unless there are some summer spates to help them in, the majority of these are apt to fall victim to the nets.

The Spey is all good fly water, though in the early part of the season most fishermen prefer to use bait. Wooden or plastic devons are probably the most popular lure, and it is easier to kill fish with these rather than on fly when the water is cold, and less hard work. But from late April onwards there is really little excuse for bait fishing, as fish can always be caught on fly, if they will take at all.

Wading the Spey is something of a problem. This is no river for disabled or inexperienced waders; they will almost certainly come to grief, and be lucky if they experience no worse than a ducking. Some of the pools are notoriously bad wading; the four worst which I know are the Rhynd at Wester Elchies, the neck of the Back of the Bog at Easter Elchies, the Long Pool at Rothes and Craig Steel at Knockando. These are all very rough going with large underwater boulders jumbled haphazard in a strongish stream; the Rhynd has been described as a series of submerged cathedral spires! Long trouser waders are absolutely essential, unless the water is high enough to allow bank fishing; and a wading staff is a great help, unless you are young and agile enough to dispense with one. You will often have to wade deep into a strong stream, if you are to cover your fish properly; and it is completely necessary for you to be prepared to do this if you are to make the most of the fishing. Admittedly you can probably resort to boat fishing, if there is a boat available together with a boatman, or if you are a good enough waterman you can run the boat single-handed yourself with a long rope and anchor. But some beats do not use boats, and many pools are not provided with them, so you should be qualified to wade when and where necessary. Curiously

The late Colonel J. P. Moreton fishing down the Long Pool at Rothes single-handed from an anchored boat.

Colour plate of OLD SPEY FLIES opposite: the names of the flies shown are as follows—*Top row* Purple King and Elchies Fancy, *Middle* Gold Speal, *Bottom row* Silver Riach and Gold Riach.

PLATE 2

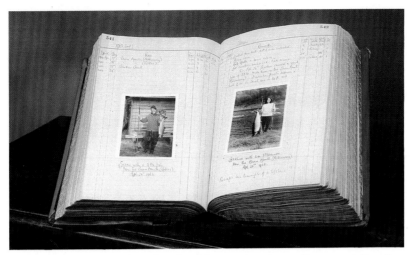

The author's fishing diary showing his two daughters, Susan and Caroline, with fish caught on the Spey in April 1963. (See page 133).

OLD SPEY FLIES

Some examples of traditional Spey flies, which are all described in Knox's *Autumns on the Spey*, published in 1872. The Purple King, or "Purpie" shown top left, was a particular favourite amongst Spey anglers of the past, and without doubt these actual flies shown here (life size) are very old.

The dressings are sombre ones, the hackles and wing feathers being all obtainable locally, (mallard, teal, and Spey cock). The method of tying is peculiar, the body hackle being wound in the opposite direction to the ribbing tinsel over the berlin wool. The wing is short, and the Spey cock hackles deliberately left long, closely resembling the whiskers of a prawn or shrimp. But for their gut eyes, doubtless now rotten, one would use them with confidence today.

PLATE 3

The Big Pouch, at Knockando, on the middle Spey.

The Trees Pool on the Aboyne Castle water, river Dee. A water colour by Julian Ashley-Cooper.

enough most wading mishaps occur not in the really difficult places, because everyone is warned about these and takes great trouble when wading them, but in much more harmless looking stretches. A fast stream, slightly more than knee-deep, gradually descending over a loose gravelly bottom into a deep downstream hole is one of the worst traps. Wading in such a place looks easy, but fall over and you will have great difficulty in getting up again owing to the strong current. The best answer is to kneel on the bottom and to get up slowly. If you wade too near the edge of the deep, the soft gravel may give way under your feet, and you will be under-weigh for a ducking before you can look round.

If, however, you have the confidence derived from experience and the ability to swim, and if you keep your head and do nothing in too much of a hurry, there is no reason why anything should go seriously wrong for you, even when wading a formidable river like the Spey. I remember once wading down a gravel spit on a well known Spey beat, with deep water both towards the bank and towards mid-river. When I had reached waist depth I reckoned the time had come to wade back upstream to where I had started and so to the bank. Could I do this? Not a hope . . . the current was too strong, and with every step that I attempted to take upstream the soft gravel under my feet gave way and I made less than no progress. What was to be done? There was no one else anywhere near who could help. I saw no reason to swim as long as my feet were still on the bottom, and I was pretty sure I could wade right through to where the water eventually became shallower some thirty yards downstream. So I carried on, first to waist deep, then shoulder deep, and finally neck deep. But then the depth slowly receded, and I once more regained shallows and then the bank. So apart from my being drenched no harm was done, in fact a lot of ribald amusement was caused amongst my friends and companions. But I treated that spit with considerably more respect in the future.

As to boat fishing, already mentioned above, there are certain pools where the use of a boat is a decided advantage in order to cover the water properly. This applies particularly to the bigger pools of the lower Spey. Sometimes the lie of the fish is too far out to be properly covered by wading, and the water where one would like to wade may be too deep. For those who cannot cast a really long line, or even for those who can, a boat makes fishing much easier. Often too, after hours of deep wading in a strong stream, it comes as a welcome relief to board a boat and fish in comparative ease. For some people, the elderly or physically handicapped, a boat may be essential—and for those not physically fit it is positively dangerous to wade the Spey; casualties or at the least duckings occur every year. Another factor is that in spring, up to mid-April at least, the water is decidedly cold, in the low 40°s or in the 30°s and not everybody is prepared to wade deep in such temperatures, however warmly clad.

If the fishery has both banks, as most Spey beats have, it is in any case a decided advantage to have a boat on any large pool if only for the purpose of crossing over and fishing from the opposite side. Some pools fish well from both sides, and need to be so fished; there are endless examples—Cairnty (Orton), Broom and Two Stones (Delfur), Gean Tree (Aikenway), Dalmunich (Carron and Laggan), Long Pool (Knockando) are only a few of them. Where there is no bridge in the neighbourhood a boat may save miles of motoring, as to wade across the Spey except in the lowest summer water is impossible.

Therefore the profitable use of boats should always be borne in mind and not despised. Every river has its own method of running boats. The normal method on the Spey is to use a heavy anchor, i.e. a solid weight of 56 lb. (anything lighter is apt to drag along a smooth bottom, and an ordinary anchor with flukes can get jammed in scattered rocks), attached to the end of about 100 yards of rope wound round cleats from side to side across the bows of the boat. With the anchor dropped overboard in the appropriate place, the boat can slowly be let down stream by the boatman on a line which enables the fisherman seated or standing in the stern to cover efficiently the lie of the fish for the whole length of the rope, or for part of it as needed. When the whole rope is out, if the full extent of the pool has not yet been covered, the boatman can pull the boat up to the anchor, coiling the rope round the cleats as he goes, hoist the anchor on board, and drop down to a new anchorage. There is considerable skill needed on the boatman's part. He must at the start

It needs skilful boat management to fish single-handed from an anchored boat.

drop the anchor in the right place, neither too far out from the bank nor too far in, he must manipulate the rope on the correct side of the prow of the boat, which ever side may be necessary, in order to get the boat to remain steady in the stream and not to otter too far to one side or another; and he must use the oars which are left hanging in the water on tholepins as a rudder to keep the boat steady without yawing. This is no easy job and demands competence, particularly when there is a strong cross or upstream wind. In this latter case, a drogue (an old bucket will do if nothing better is available) suspended in the water from the stern can be useful.

When a fish is hooked, it is normally not necessary to go through the elaborate process of pulling up to the anchor, hoisting it inboard, and rowing to the shore. The boatman can usually otter the boat near enough inshore by appropriate manipulation of the rope with the anchor still out, assisted if necessary by rowing, to enable the fisherman to get ashore and play and land his fish standing on the bank. If the fish is hooked near the tail of the pool, and he runs out of it, it is just as well if the fisherman is quickly landed, (as it will be unwise to take the boat down a rapid), and he will have to follow fast after his fish along the bank.

Normally this system works well, but boats are none too easy to handle in the strong Spey current, and the boatman needs to keep his wits about him all the time. Mishaps can easily happen, unexpectedly and quickly; for example, oars can go overboard (they should be made fast to the boat with a length of cord), or they can break without warning. A third spare oar carried in the boat at all times is a wise precaution. The boat can fetch up hard against underwater rocks, if carelessly manoeuvred, which can lead to damage, possibly a plank or bow stove in. Spey boats have to be strongly built to stand up to wear and tear of this sort, and stable enough for the fisherman to stand up in them without risk of losing his balance. Occasionally when the bottom is smooth and the current strong the anchor may start to drag. If this happens to any extent the best thing is to pull the boat up to the anchor, or at least pull the anchor down towards the boat, hoist it aboard, and row quickly ashore—to start the whole procedure again in a different way, perhaps anchoring further out of the current next time. If the boat is allowed to be drawn down into a strong rapid with the anchor still out, the rope should be cut at once and the anchor abandoned. The bow will be pulled right under by the fierce rush of a rapid if the dragging anchor jams behind a rock on the bottom as it is almost certain to do. A dragging anchor is indeed a menace, which makes the employment of a heavy 56 lb weight all the more advisable, even if it is something of a labour hauling it up into the boat.

I remember one eventful occasion many years ago when I had a boat at Creichie on the Rothes beat, not to fish from, but simply to enable us to cross the river as I had the fishing on both banks at that time. The river was moderately high, and I rowed out at the neck of the pool, heading for the opposite bank, with a passenger on board, the present Lord Tryon, who no doubt remembers the episode well! I was putting my back into the rowing as the current was strong, but I had not gone more than 7 yards out when one of my oars suddenly broke half way down its shaft. I was not particularly worried as I thought I could easily paddle or pole back to the bank with the remaining oar; but not a bit of it, the boat was heavy and the current was strong. It took charge, and away we went full tilt down the middle of the river, quite out of control, through Jameson's Cast, the Upper Slip, and Lower Slip at a rate of knots. By some extraordinary good fortune we missed all the jagged rocks that reared themselves at intervals from the bed of the river and finally fetched up on the opposite (Aikenway) bank at the Blue Stone some 500 yards downstream. I had no anchor in the boat, which was used purely for ferrying, otherwise I would have thrown that at the start and manoeuvred back to the bank on the rope. But without this and with a single oar I found I was helpless. This episode might have ended much more ignominiously than it did, and we were lucky.

Some mention has already been made of Spey salmon and their characteristics. For many years until recently the Spey was pre-eminently a spring river, with a splendid run of spring fish between February and June. But in the last fifteen years or more this spring run has, alas, sadly shrunk; and is only a shadow of its former glory. Grilse and summer salmon during July and August on the other hand seem to have increased, and the Spey in those months may still be found found full of fish almost everywhere. The rod catch for the main river and tributaries now varies between about 6000 fish in a bad year to 10,000 in a good one. The net catch both of salmon and sea trout is never disclosed but is much higher. As to weight, spring fish now average 11 lb but there is always the chance of a monster. The biggest fish I have ever seen caught on the Spey was a 38 pounder, killed by Lord Stair in the Long Pool at Rothes. The date was May 14th 1958, and there was snow on the bank that morning. Lord Stair was using strong tackle, and landed this fish in less than five minutes. He held it very hard, and it was a sight worth watching.

There were three fish of over 40 lb taken on the Rothes water during my 21 years tenancy (1948–1968), one in Creichie, one in Jameson's Cast, and one in Carnegie. My daughter Caroline had a $33\frac{1}{2}$ pounder, on a fly from a boat in the Burn Mouth, when she was only 14 years old. The photograph shown on Plate 2 shows my fishing diary open at that page. We killed a good many 30 pounders in those days when they were more common than now. It was difficult to land such fish in the strong Spey current. Always the hardest problem was to bring them within reach of the gaff. One more unexpected outward lurch in that strong stream, and they would be away out towards the middle of the river again, and all to be done anew!

One heard many stories of enormous Spey fish lost after epic struggles, no doubt basically true, as the odds were heavily weighted in favour of such fish, but some big ones were landed. Ned Ritchie, ghillie at Delfur for many years, landed one of 48 lb in the Two Stones in 1944. Ritchie was a great character, and no one who knew him will ever forget him. His language could be lurid, and he had little time for ladies or for beginners. He disliked boat fishing, and always preferred his rod to wade or fish from the bank. In the meantime he liked to employ himself by slashing down the whins or withy bushes that grew on the banks, and by creating a series of small bonfires. One could always tell his whereabouts on the river by the plumes of smoke that arose. In his youth he had served in the Shanghai Police, and he used to take pride in showing one his opium-weighing machine, a relic of China, also his snapshots of a Chinaman fishing with cormorants from a boat. These birds were trained to catch fish and bring them to the boat. They could not swallow them, as they were tightly ringed round the neck—a nice easy way of fishing for their owner. Ritchie had a scared-looking collie dog called 'Tosh', which made itself scarce when anyone approached. It was this dog which provided both material and name for the well known black hair-winged tube flies. These flies were Ritchie's prized invention in the 1950's. He was delighted with them and would have one fish with nothing else. In spite of his rough manners, Ritchie was an excellent, trustworthy, and dependable ghillie.

Another big fish was a 40 pounder killed in the Holly Bush at Delfur by the late Duchess of Northumberland. This fish was hooked on a small fly, and Ritchie said that at some stage in the fight it marooned itself high and dry on one of the big rocks that emerge from the water on the far side of this pool. Eventually it kicked itself back into the water, and all ended well. There were usually one or more 40 pounders killed every season in the Spey in the 1950s, I remember two or three being taken out of Cairnty Pool at Orton. There was a 48 pounder killed out of the Boat Pool at Wester Elchies only a few years ago, as well as a 41 pounder from Cairnty in 1977. The year 1980 produced one of $39\frac{1}{2}$ lbs, again from Orton, and a 48 pounder from Dellagyle at Upper Kinermony.

It is remarkable how really big fish seem to prefer certain pools, usually large ones with deep water in part of them which provides a refuge when wanted. Such pools are Cairnty at Orton, Broom, Two Stones, Holly Bush at Delfur, Back of the Bog at Arndilly, and the Boat Pool at Upper Pitchroy, though in high water, and when they are on the move, big fish may be met anywhere. It is noticeable however that the large majority of really big fish on record have been hooked and landed downstream of Wester Elchies. So the higher up the river one fishes one's chances of a monster appear to diminish. The biggest fish I have heard of since I started fishing the Spey was caught in the nets during the 1950s, and weighed 58 lb.

In the past, the two biggest rod-caught fish weighed 53 lb and 50 lb. These were killed respectively by Mr. W. G. Craven in the Dallachy pool at Gordon Castle in October 1897 and by Lord Winterton in the Rock Pool at Gordon Castle in the autumn of 1880. Both were caught on fly. The tally of 40 pounders probably runs into three figures, but one in particular is perhaps worth mentioning . . . it weighed 47 lb and was caught on fly from Alt Dearg on the Brae Water on September 23rd 1919, its captor being Miss Phyllis Spender-Clay, who was but 13 years old at the time! There can be no more notable triumph in the history of angling.

In my early days on the Spey, my chief fishing companions were Col. J. P. Moreton, Capt. C. P. Hazlehurst, and Capt. C. D. Burrell. Pat Moreton was a very experienced fisherman on the Wye, Dee, and Awe amongst other rivers. He had at least six 40 pounders to his credit on these rivers and was a wonderful adviser on everything to do with fishing besides being very good with beginners. Sad to say he is no longer with us. Pat Hazlehurst is the best fisherman that I know, on any type of water. Charles Burrell was a supreme fisher on big rivers. Another of my greatest friends on the Spey is Major Sir David Wills, the owner of the lovely Knockando beat. I am indebted to him for endless happy days in wonderful surroundings and will always be grateful.

I have said above the Spey spring fish were much more numerous twenty or thirty years ago than they are now, and in the summers of those days there were still plenty of salmon and grilse to be caught, even if not so many as now. Cairnty pool at Orton used to produce about 400 fish by the end of March during the 1950s. Present day catches are much fewer.

I see from my diary that from 1950 to 1960 on the Rothes beat, fishing three rods, we averaged 434 fish per season, two-thirds of them on fly. Our best year we got 633. Could this sort of thing be done now? I doubt it, and Rothes was then rated a second class beat. Delfur got over 2000 one season in the 1950s. Thanks to the kindness of the late Sir Brian Mountain I used to rent Delfur for the first two weeks of April from 1954 to 1960. We fished five rods for the first three or four years, and subsequently four. Twice we got over 250 fish for that fortnight, and never less than 140. Twice also we got 38 fish in one day, good spring fish with plenty of 20 pounders amongst them. Nowadays I fear that 50 fish for that fortnight would be thought a good score.

My personal exploits on the Spey are comparatively trivial. I have in fact landed only three fish of 30 lb or over, two on the Rothes beat and one at Delfur . . . the biggest being 32 lb. The one I caught in Creichie (Rothes) was perhaps the most exciting. It took a Mallard and Black, double hooked, size 4, and ran out a great extent of backing, with the line thoroughly drowned. Perhaps it was a tired fish, because after some violent fireworks it did not take long to land, and I was surprised at its weight. I was by myself, and gaffed it in Jameson's Cast, 100 yards downstream. It weighed exactly 30 lb and had the sea-lice still on it. No doubt I have lost several other bigger ones, and my best day for numbers was April 28th 1958, when I got eleven fish on Rothes, averaging 12 lb. Again this was nothing outstanding. Others have had much better days.

The biggest fish which so far as I know I ever hooked in the Spey was at Delfur one May morning in the 1950s. He took my tail fly (I was using this and a dropper, both of about size 6) in the tail of the Two Stones, when I was fishing from a boat with John Allan as boatman. I played him for about 20 minutes in Two Stones and when I could keep him there no longer he went down through the rapids to the next pool below called Beaufort. I followed him down along the bank, and after an hour or so he was pretty well played out, so our optimism rose. But then disaster struck without warning. A second small fish of about 12 lb (he jumped out) took or was foul-hooked by the dropper . . . and that was that. The fish were lying thick in Beaufort at that time. We saw the big fellow several times, and reckoned he was 40 lb (plus). Such events give rise to the bitter taste of catastrophe, and are the corrective of over-confidence.

My experiences on this wonderful river over the past 34 years have been so eventful and so fruitful that it would need a separate volume to attempt to describe them fully, or even a small part of them. I see from my fishing diary that I have in fact been responsible for landing over 2000 Spey fish (a goodly number though far surpassed by many other fishermen of note), and I could, with the help of my diary, give some sort of account of the capture of each one. 'God forbid', I can clearly hear my readers say and they need have no worry. I will only state that there could hardly be a more exciting river to fish or one that needs more skill and more knowledge of the salmon's behaviour. There is no British river to beat it, always providing it is holding a reasonable stock of fish.

Pollution on the Spey has always been a serious problem. Sources have been two-fold, sewage from such towns as Aberlour, Craigellachie, and Rothes, not to mention Dufftown up the Fiddich tributary, and 'burnt ale' from the many distilleries of this prime whisky producing area. Now however such pollution is largely a thing of the past. The above four towns all have efficient sewage disposal plants, and distilleries have taken considerable trouble and expense to dispose of their waste products in harmless ways. Some beats have benefited noticeably from the cessation of pollution, such as Easter Elchies and Arndilly which lie immediately downstream of

Aberlour and Craigellachie. Their catch has greatly increased during these recent years.

There is also a natural pollution, if it can be so called, in the Spey, which is the large peat content of its water after any spate or sizeable rise. In fact the Spey is an exceptionally peaty river, although it runs clear enough in low water or when the river has been steady for any length of time. Summer floods or rises, however, have always made the river run black with peat for several days on end, and nowadays it seems that this happens much more often in spring also. Some of the tributaries are liable to bring in a lot of peat; the Dulnain in particular is a bad one for this. The only effect of peat water, apart from colouring the bottom, is to sicken fish and put them off the take. Let there be no mistake about this. If the peat content goes beyond a certain point, it will put fish right off the take until such time as the water becomes reasonably clear again. The Spey is notorious for this. The Dee and a number of other Scottish rivers are not nearly so bad; but 'bog water' in many Irish rivers is even worse. (See p. 291 on the Blackwater.)

It seems to be mainly a question of degree. Slight peat content does little or no harm, and even with a moderate amount of peat in the water fish will still take fairly well. But beyond a certain point one is in trouble. Peat is extremely acid. There is nothing to be done about this and one just has to live with it. It can be very tiresome when one's fishing time is limited.

The Spey is heavily net fished near its mouth, like most Scottish rivers. At one time nets were worked as far upstream as Boat o'Brig at Delfur. Since the end of 1903 however they have been confined to that part of the river below Cumberland Ford, about $3\frac{1}{2}$ miles up from the mouth. The catch of salmon and sea-trout is large, particularly in low water years. In medium or high water a fair proportion of incoming fish get past the nets as the strong current hinders effective net working, also the river channel is divided into different branches, all of which cannot always be netted. But in low water the nets have a substantial kill of salmon, grilse, and sea-trout alike.

One last word about an unfavourable aspect of present day Spey fishing. On certain beats and stretches there is considerable evidence of over-rodding, which tends persistently to increase. The reason is not far to seek . . . a bigger return in rent to the landlord. Nevertheless it is regrettable. For example, I recently calculated the number of individual rods in action during mid-spring on the stretch of river extending for three miles downstream from the top of the Aberlour free water. This came to a total of thirty, which surely seems excessive. Fortunately other sections of the Spey are not so intensively fished, but even so many of them are now made to carry far more rods than the present stock of spring fish can justify. On the other hand on beats such as Delfur, Aikenway, Rothes, Easter Elchies, and Knockando the number of rods is strictly limited, and to the best of my knowledge has not been increased over the past thirty years, a commendable example of restraint in the face of an undesirable current trend. To over-rod a beat is always a bad mistake. If owners think that the more rods they put on the greater will be their bag, beyond a certain point they could not be more wrong. It works inversely, and a limited number of skilful rods will catch many more fish than twice their number of mediocrities. But they must be given adequate elbow-room.

Before taking leave of the Spey catchment area, some mention should be made of the Avon, the Spey's largest tributary. This small but pretty and fast flowing river is a very different proposition to the main Spey. It has a total length of around 40 miles, rising high up in the Cairngorms, and entering the Spey at the famous Junction Pool at Ballindalloch. Its water is normally extremely clear and its bed seldom more that fifteen yards wide. Except at certain limited periods when it is fining down after a spate, the Avon needs exceptionally skilful fishing if it is to be made productive. All the most refined artifices of small river fishing are needed. Nevertheless the Avon holds a good stock of fish, salmon, grilse, and sea-trout. It flows through some of the most attractive country anywhere in the Highlands. Were it a river on its own account with a separate mouth into the sea instead of being merely a tributary entering the Spey some 35 miles upstream of Spey Bay, its fishing would most probably be of far greater significance. All the same, apart from its present fishing potential, it provides much good spawning ground.

The Deveron

Mrs. Andrew Tennant fishing the Muiresk beat.

The Deveron is not nearly so highly renowned as it ought to be. Even if relegated to the second rank amongst Scottish salmon rivers, it nevertheless provides far better fishing than is generally known. Not only is it a prolific medium sized salmon river, but it also has an outstanding run of sea-trout, and its brown trout fishing over most of its course also has a high reputation.

This river has a total length of some 50 miles. It rises in the hill country of Banffshire, to the south-west of the high hill known as the

140

Buck of Cabrach (2400 ft.). For the first dozen or so miles of its course it is but a small highland stream, flowing through the typical hilly, peaty and heather covered countryside of this part of Scotland, until close to Huntly it leaves the hills, and enters a rolling lowland country richly endowed with fertile farm land.

Huntly, about 17 miles downstream from the Deveron's source, is a substantial town of some 4,000 inhabitants; and here the Deveron is joined by its first sizeable tributary, the Bogie, rising 13 miles away, near the village of Lumsden to the south. And four miles further downstream a second tributary of about equal size, the Isla, runs in from the north-west. These two tributaries do much to increase the Deveron's flow, making it into a sizeable river from this point downstream.

As far as Turriff, about 22 miles by river from Huntly, the Deveron pursues a winding course in a generally north-east direction. A third tributary of some size, the Turriff water, enters it from the east at Turriff, where the main river takes a sharp turn in a due northerly direction to fall into the Moray Firth at Banff (pop. 3,900), 11 miles further downstream.

In character therefore the Deveron is mixed. It starts as a typical small fast running and rocky highland burn, but for the main part of its course it has rather the character of a lowland river, flowing through rolling agricultural land and out of sight of any high hills, with its banks sometimes wooded and sometimes grass covered, without any falls or steep descents.

Nevertheless it is by no means slow running. Right as far as its tidal estuary at Banff the river maintains a fair stream, with a clear cut succession of rapid and pool. Seldom is there any sort of slow featureless stretch, which fails to provide a lie for fish. There are pools of all types and plenty of first class fly water.

Nowhere however could the Deveron be classed as a big river; its average width even in its lowest reaches is not more than 30 or 40 yards; while upstream of Huntly it is of much more modest size. Yet even so, salmon penetrate in numbers right up into its remote headwaters in the Cabrach. For those who prefer fishing medium sized waters, and who find rivers such as the Spey, Dee, or Tweed larger than they would like, the Deveron is a good choice. It is neither too big nor too small, with an attractive streamy flow, running through pleasant country, where the scenery, if not spectacular, is at least restful and unspoilt.

Of course it has its drawbacks, what river has not? The main one is that it colours easily, both from peat in the headwaters, and from the run-off from agricultural land further down. Heavy rain can therefore put a stop to fishing for a day or two on end. Nevertheless the two main tributaries, Bogie and Isla, do not colour easily or remain coloured for long, with the result that the Deveron itself clears reasonably quickly.

The best salmon beats on the river are probably at Rothiemay, $4\frac{1}{2}$ miles below Huntly, at Netherdale, half way between Huntly and Turriff, and at Forglen, $1\frac{1}{2}$ miles below Turriff; though there are plenty of other good ones elsewhere. A promising one amongst these is at Muiresk, close to Turriff, which now averages 100 fish for the season. Even right up in the headwaters at Edinglassie, and above, there are still a fair number of fish to be caught, though it is rare to get fresh ones so high up the river. I remember well fishing the Netherdale water in years gone by, longer ago than I care to call to mind, and what fun it was! Such a varied number of pools, and such pleasant surroundings with plenty of fish. I have never forgotten it. The last fish I caught there was a fat silvery 20 pounder covered with sea lice. This was the first genuine autumn fish which I ever caught, anywhere, and it took a Yellow Torrish, size 2/0. It made a great impression on me, unexpected as it was to see such a handsome fish so late in the season. 20 lb is no outstanding weight for an autumn fish, and I have caught many bigger ones since that long-ago time; nevertheless I have never forgotten this earliest one. The date was September 29th, and this fish was the forerunner of a good run of fresh autumn fish during the following month. I do not know whether a similar autumn run still exists now, but doubt it, as we should hear more of it if it did.

The record Deveron autumn fish was killed on October 21st 1924 by Mrs. Morrison, in the Wood O'Shaws Pool on the Mount Blairy water, $3\frac{1}{2}$ miles upstream from Banff. It weighed 61 lb, its length

being 53 inches and its girth 33 inches; and it was caught on a $1\frac{1}{2}$ inch
fly. This is the biggest fish ever caught on a fly in Britain. The story of
its capture is a strange one. It was landed in 5 minutes! Shortly after it
was hooked it swam close in under an overhanging bank, and the
ghillie probably without realising its weight got the gaff into it. He
then found himself quite unable to lift the monster out of the water,
and had to shout in desperation to a friend who luckily was nearby:
'Hey, Donald, gie us a hand wi' what's here!' Together they hauled
the huge fish on to the bank. It was wheeled up to the House in a
wheelbarrow, and was not weighed till the following day, so its true
weight might have been two or three pounds heavier—enough to
rival Miss Ballantine's 64 pounder from the Tay.

Another outsized autumn fish was caught by Colonel A. E. Scott on
October 31st 1920. This took a one inch fly, (a 'Britannia'), and
weighed 56 lb. The Deveron in those days was celebrated for its
autumn run of heavy fish, averaging 18–20 lb.   The rod fishing
season lasts from February 11th to October 31st; but nowadays,
although there is spring fishing in the early part of the year up to
May, the majority of fish are caught from June onwards. It is true that
the Deveron has no snow reservoir in the high hills, as have the Spey
and the Dee, and no loch upon its course to help it maintain a good
head of water; nevertheless even in summer it seldom falls so low as to
become completely unfishable (except in an exceptional drought year
like 1976). There are usually two or three summer spates, and after
them the water level falls away moderately slowly, so that a fair
fishing height is maintained over a reasonable period. It follows that
the Deveron could by no means be classed as a 'spate river' with its
attendant uncertainties.

Spring fish average 8–10 lb, and a 20 pounder is a large one. All the
same there was a 33 pounder killed in March 1980 on the Laithers
beat, upstream of Turriff, and a 32 pounder in September at
Dunlugas, lower down. There is a grilse run from June onwards,
which as in most rivers has increased in recent years; but the river is
usually at a low level when these fish try to enter, so that many of
them are caught in nets.

If you are going to fish the Deveron, your tackle should be of the

normal type for any medium/small river. In early spring the weather
and water can be very cold, and you will probably be bait fishing,
unless you are particularly addicted to a large sunk fly. Later on, as
the water warms up, fly fishing with a floating line and rod of around
13 or even 12 feet is perfectly effective. In summer with low water
you may often descend to using a single handed rod.

As to wading, you will have little difficulty. The current is seldom
strong, and the pools are seldom deep. Thigh waders will be all that
you need in the upper river, and they will also be long enough for
most of the pools lower down. Occasionally you may want long
trouser waders in the lower river from Rothiemay down, in certain
pools; and if you do not previously know the water it may be as well
to have a pair of these in reserve. There was a pool at Netherdale
called 'The Log Pool', where they were a decided advantage. But as a
whole the Deveron is a river where wading is neither deep nor
formidable; and there are a fair number of pools which can easily be
fished off the bank.

Turning now to sea-trout fishing, for this the Deveron is without
doubt one of the best rivers in Scotland. Sea-trout start to come in late
in May; and June and July are the best months. Their average size is
around $2\frac{1}{2}$ lb but many bigger fish of up to 7–10 lb are among them.
The record sea-trout weighed 14 lb and was caught at Inverichnie,
close to Banff, by Mr. C. Sievewright in the 1920s. Later in July and
August there are runs of finnock or herling.

The best sea-trout fishing is undoubtedly to be found in the lower
reaches, below Turriff. Such beats as Forglen and Dunlugas are
outstanding; though there are many other good ones, even as far up as
Huntly.

Any rises of water during the summer help to bring the sea-trout
in; but usually during June, July, and August the water is low, in
which case resort must be had to night fishing. A reconnaissance
should be made in daylight to see where the fish are lying thickest,
and fishing should not start before dark, in so far as it becomes dark at
all in these northern latitudes. A moonless and cloudy night is best.
Whether or not there is wind is immaterial, except that a wind helps
to keep off the midges! These can be a pest, especially in warm damp

PLATE 4

Colin Espie with a seventeen pounder from Tassach, an excellent pool at Cambus o'May on the middle Dee.

PLATE 5

Stanley Weir on the lower Tay.

The Scour Pool, river Findhorn.

weather, so never fail to carry with you some strong artificial deterrent of one sort or another. The best time in the month to fish is probably when there are high spring tides. Even if these do not coincide with a rise in water, they do encourage the sea-trout to run well into the estuary on the tide, and so to push on up the river. When fishing it is unwise to use too long a line in the dark, for fear of tangles. You should not move about too much, once you have selected a promising place; and if you do move take care to do so as quietly as possible. Fish the fly by drawing in line slowly and deliberately, and strike sharply at the slightest touch. Sea-trout of any size often take very quietly and are adept at getting rid of the fly, unless struck at once. Some experts advocate the use of two flies—to my mind one is enough, and one has tangles enough with that!

To play and land a big sea-trout on light tackle in a fair sized river during the midnight hours is a hair-raising experience. It is made more exciting by the fact that one can see little or nothing, and has to judge what is happening purely by feel and hearing. As will be realised this form of fishing is totally unrelated to salmon fishing; admittedly there is always the chance of hooking a salmon, particularly in the half-light, but for some unknown reason these fish unlike sea-trout seldom take when it becomes really dark.

Anyone who is interested in sea-trout fishing, whether on the Deveron or any other river, should not fail to obtain and read that excellent book *Sea Trout Fishing*, by Hugh Falkus, now in a revised second edition, which describes the whole business in such detail.

Brown trout also hold a prominent place in the Deveron. There have always been large numbers of them, all up and down the river. They do not average any great size, not more than $\frac{1}{2}$ lb, but the small ones can always be returned to the water in order to make the catch more respectable. Occasionally fish of between 1 lb and 3 lb can be caught. The record Deveron brown trout weighed 7 lb, and was caught on a Greenwell's Glory at Inverichnie in 1934. *Fishing Vignettes* by Cecil Braithwaite, published in 1924, gives a good picture of what trout fishing in the Deveron used to be like in the early years of this century. Braithwaite frequently records catches such as: 'April 27 to May 13. My bag consisted of 288 trout, $135\frac{1}{2}$ lb', or on another occasion: 'Six days fishing, 187 trout 75 lb.' He adds that: 'Given all the elements just right, baskets of 30 lb to one rod are quite possible.'

Anyone who is as keen a trout fisherman as was Braithwaite (and he admits at the end of his book to preferring trout fishing to salmon fishing), would probably do nearly as well on the Deveron in these present days, though he might find the fly hatch sparser. He could use dry fly or wet fly as he pleased.

But it seems that brown trout fishing is not now so popular a pastime as it used to be, and it is perhaps for this reason rather than any other that one seldom now hears of heavy catches being made. April and May are the best months for this type of fishing, when the trout are still hungry after their winter's fast.

Little mention has so far been made of netting on the Deveron. There are two stake nets in the estuary operated by two companies, which are helpful in that they take a great deal of interest in the river, are successful in keeping poaching to a minimum, and are conscientious about 'slapping' their nets at the week-end. They have a fair catch of salmon, grilse, and sea-trout, but their season's total depends greatly on the type of weather they have to contend with, as all these nets are exposed to winds coming from the north. In conclusion it may fairly be said that the Deveron is by no means excessively netted, and in this respect it is far better off now than it was in days long past, when as one learns from Grimble and Calderwood its nets were flagrantly overworked.

To end on an optimistic note, the Deveron is one of the few rivers nowadays showing definite signs of improvement over the past five years, not only in catches, but in the number of fish seen on the spawning beds. This is an encouraging state of affairs, and one only wishes that the same could be said about a larger number of rivers elsewhere.

The Dee

Tassach at Cambus o'May, middle Dee. An excellent pool.

I have already written at some length about the magnificent Aberdeenshire Dee in a previous book, *Great Salmon Rivers of Scotland*, so will not run the risk of too much repetition here. At the same time the Dee provides such outstanding salmon fishing, and apparently always has done so, that I feel reluctant to forego making due mention of it again, if only to re-emphasise briefly its main characteristics and advantages.

As most fishermen know, the Dee is *par excellence* a spring river,

147

and an early one at that. It almost certainly has now the largest spring run of all the rivers in Britain, not excepting the Tay, Spey and Tweed. Its early fish start to enter well before the fishing season begins on February 1st, and on the opening day they can be found in numbers as far upstream as Banchory, or if it has been a mild winter even higher. What is more, the Dee is one of the few rivers which at the moment seems to be on the up-grade, that is its catch of fish tends to increase rather than the opposite, a rare and encouraging state of affairs.

The present rod catch on the Dee averages around 10,000 fish each season, having risen from its lowest total of 6100 in 1977. This is a substantial number, especially as good fishing occurs only during five months of the year, and not in every part of the river simultaneously. For instance the lower river below Banchory only fishes really well (as a general rule) before mid-April, the middle river from Banchory to Cambus o'May is usually best between March and the end of May, and upstream of Cambus in May and June. At the same time it should be remembered that the Dee is fairly hard fished. Not only is there some 75 miles of river where in its due season good fishing may be obtained, but there are 45 separate beats on this river, each with a varying quota of rods, and except for late in the 8 month season (February 1st to September 30th) it is likely that most beats will be fished every day. So a pressing need arises for an ample stock of fish, if such a substantial number of anglers is to be kept happy. At present such a stock normally does exist, for which one must be grateful and live in hope that it will be long maintained.

Few fresh salmon enter the Dee after the end of May. There are a certain number of grilse in June and July, possibly on the increase, but there is virtually no run of autumn salmon, as there used to be in years long ago. Almost all the salmon caught by rod from July up to the end of the season are stale fish that have been in the river for a varying length of time. It would be of benefit if anglers made a practice of returning unharmed to the water any black hen fish which they caught during this period.

I have mentioned grilse in the Dee, and it may interest any of my readers who enjoy grilse fishing to know that Kelson in *The Salmon*

Fly (1895), p. 379, records 50 grilse having been taken by one rod in a day below the falls of Feugh. There was no shortage of these fish at that time, so it seems.

Fishing during this latter part of the season is now uncertain at best. Usually fish by then have become 'potted', and although they may be present in numbers are apt to be extremely 'stiff', taking little interest in the angler's fly. Why should they? They are almost all spring fish, and have already seen innumerable lures. If there was an extensive late-summer run, as in the Spey or Tay, it would be a different story; but the Dee does not possess such a run. Just occasionally its stale fish do come on the take, perhaps after rain or when a September frost has caused the water temperature to fall. But this is a fairly rare occurrence; generally speaking Dee fishing at this time of year is not rewarding, apart from the pleasure afforded by the delightful surroundings, and the keen angler would be better employed in looking further afield.

The average weight of the Dee spring fish is not heavy, only 7–8 lb. Anything of more than 15 lb is a good fish, and none too common. Fish of 20 lb or over number only 4 per cent of the total catch, while 30 or 40 pounders, although one or two are still occasionally landed, have become rarities. The two biggest Dee fish up to the present weighed 56 lb, caught by Mr. J. Gordon in October 1886 on the Ardoe water, 4 miles above Aberdeen, and 52 lb, caught by Mr. M. Ewen on October 12th 1918 at Park. These were both big autumn fish of the old days, when the season lasted till the end of October. 40 pounders both in spring and (in past years) autumn have been reasonably numerous, one of the biggest weighing $47\frac{1}{2}$ lb, a spring fish, caught at Durris in the 1950s. Nevertheless the Dee cannot by any stretch of imagination be called a 'big fish' river, and nowhere approaches the Tay or even the Spey in this respect.

Reasons for the present abundant stock of spring fish are many. To start with there are excellent and wide-spread spawning grounds, not only in the headwaters of the main river itself, but in tributaries such as the Gairn, Clunie, and now the Muick since a ladder has been constructed at its falls. The Dee water is remarkably pure and unpolluted. There is only one distillery on the whole of its course, and towns such as Ballater, Aboyne, and Banchory on its banks all have efficient sewage disposal systems. Even Aberdeen at the mouth, large city as it is, manages to dispose of its sewage directly into the sea without polluting the river to any extent. The peat content in the water is also minimal compared to that of many other rivers such as the Spey and Findhorn. The Dee only colours after heavy rain, and even then to no great degree; it clears quickly, although fish may temporarily be put off the take if the peat content is high enough.

A further direct reason for the prolific run of fish is the fact that the Dee is now netted on a greatly reduced scale. At one time nets were worked as far upstream as Banchory; but in 1872 the Dee Salmon Fishing Improvement Association was formed from owners and lessors of rod-fishings, with the object of improving the fishings by the leasing of net-fishings. By 1909 this Association had succeeded to a point where all netting above the Old Bridge of Aberdeen had ceased, except for two nets in the tidal water which the Association operated itself. Later it acquired further netting rights below this bridge; and since 1968 it has ceased to work any of its own nets, so that the only estuary nets now still in action are those belonging to the Aberdeen Harbour Commission from Victoria Bridge down. This is a tremendous success story, and one only wishes that owners on other hard-netted rivers had possessed as much forethought and initiative.

A further aid to the stock is provided by a hatchery at Dinnet belonging to the Dee Fishery Owners, which every year turns out large numbers of fry and parr into the upper waters and feeders. How much good such hatcheries finally achieve towards increasing the adult stocks may be problematical. If the output is large enough, however, stocking must help to some extent, and it affords an insurance against the ravages of U.D.N. or other diseases on the prospective parent fish. Another beneficial factor in the Dee is the complete absence of coarse fish, except eels and the very occasional pike, as well as a marked scarcity of brown trout. (Other east coast rivers such as the Spey, Deveron, Tay, and Tweed hold a far larger number of these last.) The result must do much to benefit the salmon fry, parr, and smolts, both through a reduced number of predators, and lack of competitors for food. Brown trout are an especially hostile element where young salmon in every stage are concerned, so the Dee is fortunate in their comparative scarcity.

The Dee rises high in the Cairngorms, and has the advantage of a snow reservoir frozen hard during the winter on those high hills, which normally lasts until well into May and keeps the water running at a fair level throughout the spring. Only the Spey amongst other Scottish rivers has a comparable advantage, draining as it does the northern and western slopes of the Cairngorms. It would be hard to exaggerate the advantage to fishing in both Dee and Spey which results from their being snow-fed in this way.

Many would say that the Dee is the most attractive of all the larger Scottish salmon rivers. Certainly its upper course from Mar Lodge to Dinnet would be hard to surpass in the delightfulness of its surroundings, dominated in the near distance by the magnificent escarpment of Lochnagar (3768 feet) to the south, coupled with the yet higher outlines of Ben Avon (3847 feet), Beinn a Bhuird (3860 feet), Ben Macdhui (4296 feet) and Cairn Toul (4241 feet) to the north-west. Everywhere is the delicious scent of pine woods, and on the higher ground of heather. Throughout its length, not only in its upper reaches but to well below Banchory, the Dee pursues a tumbling broken and rocky course, with lovely pools of all types intersected by fast streams of white water, and turbulent rapids; all combining to produce a salmon river of superlative character.

One of its main merits is that it provides ideal fly water, with just the right strength of current to make the fly swim well, plenty of good holding ground in the streams as well as in the main part of the pools, no great depth, and as already mentioned, a lovely flow of pure unpolluted water.

In size the Dee as any other salmon river naturally varies in different parts of its course. In its upper reaches above Ballater it is quite a modest stream, seldom more than 40–45 yards wide, except when in spate. It does not often need a long line for its pools to be adequately covered, and in low water thigh waders are in many places all that one may need for wading purposes. Except in early spring or in time of high water a 12 or 13 foot rod will be long enough to throw the required length of line, though personally here as elsewhere on rivers of this size I would prefer a light 14 foot rod (of carbon graphite or split cane) as giving better casting power against a wind, and better line control when the fly is fishing round.

In its middle reaches from, roughly, Ballater to Banchory, the Dee as might be expected with the influx of sizeable tributaries such as the Gairn, Muick, and Tana water, increases considerably in volume. It still however could hardly be called a big river, and is not comparable for size with, say, the middle Tweed, Tay, or Spey—nevertheless many would consider it quite big enough. What lovelier pools could one have, or more inspiring to fish than for example Tassach at Cambus o'May, Waterside at Glentana, Lummels at Aboyne, Moral at Woodend, or the Roe Pot at Blackhall? And there are many more in this category. They are fully big enough to make the angler put his back into it when casting, for hooked fish to have plenty of room for active play—not so small as to be quickly covered in a dozen or so casts, nor so large as to become monotonous in the absence of incident—but in fact of just about the right size. Could anyone ask for more?

This part of the Dee, except in a few odd places such as Cairnton and Inchmarlo, invariably requires the use of long trouser waders; and in a number of pools at any rate the ability on the fisherman's part to throw a good length of line when wanted is a decided advantage. In fact in this stretch the Dee may fairly be said to have become an excellent medium sized river, varying from a rapid and substantial flow of 45–60 yards width at high water, to a reduced but still brisk moving stream at low summer level.

Below Banchory, where its last main tributary the Feugh enters, the Dee becomes a fairly big river, especially when running high. But its attractive character remains unchanged. Where for instance are to be found finer pools than those at Crathes and Park, such as Park Inn or the Durris Stream, to name but two? Not before Drum and Tilbouries does the current begin to slow up to any appreciable extent; and down here boats are sometimes used for fishing purposes, especially in the early part of the season—a welcome relief from wading when the water is icy or even moderately cold!

So over its widespread extent from Mar Lodge down to Kingcausie

Queen's Pool at Crathie, upper Dee; everywhere the delicious scent of pine woods.

(just short of Aberdeen itself), the Dee provides every sort of water large or small to suit the varying tastes of fishermen of all persuasions. They would have little need to look further for something to their liking than to some point on this 75 mile stretch.

As is well known there is an understanding amongst Dee fishery owners and tenants that after mid-April 'fly only' shall be the general rule. On most beats this understanding is strictly observed, and it is an admirable one on such a perfect fly river. There are however one or two owners and tenants who do not subscribe to it, which seems a pity. Deviations from an accepted standard are always liable to widen rather than contract, and thus to cause ill-feeling. One or two other beats in contrast fish fly only from the start of the season, and do quite well enough. It would be a good move if their example was more widely followed.

I know that as far as I am concerned I would never want to fish anything but fly in the Dee, however early in the season it might be.

This river provides the most attractive fly water, and it seems a shame to use anything else in it. Most people would undoubtedly say that small fly fishing with a floating line, as popularised by Mr. A. H. E. Wood of Cairnton in the 1920s, is the most attractive method. Though no one would deny its merits, I am not sure that I altogether agree. I do find that fishing a medium sized fly on a floating line with a sinking tip is a most enjoyable and effective method, at a time when many fishermen are falling back on bait. If the water is cold I am only too glad to use a sunk line with a biggish fly. This method, once used so extensively, seems to have passed almost completely out of fashion. It is the most difficult of all forms of fly fishing (though much helped by the recent invention of both fibre-glass and carbon-graphite lightweight rods), while floating line fishing is the easiest. Few people realise how deadly a sunk fly can be in the hands of a skilled performer.

The way fresh fish distribute themselves on entering the Dee is worth notice. Granted that odd fish may be found anywhere in the river at any time in the season, but the large majority of the incomers will head for a certain area, dependent on water temperature, time of year, and where they find the bulk of the previous entrants already settled. All salmon prefer to move and lie in shoals, but it seems as though Dee salmon have a particular inclination in this direction.

During the early part of the season up to somewhere around the end of March most of the fresh fish are likely to stop in the lowest part of the river, below Banchory. Then early in April, the actual date of course varying in an early or late year, there is likely to be a mass movement of fish out of the lower reaches and into the middle river between Banchory and Dinnet or Cambus o'May. Fresh fish entering the river at this time are inclined to push straight up to this area, without stopping in the lowest part of the river where only some old stagers, the remnants of the early spring run, will be left. Later in the season, towards the end of May, there will be a similar wholesale movement of fish from the middle reaches to the upper ones above Ballater. Any fisherman who has his wits about him will consequently appreciate how important it is to fish at the right place and at the right time as far as the Dee is concerned—neither too early nor too late. If he allows inexperience to colour rosy anticipations, and goes optimistically to any beat, even one of the best with a large yearly catch, outside of its good fishing period, he is likely to be sadly disappointed. This principle seems to apply more closely to the Dee than to some other of the larger rivers. Certain beats on the Spey and the Tay for instance will produce good sport over a much more extensive period—consider, say, either Islamouth or Delfur, which continuously fish well from March to September inclusive. In contrast there are few beats on the Dee which have more than $2\frac{1}{2}$ months of good fishing.

Another justifiable criticism of Dee fishing, if one wants to be critical, is that there are few beats which have sole fishing rights on both banks, only about five to be exact. With the intensive fishing of modern times it is always an unmixed blessing to have such rights, would not my readers agree? Often reciprocal arrangements can be made between opposite neighbours, to avoid mutual interference so far as possible; this is everywhere and at all times a good plan. But sometimes agreement is not achieved, or even attempted, and friction can then result to everybody's discomfort and disadvantage.

I have emphasised above the exceptional clarity and purity of the Dee's water. It comes therefore as a surprise that the foul disease U.D.N., which originated in the south-west of Ireland in 1965, even today still persists in this river. Every year it seems to break out when the water is cold during winter, and to last for a varying time into the spring. The trouble is partly that, as in other early spring rivers, there is no time of year when fish, either salmon, grilse, or kelts, are not present in the Dee; so that the chain of infection, even if the disease at times is dormant, can still be carried on. One wonders how long it will last. The harmful effects of U.D.N. are of course not confined to the actual mortality amongst fish. Time and again, during or after a bad outbreak of this disease, one has seen the surviving stock of fish extremely 'dour' and unwilling to respond to any lure. This can have a decidedly unfavourable effect on fishing, and a river can as a result be obviously full of fish yet except for sea-lice fish be barren of takers. Fortunately this disease is largely, though by no means entirely confined to cold water conditions; and it is apt to disappear as the water becomes warmer in April and May. (Though this may be the case on the Dee, it is noticeable that in other smaller east coast rivers further north U.D.N. can proliferate badly during these months, and even later, particularly if the water is low and fish become concentrated in small pools). And there is no doubt that, in spite of the worst ravages of U.D.N., most of the fishing on the Dee can decidedly be classed as excellent. Let us hope that after 16 years the potency of this affliction is finally on the wane.

My own experience on the Dee has been reasonably extensive, though I would dearly wish it larger. I caught my first salmon ever at Abergeldie in 1931, where as a boy thanks to the generosity of H.M. King George V I was allowed to fish for 11 years on that delightful stretch of river. I still remember vividly every one of its pools from the Clachanturn to Polhollick, they were stuffed with fish in those days—very red of course during August and September, and rarely edible; but what did that matter to a boy in his teens? The excitement of fishing was intense, all the more so because fish used to jump incessantly in every pool. The whole spawning stock of the Dee must have been concentrated in the upper river at that time of year. I often wonder how it would seem if one went back there now. I feel that fishing in April, May and June, for fresh fish, would be highly enjoyable, if less productive than in the lower parts of the river; but I am sure one would no longer want to kill very red spring fish during August and September (though one could of course put them back). The river too, whenever one now looks at it up there, seems small compared to one's youthful memory of it—like many other things in life.

In later years I have also been lucky enough to have fished for odd days or weeks at Crathie, Monaltrie, Cambus o'May, Aboyne, Woodend, Blackhall, Lower Crathes, and Park. It has all been a wonderful experience for which I am grateful beyond measure; I have fervently enjoyed every minute of it, and only wish that my future activities on the Dee, in the company of my friends, may be even more extensive.

The North Esk

Morphie Dyke, a notable feature on the river, low at this time, about two miles up from tidal water.

It has often been said that the North Esk would be one of the best small salmon rivers in Scotland if it was not for the heavy netting in its lower reaches. To a certain extent this may well be true. This attractive east-coast river *is* subjected to severe netting; though this has been greatly reduced over recent years, and its rod fishing has consequently improved.

The North Esk has a catchment area of 288 square miles which for size puts it on a level with the Awe, Beauly, or South Esk. It is

157

therefore a river of some significance, bigger than the Naver, Thurso, or Helmsdale, though slightly smaller than Findhorn, Deveron, or Beauly. It rises in Invermark Forest in the county of Angus, on the borders of Aberdeenshire, where its head-waters unite to form the $1\frac{1}{4}$ mile long Loch Lee, close to Invermark Lodge. Just over a mile downstream below its outlet from Loch Lee, the North Esk is joined by a main tributary, the Water of Mark, which flows in from the north-west. From here the river has a fairly direct south-easterly course of around 33 miles to its mouth into the North Sea near Kinnaber, 3 miles north of Montrose. Its other chief tributary is the West Water, which rises near Hunthill in the high ground to the south of Loch Lee, and unites with the main river near Stracathro, $2\frac{1}{2}$ miles downstream of Edzell.

In its upper reaches the North Esk is a typical small east-coast highland river, with a fast and rocky course through hilly heathery country. Its fall is fairly abrupt for the first 15 miles of its course from Loch Lee to The Burn, during which it falls some 450 feet, i.e. an average drop of 30 feet per mile. This may seem steep, but except when in spate the flow of the North Esk in this upstream area is of scant proportions. Salmon and grilse can and do penetrate right as far as Loch Lee, though in reduced numbers and seldom when fresh run. The loch also holds brown trout and char. These upper reaches are highly delightful in character, situated as they are amongst some of the best grouse ground in Scotland, with magnificent views in all directions. One always notices too how much more invigorating is the climate in these areas compared to that of the west-coast. The same seems to apply all over Britain from north to south. One appreciates this at any time, but particularly on a summer's morning if one wants to rise in the early dawn for some pre-breakfast fishing.

Close to The Burn, about midway down its course, the North Esk enters a rocky gorge of about one mile in length. Near the head of this gorge there is a fall, known as 'The Loups', which is quite a spectacular drop of about 12 feet. All the same, fish can ascend it fairly easily when they want to, owing to the broken nature of its descent and the deep water immediately below it which forms a good starting point for their initial upstream leap. While the water is still cold in spring, however, few of them attempt to surmount this obstacle, in spite of the fact that there is now a fish-pass to help them.

Below Gannochy, which lies opposite The Burn, the river increases in size, and between here and Kinnaber at its mouth the most productive of its fisheries are to be found. Although it has now left the hills and runs through rolling agricultural country, it still maintains a good rate of flow right as far as its tidal estuary. It has plenty of rapids and pools of different types, some rocky and some gravelly, with few sluggish stretches, all combining to form a moderate sized salmon river of very pleasant character. Its water is clear and unpolluted, though liable to run dark with peat after heavy rain.

There are around ten beats on this part of the river. The best of the middle part of the river is probably at Edzell and belongs to Lord Dalhousie, but there is good water at Stracathro also. The best beats of all however are undoubtedly those which lie immediately below Morphie dyke on the lowest two miles of river above the high tide mark. It should be explained that 2 miles upstream from the mouth there is a weir from bank to bank across the river, similar to a 'cauld' on the Tweed, but the local name for it here is a 'dyke'. This is at Morphie; and a further $2\frac{1}{2}$ miles upstream there used to be a second similar dyke at Craigo. Both these dykes, at least in spring when the water was cold, and in spite of being provided with ladders, did present a considerable obstacle to the passage of fish, so that the early springers accumulated in numbers downstream of them for some distance. Moreover the Craigo and Morphie beats, which lay below them, were regularly net-fished from the start of the season on February 16th. So a large proportion of the spring stock was undoubtedly caught by net, and spring rod-fishing was indifferent.

Now the situation has changed. Craigo dyke has crumbled and is being allowed to disintegrate. It no longer checks the fish to any extent. Morphie dyke which provides lade water for Montrose water supply remains, but the fish passes in it have been made easier. Net fishing now takes place only below Morphie dyke (apart from the coastal nets), and the rod fishing on the river upstream has considerably improved. Rod-fishing is also carried on at the start of the season on the two miles of river below Morphie dyke, until the net fishing which starts in the dyke pool is extended downstream to supersede it; and very prolific this rod-fishing is. So speaking generally for most of the river one can fairly say that the spring fishing is now potentially better than ever before.

By about mid-April the snow on the hills is mostly gone, and the river drops to a progressively lower level. The run of salmon dwindles, and few fish in summer get past the nets at the mouth. Those already in the river become 'potted' and disinclined to take. Weather on the east coast of Scotland is apt to be consistently dry during summer, and spates then are rare, though they do occasionally occur. Lord Dalhousie tells me that he once caught an 8 lb fish with sea-lice in the Millden water (above the Loups) in June after a summer spate. In the old days there used to be much talk of Lammas floods in early August, but these too now seem to be infrequent. Summer fishing as a result is patchy and spasmodic, often hardly worth while. A certain number of grilse come in from mid-June onwards. A few are caught in the main river, and some up the West Water whenever there is enough flow. They penetrate far upstream, whenever there is rain enough to help them on their journey. There is also a run of sea-trout, and particularly of finnock or herling, the sea-trout equivalent of the grilse. Night fishing in June and July is best for these, up the West Water as well as in the main river.

The salmon rod-fishing season lasts until October 31st. There is a reduced autumn run of fish—they come in at any time after the beginning of September, when there is enough rain to cause a rise in water. Some of these are bright silver fish, but many of them are starting to colour before they leave the sea; and as the October days shorten most of them are in varying stages of redness. The three beats below Morphie dyke always provide the best fishing on the whole river at this time of year. The Craigo beat used also to be first class, but since the dyke has crumbled fish do not stay in it to anything approaching the same extent as they used to do. Up-river as far as the Loups autumn fishing can be quite good at times, but further upstream is barely worth while.

Some mention should be made of appropriate tackle for the North

Esk. In spring, that is from the start of the season up to mid-April, the weather is likely to be very cold and probably frosty. Water temperature is not likely to be above 45°F and may well be in the 30°sF. Most fishermen in these circumstances use bait, wooden devons or something similar. Fly can also be good, particularly if the water is fairly low and clear. A hair winged tube fly with a sunk line is best. Whether fishing fly or bait the angler is unlikely to find a long line necessary, so nothing outsized in the way of heavy tackle will be needed. An ordinary light spinning outfit, or a fly rod of 14 feet (perhaps 15 feet on very windy days) with appropriate line and flies is all that he will want.

Even when in spate the North Esk is still of no great size, and often it is possible to cover pools off the bank or by wading no more than knee deep. Long trouser waders are however advisable, at least in spring. Not only is it an advantage to be able to wade deep if necessary, but such waders are in any case a good protection against cold winds and driving rain.

For summer fishing, such as it is, light tackle will be enough—for instance a 12 foot rod, 10 lb breaking strain nylon leader, floating line, small flies, and thigh waders—or even a single handed rod of 10 feet or so.

In autumn one reverts back to stronger tackle as soon as the river becomes higher and colder, until towards the end of October one can be using much the same outfit as in early spring.

As to the size of fish, the North Esk as a general rule is not a big fish river. Springers average 9–10 lb. A 20 pounder is a large one, and above that weight not many are caught.

In autumn there is a better chance of a 30 pounder or heavier, though less now than in days gone by. Such a fish will in any case probably be an old red kipper cock. The record North Esk fish weighed 53 lb and was caught on a fly at Morphie in the autumn of 1902. Big fish were obviously more frequent in those days, on this river as elsewhere, and it is useless nowadays expecting to kill one as big as this.

For an angler visiting the North Esk and in need of accommodation, there are good hotels in the neighbourhood, in or near Montrose, or else at Edzell which is about half way up the river.

As to my personal experiences on this river, they have not been as extensive as I would wish. In years gone by my good friend the late Captain John Stansfeld of Dunninald used often most kindly to let me fish on the lowest part of the river below Morphie Dyke. In February, before this section of the river was netted, the rod fishing here was often excellent. I have a note in my diary that on February 24th 1950 I caught 6 fish before lunch on the Flats at Kinnaber, biggest 22 lb. This sort of thing was in no way outstanding in those days, except that these particular fish were all caught on fly, an unusual occurrence so early in spring, when most people prefer to spin.

The bridge at Kinnaber crosses the river at the head of the tidal water, with the open sea about a mile downstream. The river is low.

The late Lord Dalhousie was a 'fly only' man, and a most skilled performer. He was said to have had extensive kills on this water, up to even 20 fish in the day, before his unfortunate death at an early age.

It is sad that the art of sunk fly fishing seems largely to have been lost in these present days. Spinning is so much easier, but how prosaic by comparison! How much more inspiring it is to see a proficient Spey caster putting out a steady 30 to 40 yards of line, apparently with so little effort, and with repeated response from the fish, given any normal degree of good fortune. I remember John Stansfeld, who sad to say was a semi-invalid at the time, being impressed by this method of fishing and speculating as to whether his light 12 foot fly rod and correspondingly light line would be effective for it. My counsel was a definite though regretful 'No', which was undoubtedly the correct response. A long rod and heavyish line are essentials for this form of fishing, though the advent of fibre glass and more still of carbon graphite as rod materials has revolutionized the position vis a vis suitable rods since those days. No longer does one have to put up with the weight of a 15 or 16 foot Grant Vibration, while a carbon graphite rod of that length is a delight to use and weighs no more than a 12 foot split cane. At the same time a rod of this type can handle with ease the necessary heavy line and big flies for spring fishing, even when a contrary wind blows most foully.

Before leaving the subject of the North Esk and its fishing, I would once again like to emphasize the outstanding potentiality of this small but delightful river. No doubt the wealth of favourable spawning grounds in its headwaters and tributaries is largely the reason behind this. In the West Water for instance, grilse and small salmon, as the spawning season approaches, push on to near its source, past Hunthill, where it is no more than a hill burn. There is good gravel for spawning in many places all the way up this 13 mile tributary, as well as in the main river itself and in its many other smaller tributaries. In addition the whole river is liberally stocked (artificially) with eyed ova each year.

Grimble in his *Salmon Rivers of Scotland* (1899) writes: 'For its size this river (the North Esk) is the most prolific of all the Scotch streams.' No doubt in those days this was a fair statement of fact, even though the large majority of the fish were net-caught; but in modern times too I would hazard a shrewd guess that it is little less true.

The South Esk

It maintains a fair stream for fishing purposes right down to its tidal reaches. This is the Arn Pool, Kinnaird water with the river at summer level.

The South Esk is another Angus river of much the same size and character as its counterpart and neighbour, the North Esk. It rises high up in Glen Clova, on the borders of Angus and Aberdeenshire, the little Loch Esk on its headwaters being only 4 miles due south of Lochnagar. Its general course lies south-eastwards, passing close to Cortachy, Tannadice, and Brechin, to fall after 49 miles into Montrose Basin, and so into the North Sea at Montrose. This river drains 245 square miles (first of hill country and then of flatter agricultural land), which makes it very similar in size to the North Esk. It is another charming though comparitively small river, of no great size even when in spate, easy to fish, and with a good flow in spring and sometimes autumn, but liable to shrink to decidedly minor proportions in summer.

Its upper course through Glen Clova has the typical steep descent of a small highland river, rocky and tumbling, with short pools and fast streams. This part of it is of more significance from the spawning angle than that of fishing. Immediately below Cortachy it is joined by its biggest tributary, the Prosen Water, which also rises in the hills to the north west. It provides better and more extensive spawning ground than the South Esk upstream of their junction. The South Esk as a result of this influx is considerably increased in size, and now leaves the hill county to enter the rich farmland of Strathmore. It then runs more or less directly eastwards towards Brechin, though winding to a fair extent in places, and so to Montrose Basin. One other sizeable tributary, the Noran water, joins it from the north-west four miles upstream of Brechin. This too provides ground for extensive spawning.

The flow of this river is reasonably rapid and it maintains a fair stream for fishing purposes right down to its tidal reaches, which is rather surprising considering the lowland nature of the country through which it flows for the main part of its course. In spring at any rate, unless there is prolonged and exceptional frost, the flow is all that a discriminating angler would desire, as it is too in autumn provided there is a fair amount of rain. In summer, however, the flow does become considerably reduced and loses its impetus. With the river thus diminished, fishing deteriorates correspondingly during this part of the season.

There are a number of what are locally known as 'dykes' on the South Esk, i.e. weirs, or 'caulds', call them what you will. The main one is at Kinnaird, $1\frac{1}{2}$ miles downstream from Brechin. Others were at Brechin itself, and at Kintrockat, 3 miles further upstream; also there were formerly three or four more further up-river. The purpose of these dykes was originally always the same—i.e. to provide a head of water to empower mills, or else to provide a local water supply. Now they are mostly redundant, and have been allowed to disintegrate partially or wholly. The only dyke which still has a significant effect on fishing is the one at Kinnaird. The drop here is an appreciable one of seven to eight feet, and though amply provided with improved ladders and redesigned lately, this dyke does tend to check the ascent of fish when the water is cold during the spring. It is not that they *cannot* surmount it, or even that they find the passage difficult, (they pass up it freely enough later in the season); it is simply a case of the old story that when the water is cold fish are unwilling to face even a minor obstacle and prefer to rest downstream of it. It should not be forgotten that in early spring the temperature of the river water is almost certainly a good deal colder than that of the sea. An early spring fish entering a cold river no doubt has his energy reduced towards semi-paralysis, one notices for instance what a poor fight fresh run salmon usually put up when hooked in very cold water. No doubt their instinct in any case is to conserve all their energy to combat the cold, rather than to squander it, and the spawning season is still eight months away, so there is no pressing need to travel fast up-river. So perhaps it is not surprising that they await a recrudescence of energy, induced by a rising water temperature, before they tackle any sort of obstruction. The dyke at Brechin (now done away with) for some reason never formed any appreciable obstacle to the passage of fish, nor does the one at Kintrockat, but the Kinnaird dyke does go far to ensure very good fishing for half a mile or more downstream up to about mid-April.

There is little or no pollution in the South Esk, except that, anyhow in bygone days when I last fished this river, a good deal of sewage reputedly from Brechin used to seep in. This trouble may well have been rectified by now, I do not know. It certainly needed rectification then, as in low water it made the river pretty foul and produced fungus on the fish. There was also apt to be 'pot-ale' distillery pollution from time to time. I gather the general position is still not entirely satisfactory. Otherwise the South Esk's water is adequately pure, except that after heavy rain it colours with peat and agricultural drainage to a certain extent, as might be expected.

The rod-fishing season opens on February 16th, and lasts till

October 30th. There is a good spring run of salmon, particularly due to the fact that there is little netting carried on at the mouth. Kinnaird, for the reasons explained above, always has much the best of the fishing. By April however a lot of fish are past Kinnaird, and the upper beats do reasonably well. As on the North Esk the river level from mid-April onwards is likely to fall steadily as the snow on the hills disappears, and by mid-May except in a late year the water is likely to be approaching summer level. Fishing deteriorates correspondingly, and all through the summer except at time of spate, which is rare, there is little to be done, except in the way of night fishing for sea-trout and herling. This can be very good in the lower reaches.

There is quite a good run of grilse, but the autumn salmon, which at one time were plentiful, have now dwindled. Only an odd one comes in, and can be caught provided there is adequate rain to raise the river and keep it running at a good fishing height. This is a necessity. There is little hope of a worthwhile bag as long as the river remains in its diminished summer condition.

Kinnaird is a splendid beat to fish in early spring. I remember well the excitement of fishing the long stretch of streamy pools below the dyke, and knowing that with every cast one's fly was covering a large number of fresh fish. They lay thick in all the pools, and there was no difficulty in locating them! It was just a question of whether they would take or not, and often they would. There were few hazards. High flood from melting snow was of course one of them, but such floods rarely lasted for more than a couple of days at most. A more serious one was exceptionally hard frost, and a low river frozen along its banks, and full of 'grue' or floating ice. As long as this lasted, and it could persist for some time during February or early March, there was little to be done. Apart from this, one could hardly go wrong.

Other than at Kinnaird the best fishing in those days was to be found at Cortachy, Inshewan, or Finavon. I don't know how things are now, but doubt whether they are much changed.

The average size of spring fish, as in the North Esk, was 9–10 lb and there were few over 20 lb. In autumn one had a better chance of a big one. There was however a 47 pounder killed in May some years ago.

The record fish for this river attained the astonishing weight of 59 lb. It was caught by Mr. J. K. Somerville in October 1922. I wish I knew the story of its capture and could relate it here. It must have been highly dramatic. What can have induced such a monster to run up this comparatively small river? and it must have looked like a veritable porpoise in such restricted surroundings.

Tackle and methods of fishing suitable for the South Esk are in every way similar to those recommended for the North Esk (see page 161). In fact the two rivers resemble each other closely, except in one important respect which is that the North Esk produces a considerably bigger head of fish. It has much better and more extensive spawning grounds, both in main river and tributaries: indeed it would not be an exaggeration to say that if the South Esk under present conditions produces a better rod catch than the North Esk, this is predominantly due to the latter being more heavily netted.

For visiting fishermen who look for hotels, there are several adequate ones in Montrose, which is a pleasant sea-side town with good shops, and very much a centre of the salmon net-fishing industry all along the coast. Half-way between Montrose and Brechin there is another country hotel called the House of Dun, which offers its guests some fishing on the lowest stretches of the South Esk, below Kinnaird.

The Tay

Fast water on the river at Islamouth.

The first thing that impresses anyone about the Tay, I am sure, is its sheer size. Apart possibly from the Shannon, the Tay below its junction with the Tummel at Ballinluig is by far the biggest salmon river in the British Isles. The Tweed, Spey and Ness are its nearest rivals in Scotland but not nearly so large. The Severn may be longer but its fishing, by comparison, is very limited and only in the upper part of the river.

In its tidal reaches at Perth the Tay is a good 150 yards wide, and thirty-two miles upstream at Dunkeld it still has a width of 80–90 yards, or more when in spate. By British standards this is a large river indeed, and I am sure that any angler seeing it for the first time will fully agree with me about this.

The effects on fishing are manifold. First, the wide extent of the water makes the use of boats, whether for harling or casting, frequently and almost everywhere an indispensable need, and second, if wading is attempted one certainly has to be prepared to wade deep and in a strong stream and to be an accomplished performer, otherwise one may well drown or at least undergo an unpleasant ducking. A third result, incidentally, is that for an angler, whether fishing from a boat or more still if wading, the ability to throw a really long line, whether with fly or bait, is a decided advantage. All the statements in this paragraph apply primarily to the Tay below Ballinluig, where the Tummel enters. Upstream of that point both Tay and Tummel are only about half the size, so that fishing requirements and conditions are different.

Almost invariably, when one is fishing elsewhere, one curses prolonged dry weather, and prays for rain and a consequent spate and run of fresh fish. It is an axiom among the unenlightened that fishermen are curious beings who delight in rain and generally foul weather. While this is true to a certain extent, it being of course the results of rain that the fisherman welcomes rather than the rain itself (it is as unpleasant fishing in pouring rain as it is doing anything else), on the Tay the opposite holds good. It is fine weather and low water which as a rule produce much the best sport. This is a happy thought when there is lack of snow in winter, or during prolonged dry weather in summer—both of which are apt to spell disaster on other rivers.

The mighty Tay never falls too low for fish to run. In low water fish are more inclined to linger below Ballinluig rather than to run through into the upper river, or into Loch Tay, or the headwaters, or tributaries, so the lower and main part of the river thus benefits.

Another result of the Tay's large size (and this time an unfavourable one) is that with a high river the only really effective way of covering the water is by harling. As my readers no doubt know, harling is a system of boat fishing whereby one or two anglers sit in a boat with three rods trailing various lures on varying lengths of line downstream from the boat. The boatman, nowadays using an outboard motor, works the boat to and fro' across the width of the pool, dropping slightly downstream on each crossing or 'harl'. Any skill in the process lies entirely with him. All the fishermen have to do is to see that their lures are fishing properly, i.e. that they do not foul the bottom, or collect any weed or leaves, or become entangled. The fish, when they take, either hook themselves or not, as the case may be. If they are hooked, the fisherman's part then is simply to hold on hard with the strong tackle that is normally used and land the fish in the shortest possible time so that the process can be renewed.

I must admit that in my young days I harled briefly both on the Tay and in Norway but it is not a form of fishing to which I feel in any way attracted, and I would never do it again unless in my old age I became physically incapable of any other method. Nor would I recommend anyone else to try it. The only way one could get any amusement out of it might be by managing the boat oneself, though one's boatman would not be likely to favour this. Otherwise it is boring to a degree, and I feel that trolling for pollack on the open sea would be about as entertaining! One possible excitement is if two or even three fish become attached at the same time, which is a greater likelihood when there are kelts about. My friend Colonel A. M. Lyle tells me that, conversely, when harling as a boy he had one single fish attached to two different rods! There seems to be a number of alternative possible combinations.

One indirect consequence of the Tay's size is that it is the best producer of big fish of any river in Britain. There have been three fish of 60 lb or over killed on rod and line in this river, the biggest being Miss Ballantine's 64 pounder from the Glendelvine water on October 7th 1922.

I have given a detailed account of the capture of this record British rod-caught salmon in a previous book *Great Salmon Rivers of Scotland*, so will say little more about it here. This fish was caught by harling, on strong tackle, and an artificial mottled brown spinning bait known as a 'dace'. Miss Ballantine's main task was simply to hold on as hard as she could for the next two hours and keep her prey clear of all obstructions. The fish was hooked at 6.15 p.m., at dusk, high up in the Bridge Pool above Caputh Bridge, and was not landed till shortly after 8 p.m. when it was quite dark. Miss Ballantine had by then been taken about half a mile downriver and under Caputh road bridge. When the time came for gaffing, Mr. Ballantine her father, who was acting as boatman and was 70 years old at the time, slid the gaff down the trace knot by knot until he had reached what he judged to be the right depth. He then got the gaff into the monster, but this was not the end of it . . . . Colonel A. M. Lyle of Glendelvine tells me that the Glendelvine records show that the shock of this fish's weight was so great that the gaff not unexpectedly slipped out of Mr. Ballantine's grip, and the fish went off carrying the gaff with it. Fortunately it remained firmly hooked, and Mr. B. had to hurry back to his cottage and collect another gaff. Next time all went well. . . !

Caputh road bridge, looking down river, scene of Miss Ballantine's famous encounter with her 64 pounder.

There have been a further twenty Tay rod-caught fish of 50 lb or over, other than the three above, which I have so far managed to trace, and this may well not be a complete total. No other British river can rival this score, only a Tana or Alta or Aaro. For some reason as a general rule big fish prefer big rivers, and the Tay's head of such fish bears this out. There are exceptions, of course. The Awe has produced at least eleven 50 pounders, the Deveron one of 61 lb and one of 56 lb, and the South Esk one of 59 lb; and these are all rivers of modest size. But in general the principle holds good.

The biggest Tay fish on record weighed 84 lb and was caught in a net by one Wullie Walker in 1869, low down in the estuary. P. D. Malloch of the Tay Salmon Fisheries Company writing in 1908 gives the average yearly weight of the heaviest Tay salmon caught by net over the previous 14 years as 60 lb. He says that fish of between 50 and 60 lb were often caught and a fair number of between 60 and 65 lb, but that over 65 lb they were scarce. He has seen as many as 40 fish of over 40 lb netted in one day. It makes one's mouth water!

In present times, in spite of consistent netting in the estuary during spring and summer, the Tay yearly rod catch is good, totalling around 10,000 fish.

There is still a sizeable spring run of fish averaging 11 lb, with the chance of a big one of perhaps 40 lb amongst them but the average size of Tay fish has shown a gradual but steady decrease over the last fifty years. In 1924 it was as high as $19\frac{1}{2}$ lb. The number of big fish of 30 lb or over has also shown a steady reduction.

Good spring fishing lasts until early May, the best month invariably being April, though the last part of March can also be good in an early year. By mid-May the best of it is over. The river level is likely to fall and the majority of incoming fish are caught in the nets. The rod fishing season actually opens on January 15th, but weather conditions early in the year are likely to be sub-arctic, real 'brass monkey' weather as it is sometimes vulgarly described, and fish none too plentiful. Also, one's boatman is almost certain to recommend harling as the only worthwhile method, so generally speaking one would be well advised to postpone one's start to the Tay season at least till the last week of March. From then onwards casting from an anchored boat, either with bait or sunk fly, should offer a reasonable chance of success on most beats. If the water is low wading may also be possible to a limited extent. But do not count on any warm weather till at least the end of April, or even later, if you are hoping to fish fly with a floating line.

During summer, as indicated above, the run of salmon is apt to dwindle, and only the best beats such as Kinnaird, Islamouth and Taymount still produce a fair catch. But from about the last week in June grilse averaging between 5 and 7 lb, start to arrive in numbers. July is the best grilse month, when in certain beats they congregate thickly and produce most entertaining fishing. However, one factor essential for the provision of a good grilse fishery is the presence of shallow and streamy pools. If your beat has none of these, you will catch few if any grilse, as these fish are extremely choosy where they lie and this is what they like. Islamouth is by far the best beat for grilse, and Taymount and Kinnaird are good also. Otherwise one has to look for streamy pools elsewhere, such as at Grandtully, or even up the Lyon. There are not many really good grilse beats other than the above.

Is there any method by which, when grilse fishing, one can avoid losing nearly half the fish one hooks through their coming unhooked after a minute or two's play? In spite of every precaution in the way of fine and sharp hooks, fine gut, a light hold during play, and a light and lissom rod, one still seems to lose far too many. It no doubt adds to the fun, but it can be exasperating. If any of my readers have suggestions I should be glad to hear from them.

The autumn influx of salmon into the Tay is probably the biggest run of all. It is apt to start in middle or late August, and has an unrestricted entry after August 20th when the nets cease to operate. Fresh run fish with sea-lice are common in the first half of September. They average 11/12 lb and there are bigger ones amongst them, often up to 20 lb and over, with an occasional 30 pounder, and sometimes even a 40 pounder. One usually hears of one or two of these last killed during most seasons. I have myself seen two 33 pounders killed by friends during these last few years, and my own biggest weighed 31 lb, though Islamouth where we do most of our fishing is not a good beat for really big fish. It is too shallow and streamy, and the leviathans prefer deep solid pools. The biggest fish of recent times was caught some eleven years ago at Ballathie. It weighed 54 lb.

Towards the end of September fresh fish become scarcer, and during October, when the fishing season lasts till the 15th, only an odd one is caught, though the old stagers which are getting red by then take freely.

Weather during this period can vary from warm summer conditions in late August to cold or flood in early October so the angler, whether he is going to use fly or bait, should be diversely equipped. Weather at this time of year is always uncertain, and can change quickly. In the inventory of flies and baits any size may be wanted from $\frac{3}{4}$ of an inch to $3\frac{1}{2}$ inches. It is as well to have a wide selection, as one can never foretell exactly what one will need.

Without doubt there is a better chance in the Tay at this time of year of catching a 40 pounder than in any other river in the British Isles, not excluding even that renowned big fish river the Wye. It follows that the angler should use reasonably strong tackle at all times, and when by himself should always have a gaff handy. If he does not, and encounters a fish in this category, or even a 30 pounder, he is likely to regret it.

The Tay's water is usually pleasantly clear and free from peat or other impurity. This is an advantage resulting largely from the many lochs in its catchment area, and on its upper course. The two biggest of these are Loch Tay, $14\frac{1}{2}$ miles long, and Loch Rannoch, 10 miles long, but there are also Lochs Ericht, Lyon, Tummel, and the artificial Loch Faskally, amongst others, all of which help to feed the Tay. These lochs provide advantages in more ways than one, as they all act to a greater or lesser degree as a settling tank for discolouring matter and help greatly to keep the main river clear. Lochs Tay, Faskally, and Tummel provide a sanctuary for fish to some extent (although a good deal of fishing is practised in them).

The Isla, a large tributary which enters the main river immediately downstream of Kinclaven Bridge, is on the other hand a bad source of discolouration. Although when low it is perfectly clear, this river, 47 miles long, flows for much of its course through the low lying agricultural land of Strathmore. After heavy rain it is apt to colour badly, and for a day or two can dirty the whole 14 miles of the lower Tay as far as the estuary, to the annoyance of fishermen on that part of the river, while their fellow anglers upstream are still finding the upper Tay agreeably clear. Here, as elsewhere, there is no doubt that fish take better in clear water, and the dirtier it becomes so the fish become progressively less co-operative.

The confluence of the Isla with the main Tay.

As to artificial pollution, this is negligible. There are few distilleries, and all sizeable towns on the main river or its tributaries, such as Blair Atholl, Pitlochry, Aberfeldy, Dunkeld, and Perth have their sewage disposal well under control. So the Tay is fortunate in the pure quality of its flow, rather unexpected in such a large river, and better in this respect than two other of the major Scottish rivers, the Spey and the Tweed.

I have already mentioned the large size of the Tay, and the general effect of this upon its fishing. There are other characteristics of this river, however, of which the would-be Tay fisherman should be aware. As a whole the current of the Tay is not particularly fast, not nearly so much so as that of the Spey for instance, or of some other highland rivers. Loch Tay is only 350 feet above sea level, and the course of the Tay from Taymouth (at the eastern end of this loch) to Perth is 49 miles in length, so the average fall per mile is 7 feet, not a particularly steep rate of descent for a Scottish river. This results in many stretches of river having a rather dull and solid flow, without incident in the form of rapids or broken rock formations. Such stretches do not normally provide good fishing, though some fish are taken in them when their stream quickens in time of high water.

From time to time, however, and in various different stretches, there are some very fast and powerful streams, and generally speaking it is the beats with streamy water and a quick flow which are the most productive in fish. Islamouth is the best, but there is also fine strong water at Grandtully on the upper Tay, at Kinnaird immediately below the Tummel mouth, at Murthly and Glendelvine, at Taymount and at Stanley, Benchill, and Redgorton. Kinnaird and Islamouth are additionally fortunate in each having the influx of a sizeable tributary, the Tummel and the Isla, up which many fish in due course travel. Junction pools and the stretches below them always seem to hold fish in liberal quantities, and these two beats are no exception to this rule. The Islamouth beat reached its full capacity only after an obstruction in the Ericht (a tributary of the Isla) was removed about 15 years aso. This obstruction was caused by a landslide in 1897. It seems that the Ericht fish have increased in numbers as a result, and that many of them are inclined to linger in the Islamouth beat of the Tay before running further towards their parent stream.

In general the above mentioned beats are the most prolific on the whole river.

The best method of fishing with the river at a reasonable height is from an anchored boat, casting one side or the other with either fly or bait. The Tay pools are so wide that two fishermen can often operate together, casting one on each side of the boat—and although it sounds rather an odd procedure, this method is frequently and successfully adopted. If the river is fairly low wading may be possible, though it is never easy. One or two pools, for example the March Pool at

Meikleour and Catholes at Stanley, can be fished even from the bank; but pools of this type are few and far between. With a medium or low river all the above beats provide good fly water, fast running and shallow enough in most places, and at any time from April onwards fly will kill well, though your boatman (with an eye to a more easily obtained bag) may well try to persuade you to use bait. Only if the water is high does bait hold a decided advantage.

A drawback in time of medium/high water is that the Hydro at Pitlochry finds it necessary to let surplus water down the Tummel early every morning. This can result in a rise of a foot or more carried all the way down the Tummel and the Tay below Tummel mouth, as far as the estuary. This rise in water is apt to reach Islamouth every day at about 12.30 p.m., and the lower beats proportionately later. It is probably not so disruptive in its effects as would be a natural rise caused by rain water, nevertheless it must disturb and move fish to a considerable extent and can be maddening when it arrives to raise yet further a river level already too high for one's liking. (In low water this daily Hydro rise is hardly apparent, and amounts only to a matter of an inch or two, which has little effect on fish in so large a river. The reason is that surplus water is released through the Hydro dams only when the level has reached a certain height overnight.)

My own experience on the Tay has been limited chiefly to Islamouth and the Meikleour Home Beat, thanks to the kind hospitality of Lord Lansdowne. Islamouth in particular is delightful water to fish with the river at a medium or low level. It is a fast streamy stretch resembling closely many parts of the lower Spey, except of course that the Tay is a much bigger river. I have been lucky enough to have fished there for seven or eight years now, but have also fished at odd times in the past at Stanley, Benchill and Redgorton. Apart from this I have no first hand experience of other reaches of the Tay, except by looking at them and hearing much about them from others.

My biggest fish in this river up to the present weighed 31 lb. It was caught in the New Shot at Islamouth on September 22nd 1975. It took a double-hooked Blue Charm size 6, and I caught it when casting from a boat. It was fairly fresh, and had not from its appearance been in the river for more than a fortnight ... not that there is anything outstanding about a fish of this size from the Tay, and bigger ones are caught every season, But it happens to be my best, though I have caught many in the 20 lb class. My best day for numbers was September 15th 1975, when between 10 a.m. and 4 p.m. I caught 13 fish at Islamouth, all on fly. These fish averaged 10 lb and the biggest was 16 lb. This is in no way exceptional for the Tay, though one should be pleased enough with it in these modern times.

At Islamouth. Colonel Kidston-Montgomerie and Mrs Fearfield after a successful morning's fishing.

My remarks in this chapter are applicable mainly to the lower Tay. The upper Tay above Ballinluig is obviously a much smaller river, and there would be less boat fishing and more wading or casting from the bank or from croys. Some of it looks attractive water, particularly in the Grandtully area, where I hope perhaps to fish in the future.

The Tay has extensive headwaters and tributaries, most of which provide good and widespread spawning grounds. Some of these tributaries, for instance the Tummel, Lyon, Dochart and Ericht can sometimes provide quite good fishing. The Tilt, a small tributary which joins the Garry at Blair Atholl, also provides fair summer fishing and and holds a reasonable stock of fish.

The only one of these which I have myself fished is the Lyon, and that not frequently. It seems a pretty river which holds quite a number of small salmon and grilse, but has been badly affected by Hydro operations, and now lacks natural spates and an adequate flow. I believe it used to be an excellent small salmon river before the Hydro was installed. What a pity it is. One can but be thankful that all future plans for Hydro installations in Scotland have now been scrapped.

One advantage not so far mentioned is to be found in the sensible arrangements in most parts of the river about beats. Some fishery owners have sole rights on both banks, or at least rent an opposite bank, which has the same effect. But where opposite banks are in different hands an understanding has almost everywhere been reached over the way in which the fishing should be divided, so that

This railway bridge is at the bottom of the Islamouth beat. Fish often lie right underneath it.

the least possible mutual interference between fishermen should occur. This sort of thing is always a good plan, and well worth while.

U.D.N. has for many years past been present in the Tay, but although it was bad in its early stages, it has now so far dwindled as to give little cause for concern. Only in late autumn as the water becomes cold and the spawning season approaches is an odd diseased fish still to be found. One can but be thankful for this mercy.

There are numerous good hotels on Tayside, as can be discovered in any directory. The two best and pleasantest which I have so far found are one at Dunkeld, on the river there, and one at Ballathie, also on the river. There is excellent chalet accommodation to be had near Butterstone (close to Dunkeld), for those who prefer this.

I now bid farewell to the Tay, so far anyhow as this book is concerned, and until next fishing season. It is undoubtedly Scotland's greatest river, in all senses, and I wish any of my readers who go to fish it as much excitement and wonderful sport as I have been lucky enough to have enjoyed on it for many years.

The Tweed

The Tweed at Rutherford looking upstream towards the Eildon hills, legendary burial place of King Arthur.

More has probably been said and written about the Tweed than about any other river in Scotland. For this reason my present script about this magnificent river will be short.

The Tweed has provided inspiration for a wealth of books; but none of them is more outstanding than that masterpiece *Days and Nights of Salmon Fishing* by William Scrope, published in 1843. No keen Tweed angler should fail to study this book. It is wholly delightful, witness the assertion of James Robb in his *Notable Angling*

Literature: 'Scrope's name is beloved wherever the literature of the salmon is known.' Howard Walden in his *Upstream and Down* declares in similar vein: 'Only books like these survive as pinnacles of angling literature, timeless and unchanging, because they deal with those fundamentals of angling that are also timeless and unchanging, the fisherman and the fish. Books that deal with tackle and tactics and the endless trivial detail of 'how to do it' proliferate like weeds and like weeds perish.' How very true, and even after 150 years one can still feel a vivid thrill in Scrope's angling adventures, as though they occurred but yesterday.

The Tweed's surroundings and characteristics are perhaps unique in their variation. This river's upper reaches run through a heathery hill country not unlike that of say Banffshire or Angus, as do its tributaries such as Ettrick, Yarrow and Teviot. Over its middle course from Ettrick mouth to Kelso, its valley opens wider, with rich farmlands bordering its still briskly flowing and wider stream; while only below Kelso, and still more below Coldstream or Tillmouth, does the Tweed assume the character of a substantial lowland waterway. Everywhere along the lower half of the Tweed's course the horizon is dominated by the triple peak of the Eildon hills or by the long blue ridge of the Border hills culminating in the Cheviot. What river could boast a more picturesque setting?

In its historical associations the Tweed as a river is unrivalled. Being a border river it has featured prominently in British history as far back as Roman times, while its place in romantic story is assured by the countless ballads, legends, and fairy stories which illuminate its background.

As a salmon river, both for net and rod fishing, one can be quite sure that in the past the Tweed has been second to no other in Scotland, though in present days this pre-eminence could well be queried.

No less than eight fish of 50 lb or over are on record as having been caught from the Tweed by rod and line during the last 100 years, the last of that weight having been killed in 1925. All were caught on fly, and all were autumn fish. The biggest weighed $57\frac{1}{2}$ lb and was caught on the Floors water on October 27th 1886 by a Mr. Pryor. This fish took a Silver Wilkinson size 4/0 and a model of it is still to be seen in the Ednam House Hotel at Kelso. Mr. Pryor caught 15 fish altogether that day. The big one was not weighed till the following morning, so it may well have scaled 60 lb when first caught.

The Tweed is the second largest salmon river in Scotland, after the Tay. Three quarters of its course and catchment area lie in Scotland, while for the bottom 19 miles of its course it forms the boundary between England and Scotland until Gainslaw, $4\frac{1}{2}$ miles above its mouth, where it passes wholly into England. It has a course of 96 miles length, rising in Tweed's Well in the hills near Moffat, and runs in a generally easterly direction via Peebles, Melrose, Kelso, and Coldstream to Berwick. It is augmented en route by many tributaries of all sizes, of which the Ettrick, Gala, Leader, Teviot, Till, and Whiteadder are the most notable. Its catchment area is one of approximately 1500 square miles, (compared to the Tay's 2000 and the Spey's 1100.), of which 300 are in England and the remainder in Scotland.

I first fished the Tweed in 1950, thanks to the kindness of my friend Sir John Milburn who took me over for a day at Carham. This was on October 23rd and I was lucky enough to catch a good 17 lb fish in the Kirk End pool. This was indeed lucky because autumn fish were scarce in those days. Since that long ago date, and owing initially to the kindness of Capt. John Moller and subsequently for many years to that of Capt. Charles Burrell of Broome Park, I have fished this river both in spring and autumn and at many different times and places during almost every season since that date. How grateful I am for this.

Most of my fishing has been done on the Floors Junction beat, the Lower Floors beat, and at Rutherford; but I have had odd days at Upper Mertoun, Makerstoun, Upper Floors, Birgham, Carham, and Lower Birgham, so have been lucky enough to have had a reasonably wide experience of the main part of the river. It is all delightful in many different ways, but the best of it seems to me to lie upstream of Kelso. The river there is smaller, lacking the influx of the Teviot, but all the same by no means too small; it is also streamier and rockier, and its surroundings are more impressive. More important still, in autumn at least it normally seems to hold a bigger head of fish. Nevertheless I would be happy to fish almost anywhere on this lovely river, though I must confess to a preference for the magnificent Floors water, where I am lucky enough to be a tenant of the Duke of Roxburghe. There could be no better beat on the whole river, though even here the spring fishing in present days is sadly fallen away.

Tweed rod fishing used to be exceptionally prolific during spring and early summer in earlier times. Up to the end of the 1950's there was a massive run of small spring fish averaging around 7–8 lb in weight. Any fish over 14 lb was a big one, and 20 pounders were almost unheard of. But this class of fish emphatically made up in numbers for what it lacked in weight. For a single rod to catch double figures in a day was then commonplace, whether with fly or bait. For instance, I have a note in my diary that on February 15th 1956 I caught eight salmon in eight successive casts at Teviotmouth in the Junction Pool at Kelso. There was little or no skill in this, as the fish were lying there thick, but I still remember this incident, as it seemed almost miraculous on one's first day's fishing that season. These were the days too when Capt. Straker Smith of Carham caught 22 fish in one afternoon, and then stopped because he thought he had had enough!

In those days I used often to fish on the famous Junction Pool early in the season. Two rods then would have had no difficulty in catching 30 fish or more on fly only, during the first fortnight of the season, provided the river was in order.

This sort of thing is now completely past history, alas! The spring run over the last ten or fifteen years has dwindled to a shadow of what it was, and catches are pitiable by comparison. There is no recent sign of improvement, if anything the contrary, (and yet there are more fishermen than ever). There is not now one spring fish for twenty that there used to be twenty five years ago. The reasons? No doubt there is no single one, and they are multifarious. Over-netting in the river itself, as well as all along the neighbouring Northumberland coast coast is probably the main one, though no doubt the Greenland and Faroes fishing also plays its part. In addition there must be taken into account the ravages of U.D.N., illegal fishing both in the river and at sea, over-fishing by rod for fish spawning or about to spawn (the Tweed rod-fishing season lasts till November 30th), and last but not least the havoc wrought by the ever increasing population of seals.

So much for spring fishing and the present dearth of spring fish.

The Junction Pool at Kelso. The boatman on the bank (out of the picture) is 'ottering' his rod downstream at the end of a length of rope, an alternative to rowing which is sometimes used on the Tweed.

Summer fishing is worse, and is simply not worth while, except in the rare event of continual high water. The nets, which fish till mid-September and to nearly as far upriver as Coldstream, take a prohibitive toll.

Autumn fishing in the 1940's and 1950's was very poor; in these latter years it has certainly improved, but is still nothing like as good as it was in the early years of the century. Moreover the 30 and 40 pounders, formerly fairly common, have now practically disappeared. They turn up only very infrequently in present days. Autumn weather too is unpredictable and can change remarkably quickly, while the quick drainage of the whole catchment area causes the Tweed to colour easily, so putting the fish off the take, and to rise and fall unnaturally quickly. So autumn fishing becomes a remarkably chancy business, and one is lucky if one has the water in good fishing order for an average of three days out of six.

For many years up to 1981 the beats below Hendersyde and Sprouston have, for some reason unknown, failed to hold any number of autumn fish. They have simply failed to stop in this part of the river. Beats above Kelso however have been considerably better. But in 1981 for some reason, again unknown, the fish were far more inclined to stay in the lower part of the river from Floors downstream, while one gathered that the upper beats had a progressively worse catch the higher upriver one went. Regretfully it must be admitted that there are plenty of problems connected with Tweed fishing, though personally I am extremely grateful for the privilege of casting a fly in such a lovely river, whether I catch anything or not. It holds a very high place in my affections.

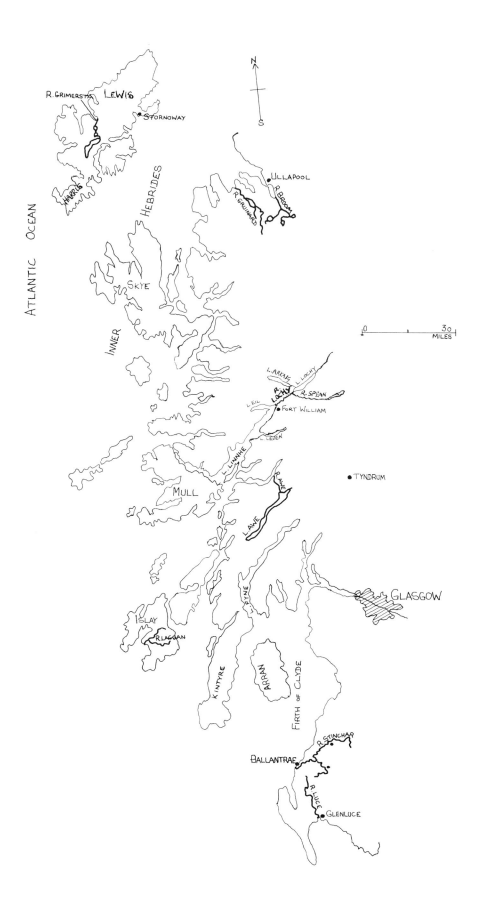

Labels on map:

ATLANTIC OCEAN

LEWIS
R.GRIMERSTA
STORNOWAY
HARRIS
HEBRIDES

N
S

ULLAPOOL
R.GRUINARD
R.BROOM

INNER
SKYE

L.ARKAIG L.LOCHY
R.LOCHY R.SPEAN
L.EIL
FORT WILLIAM
L.LEVEN

30
MILES

TYNDRUM

MULL

L.LINNIE

R.AWE

L.AWE

ISLAY
R.LAGGAN

GLASGOW

KINTYRE
ARRAN
FIRTH OF CLYDE
L.FYNE

R.STINCHAR
BALLANTRAE

R.LUCE
GLENLUCE

SCOTLAND

Rivers of the West and North-West Coast

Luce—Stinchar—Laggan (Islay)—Awe
Lochy—Gruinard—Broom—Grimersta

Except for the Lochy the rivers here are all of comparatively small size, many of them having the character of 'spate' rivers. There is no worthwhile spring fishing in this area, in fact all good fishing occurs only from about mid-June onwards. Big fish in all these rivers are now a rarity. Nevertheless in their due season they can all provide the greatest fun, their best fishing period as might be expected being during the first few days of run-down after rain and high water.

The Luce

Lord Stair at the Turnweil Pool in high water.

The Luce is the westernmost of the Solway rivers, its two chief headwaters, the Main Water of Luce and the Cross Water of Luce, rising in the high moorland where Wigtownshire meets Ayrshire. Both these streams, being of almost identical size, have a southerly course of about 13 miles, nearly parallel with each other, until they converge at the village of New Luce to form a united Luce. This larger river continues to run southwards for 7 miles, passing by the small town of Glen Luce, until it flows into the Solway at the head of Luce

Bay. It is thus a Wigtownshire river throughout its course, besides being the biggest and most productive of fish in that county. Although the county name is now obsolete, to me it will always be 'Wigtownshire', a name it has borne at least since the 14th century. One outstanding feature of the Luce, including both the Main Water and the Cross water, is that all its fishings, both rod and net, belong to a single owner, (the Earl of Stair), except for one short stretch of the headwaters of the Main water with separate ownership. There must be few other rivers of any consequence in Britain which can boast as much, and indeed the Luce is fortunate in this respect. There could be few owners of salmon fishings as knowledgeable about everything to do with salmon and sea-trout as is Lord Stair, and certainly none who is a better fisherman. On either Luce or Stinchar Lord Stair can catch fish whenever he wants to, be the river in as low or impossible a state as can be imagined. After the manner of the heron or seal, he is a master-fisherman!

The benefits of this undivided ownership are many. For instance it is hard to find a river elsewhere where local fishermen are given a bigger share in the available fishing. The Stranraer Angling Association has a lease of all the fishing on the 13 miles of the Cross Water throughout each season, as well as on a number of lochs in the neighbourhood. A local syndicate rents the rod-fishing on the bottom 4 miles of the Luce down to the tideway. The fishing on the upper part of the main water of Luce is also let. Lord Stair keeps for his own use but two miles of fishing from New Luce downstream, from a pool called the Turnweil where the Main Water and Cross Water unite, down as far as the Red Brae. The netting rights in Luce Bay are also leased to local fishermen, but are not over-exploited.

Thus under this single and efficient ownership, there is wise control, a generous distribution of fishing, and general peace and harmony. How seldom, unfortunately, does one see the like when fishing rights on a river belong to a variety of different owners—each with a different set of ideas of how fishery matters should best be managed. There is no need to elaborate further on this theme.

The Luce is a small river, with a catchment area of only 73 square miles—half the size of that of the neighbouring Stinchar. It rises and falls very quickly. Heavy rain will bring it out in flood in a mere matter of hours, and like many other small upland rivers, when it is running at four or five feet above summer level for the time being it gives the impression of considerable size. When the rain ceases however, it quickly falls away again; and when it is down to low water level it at once becomes apparent that after all this is a river of modest dimensions.

The Luce thus has the typical flow of a small west-coast or Solway river, fast and powerful in spate, but down to little more than a rivulet in low water. No doubt here as elsewhere hill drainage has accelerated the natural rise and fall of the water. Spates, in summer at any rate, are none too frequent. The Wigtownshire yearly rainfall is little more than 50 inches, a moderate amount for the west coast of Scotland; and for the Luce fisherman an abnormally wet summer is always an unlooked for but welcome bonus.

The Main Water and Cross Water are both high moorland streams, with a quick rate of descent, and a series of small rocky pools. Salmon and grilse manage to penetrate right to their headwaters, given enough water to help them upstream. When low, as can be imagined, these two small rivers do shrink to a very reduced size, and fishing is liable to come to a standstill until the next rise in water. The Luce below New Luce is naturally about double the size of either the Main Water or the Cross Water, and does not contract to quite the same extent as these two latter; nevertheless at low summer level it too does become very small. Fishing here also comes virtually to a stop under such conditions, although never quite hopeless once a stock of fish is present.

Much the best fishing time is invariably when the river is clearing and fining down after a rise, as is the normal rule on spate rivers of this sort, and when for the first time after a flood it comes into what could be termed 'good fishing order.' It is as well to let no time be wasted on such occasions.

Returning to the description of the river and its surroundings, there are few trees to give shelter upstream of New Luce, but from there down the banks of the river are frequently wooded, which is a benefit in forming a wind break and providing shade over the water on bright sunny days. The river valley is a very pretty one, narrow, quiet and peaceful, with farmland along the lower reaches, where the stately ruins of the mediaeval Glen Luce Abbey are also in evidence. There is only one minor road close to the river for most of its course, and traffic on it is negligible. The river has a gravel bottom in most places, with occasional outcrops of solid rock; its flow when other than dead low is fairly rapid, with a quick succession of streams and pools—and there are two small falls on the Main Water, which present little obstacle to fish. There is no denying that the spate water as a rule is very coloured and peaty (Wigtownshire moors being of solid heather covered peat), and it may take two or three days to clear. How far this affects fishing is difficult to say—Luce fish *do* take in peat water; but I would hazard a guess that if this river ran out of a largish natural loch, or series of lochs, as do the Grimersta, Awe, and Naver, they would take a good deal better as the result of a much clearer flow.

The rod fishing season lasts from February 20th to October 31st. As in the Stinchar and most of the Solway and Ayrshire rivers (though not all of them), the first part of this season is purely academic, there being no spring run in this river. Once cannot expect fresh salmon to arrive before June, and then only if there is rain and enough water to bring them in. But at any time from mid-June onwards a spate should make them enter. The best fishing period depends mainly on the weather; whenever the water is at a medium or high level fishing should be good, but when it is low or consistently low there is little to be done. It follows that September and October are likely on average to be the most productive months, simply because there is more chance of rain then, though it does not always work out that way. By late September too the fish are becoming coloured, and more so in October, though an odd fresh one can still be found if one is lucky. I should have mentioned that 'fly only' is the permanent rule on this river; no bait fishing of any sort is allowed—a commendable restriction for a river of this type.

Salmon and grilse come in together, the latter outnumbering the salmon to a considerable extent. Salmon are small averaging 8 lb, and grilse smaller. A 15 lb fish is an unusually large one for the Luce, and few are now caught of that size or over. This apparently was not

The river valley is a very pretty one. Cloisters Pool.

always the case. Sir Herbert Maxwell writing at the end of the last century constantly referred to Luce fish of 20 lb or over. He also emphasized that the Luce was a late river in character, which is still true to this day, but the big fish have largely disappeared. Calderwood writing in 1909 also remarks on the comparatively large size of fish to be found in the Luce, and mentions the capture of a 35 pounder, an almost incredible weight for so small a river; but unfortunately he gives no relevant details. The biggest Luce fish of recent times weighed 27 lb and was caught on Lord Stair's beat in the Ash Tree pool by the Hon. Mrs. H. Bridgeman on Oct. 16th 1956. This too was an outsized one for this river.

The yearly rod-catch of salmon and grilse varies from a total of about 80 in a bad year to 200 in a good one; but the river is not hard fished, in fact for fair periods of time it is hardly fished at all, far better treatment for a small river than the constant and merciless over-fishing which one so often witnesses elsewhere.

The best pools are perhaps the Turnweil, already mentioned, which is a sure hold for fish, the Broad Weil, the Ash Tree, Cloisters, the Red Brae, Boreland Bridge, the Jackdaw, and the Puddle Hole, amongst many others. This last is a well known one, below the old railway bridge near Glen Luce. There used to be some sort of weir or 'cauld' at the neck of this pool, which has now disappeared; but Lord Stair has built a new one across the river at the tail of the pool, which has served efficiently to step up the water level upstream by a foot or two, and thus to make it better holding water.

The Luce fisherman does not need heavy tackle. A 13 foot rod will be long enough, even with the river in spate, and a floating line with or without a sinking tip will be all that he wants. If the water is high and coloured, fish will take quite large flies up to $2\frac{1}{2}$ inches in length (thinly dressed and straggly hair wings are best), but as it falls away and clears the fly should be correspondingly reduced in size as one would expect. With low water and a reduced stream, it is advisable to 'strip' the fly fast through the pools, and fish can often be induced to follow and take if this is artistically done. A $9\frac{1}{2}$ foot single-handed rod will be the best implement for this. Thigh waders at anytime are long enough.

Apart from its salmon and grilse, the Luce is a noted sea-trout river. The run of these fish was at one time extensive, and even if it has fallen off to some extent in present days it is still worthy of note. Big sea-trout, up to 6 or 7 lb in weight, run from June onwards, and they are followed by large numbers of herling, the grilse of the sea-trout, which will run up-river however low the water may be. In medium or high water sea-trout can be caught at any time of day, but in low water night fishing gives by far the best chance. One used to be able to catch 10 to 20 herling during an evening in days gone by and without much difficulty; if one had tried hard and for longer hours one's bag would undoubtedly have been greater. One needed a fairly small fly of sea-trout size, pattern didn't much matter, and one had to pull it slowly through the water, having waited for darkness to descend, and to strike at the slightest touch. It was an intriguing form of fishing, as one never quite knew what one was going to encounter. It could be a $\frac{3}{4}$ pound herling, or a 4 lb sea-trout (or larger), or even a grilse or salmon, though the latter seldom took in complete dark. But the midges on the Luce as elsewhere could be formidable, particularly on a warm and damp evening. If a smoker, one needed clouds of one's most asphyxiating pipe or cigarette smoke as a deterrent, or failing that copious applications of one of the many odorous anti-midge ointments now obtainable.

If anyone is inclined to decry sea-trout fishing as a somewhat petty sport, let him consider Major G. L. Ashley-Dodd's great exploits on the Luce, described in his book *A Fisherman's Log* (1929). He writes:

> The three biggest bags of these fish I ever got, (168, 166 and 145) were made in hot sultry weather and dead low water, by fishing at night, when there would have been no chance by day.

These catches were in fact made in the Puddle Hole mentioned above, and they were by no means all of herling, there being plenty of sizeable sea-trout amongst them. Nor were they made on consecutive nights. On another occasion Major Ashley-Dodd caught 48 sea-trout and six salmon and grilse on a 10 foot rod. The biggest sea-trout weighed 13 lb and 11 lb. Can all this fairly be written off as 'insignificant' fishing? Surely not, as even the most dedicated salmon fisher must admit.

In August 1943 a 10 lb sea-trout was caught in the pool called Birkbank by Major the Hon. Colin Dalrymple, and no doubt there have been many other big ones from time to time.

My own achievements in the Luce have been insignificant, and I have always found its fishing extremely difficult. In September 1981, however, I had the good fortune to kill a 15 lb salmon and a 6 lb grilse on the same morning in a rocky pool called Linn Craig. The former was a big fish for the Luce. I was by myself, and he gave me a great fight on light tackle, running wildly all over the 40 yards long pool. The antics of sizeable fish hooked in small rivers often seem more formidable than in big rivers, though in fact there is probably less danger of their breaking free. Anyway it is certainly unexpected windfalls like this, even if they are in no way outstanding, which provide fishing with its spice of life.

The Stinchar

Fishing the pool at Ballantrae Bridge, $\frac{3}{4}$ mile upstream from the open sea.

Many fishermen are unacquainted with the wonderful district of Carrick, which lies in the south-west part of the Scottish Lowlands. It is a lovely wild and unspoilt region of hills and heather, with a magnificent coastline looking across to Arran, Ailsa Craig, Kintyre, and County Antrim. It is in this part of the country where in March 1307 Robert the Bruce, at the battle of Glen Trool, began his campaign of independence against the English overlordship which was to culminate seven years later in the great victory of Bannockburn.

Its main river is the Stinchar, which rises high up in Carrick Forest, its headwaters are burns flowing off the north side of Shalloch Hill (1777 feet), close to the source of the Girvan, and it runs for 30 miles in a south-westerly direction via Barr, Pinwherry, and Colmonell, to fall into the sea near Ballantrae, a village 12 miles south of Girvan, on the South Ayrshire coast. The Stinchar is a very pretty small river, a moorland stream to begin with, but developing considerably in size with the influx from the south of two tributaries, the Duisk at Pinwherry, a sizeable subsidiary flow with a course of 10 miles, and lower down the Tig, which is smaller.

The Stinchar drains an area of 133 square miles, which makes it the biggest of the many rivers in this district. It flows through a lovely valley, often wooded, and always peaceful and unspoilt, with a succession of hills of moderate height on either side. Every now and then, on the lower part of the river, one catches a glimpse of the open sea at the south extremity of the Firth of Clyde, and the whole setting is delightful.

Resembling many west coast streams, the Stinchar has a markedly quick rise and fall—as a result of the hilly surroundings of its entire course. After heavy rain it colours considerably with peat, and takes two or three days to clear; but when at a medium height, or lower, it runs clear enough. It has a reasonably fast rate of flow when other than dead low, and a good succession of rapids and pools of all different types, which makes it good fly water. Much gravel is to be found in it, an asset for spawning, but which can lead to substantial changes in the configuration of pools after big spates. It also has built up a high bar for some distance along the sea shore, adjacent to the mouth of the river, which on occasion in the past has almost closed the fresh water outlet; and the actual position of the mouth has changed periodically.

It may be a point of interest to those anglers who are also concerned with bird-life that this bar provides the only mainland nesting ground for the Little Tern on the west coast of Scotland. The Common and Arctic Tern also nest here regularly, while the Sandwich Tern has been recorded occasionally.

The Stinchar has been described as a 'spate river.' I suppose this is a fair description. When it is low, even if fish are present in good numbers, it becomes extremely difficult to catch any of them, and only the lowest beats on the river, in the neighbourhood of Ballantrae and Knockdolian, are likely to be of any use. Unfortunately, in summer, this river often does remain low for considerable periods of time. The annual rainfall in this part of Scotland is modest compared to that of the west-coast Highlands further north. And a good deal of this rain naturally falls outside of the fishing season. So good fishing periods in June, July and August are likely to be rare, except in an unusually wet summer. During September and October there is more chance of heavy or continuous rain, and it is hard to have too much of it on the Stinchar for fishing purposes. When rain does come and the water rises, the angler should take every opportunity of making the most use of it. He should be prepared to be on the water at all hours, early or late, and miss no chances. It may well be that the river will remain in good fishing order for only a short time, one can never tell; so no outside distractions of any sort should be allowed to interfere with his being completely absorbed in the good fishing for as long as it lasts.

In times of low water fresh fish certainly come in to the bottom beat of the river at Ballantrae, which formerly belonged to the Earl of Stair and is now the property of Mr. Robert Dalrymple. Part of this beat is tidal, as far as the road bridge at Ballantrae. It is liable to hold a big stock of fish if the water is continuously low over a long period, though they are unlikely to move much further upstream on the reduced flow. It is extremely difficult to get them to take under such conditions, in spite of their numbers; and the current becomes greatly diminished. Lord Stair and Major Hew Dalrymple are past-masters at this type of fishing. I know of no one else who can emulate them. Fishing on this beat is very wisely limited to 'fly only'. It is possible on occasion to count as many as 500 fish and more off the old road bridge at Ballantrae, lying below in the Bridge Pool.

In any height of water, however, there is little doubt that the Ballantrae beat, also the Knockdolian beats, $3\frac{1}{2}$ miles upstream, which belong to the Duke and Duchess of Wellington, are the best on the river. In my own case, thanks to the unlimited hospitality of Lord

Stair and of Major Hew Dalrymple, I have been lucky enough to have fished frequently at Ballantrae, and have found it a never ending source of the greatest interest and enjoyment. Sometimes I have drawn blank, but not always so, and sometimes have had magnificent sport. There is no small river where I would rather fish. Another good beat, though I have never fished it, lies at Dalreach, half way between Colmonell and Pinwherry.

The rod season on the Stinchar lasts from February 25th to October 31st, but the early part of this season is theoretical only. A very occasional odd spring fish can be seen in The Bridge Pool at Ballantrae, and an even rarer one can be caught, but in fact no worthwhile numbers of fish enter the river before June, and then only if there is a rise in water to bring them in. By July the river should be holding a fair stock of fish, and from them till the end of the season their numbers should progressively increase; but the date of their entry does largely depend on the weather—plenty of rain and high water, and the whole river will stock up in July; but continuous low water, and only the lowest part of the river will hold any number of them, until such time as there is a spate to help them on their way, even if this is long delayed into August or September. In July and August most of the fish, whether salmon or grilse, will be fresh-run, often with sealice; but in September and October more and more of them become coloured, until by mid-October a fresh one is rare indeed . . . nevertheless the Stinchar can fairly be classed as a 'late' river in that its best fishing period is from July onwards.

The average size of Stinchar salmon is not large, 8–9 lb, and 20 pounders or over are now scarce. This did not use to be the case, as this river in times gone by in proportion to its small size produced a remarkably large number of big fish—20 pounders were common, and the heaviest rod-caught fish that I have been able to trace was one of 46 lb caught by Mr. Robert Paul, keeper at Balnowlart, in the early 1920s. Another large fish of 42 lb fell to the rod of Mr. Robert Walker in the Bridge Pool at Ballantrae some 40 years ago. I remember Walker telling me about this fish; he had seen it some days previously, and Major Hew Dalrymple says he also saw it, after capture, and that it was slightly coloured which was surprising so early in the season (it was July). This latter fish was certainly caught on fly, though I am not certain about the former. In 1980 a 21 lb sea-trout was caught in the sea-nets at Ballantrae. It was $37\frac{1}{2}$ inches long. Grimble and Calderwood both give a long list of big Stinchar salmon caught by rod and net. Grimble actually mentioning a net-caught one of 62 lb, and he says: 'For its size, this river yields larger fish than any other in Scotland.' However this was all in days long past; and this statement would, I fear, no longer hold good in our times.

The average catch for the whole river at the present is 400–500 salmon and grilse, the latter from July onwards being as plentiful as salmon. There used also to be an extensive sea-trout run, mainly of herling; but these fish have become scarcer, and are now no longer to be caught by tens and twenties in an evening, as they used to be.

The salmon and grilse stocks as a general rule are plentiful for a small river of this size—partly due no doubt to good and extensive spawning grounds, and partly to the fact that for long years past there has been no netting in the river itself, and only spasmodic netting along the gravel bar outside the river mouth, in the open sea. Once fish get into the river they are therefore safe from all legal nets.

This leads to the subject of poaching. In low water during summer there is unfortunately always a risk of this. It is carried out mainly by gangs from north and central Ayrshire, only one hour distant by car. Many Stinchar pools are shallow and it is easy work to run a net through them on a dark night. The high profits to be obtained by the sale of a good haul of poached fish are a substantial temptation, particularly in these days of high unemployment.

U.D.N. has not affected the Stinchar to any extent. It did arrive there some 14 years ago, and a substantial number of salmon and grilse died during the subsequent two or three years. But, as in so many west-coast rivers which have virtually no spring run, it quickly and fortunately ceased to have much impact. If it is still present now, it has become of little consequence. Sea-trout were harder hit, and for a time their numbers were greatly reduced. Now however they are beginning to recover.

As to the tackle the reader will require if he is going to fish the Stinchar, he is unlikely at any time to need a fly-rod of more than 14 feet, even in the highest water—13 feet or 12 feet will be enough in medium or low water, and many would say that in low water a single-handed rod of $9\frac{1}{2}$ or 10 feet would be better. He will at all times want a floating line, or a floating line with a sinking tip if he prefers this; and all the usual flies from $2\frac{1}{2}$ inches long in high coloured water to $\frac{3}{4}$ inch when it is low and clear. A successful method of fishing in low water, when there is little stream, is to pull the fly quickly over the fish, drawing in three or four yards of slack, to be 'shot' with the next cast.

On some beats bait fishing is allowed; though this seems a pity on such a small and well stocked river, which provides good fly-water. For wading, all that will be needed in medium or low water is thigh waders. As the river increases in height, however, the angler will be better off with trouser waders, if only to give him more scope to wade deep where he wants to, or to wade across the river if necessary.

There are two pleasant hotels on the Stinchar for those who want such accommodation, one at Ballantrae, and one at Colmonell—and if the river is hopelessly out of order there are various alternative diversions in the shape of sea-fishing, sailing to Ailsa Craig, visiting the many magnificent gardens in the neighbourhood, such as at Castle Kennedy, near Stranraer, or even making a day's voyage from Stranraer to Larne and back. The crossing takes little more than $1\frac{1}{2}$ hours.

The Laggan (Islay)

Small flies, a floating line and a light rod are all that are
wanted.

Most anglers are unaware that on the island of Islay, the southernmost
of the Western Isles which lies close to Jura and westwards of the
peninsula of Kintyre, there exists a small but unusually prolific
salmon and grilse river called the Laggan. Islay is not a large island,
being 25 miles long by 19 wide at its greatest extent, (i.e. slightly
larger than the Isle of Wight), so there is no scope in it for a long or
large river. The Laggan, which is Islay's only sizeable stream, has in
fact a surprisingly large catchment area in the circumstances,

amounting to 37 square miles, the equivalent of the Broom in Ross-shire, though smaller than the Borgie in Sutherland. Even when in spate it cannot be classified as anything other than a small river, seldom more than 10 yards across at its widest.

Its length is around $9\frac{1}{2}$ miles, and it rises in the hills on the east coast of Islay, the highest of which rises to some 1600 feet. Its course runs south-westwards, till it falls into Laggan Bay on the south-west coast of the island. Many small tributaries join it on both sides.

I have not fished the Laggan for 10 years now, but this type of river is apt to change very little, so I should be surprised if the Laggan is in any way radically different from when I was last there.

It should be made clear at once that this is no river for an angler who likes to wade in and throw a long line, to catch large fish, and to be run out onto his backing by hooked fish. But for those who love wild and unspoilt surroundings, who are satisfied with salmon and grilse of 12 lb or less in weight, who do not expect to wade more than knee-deep and are content to fish with fly only, there could be many worse rivers than the Laggan.

Islay is not a hilly island, unlike its close neighbour Jura. It is comparatively flat, though as already mentioned there are a series of minor hills on its eastern coast. There is much rough grassland, and on the higher ground heather-covered slopes. Trees are conspicuously absent, except close to Bridgend, and near Port Askaig opposite Jura. Magnificent views can be obtained in all directions, from any piece of ground higher than the ordinary. The high hills of Jura, rising to 2500 feet, show up starkly to the north. In the opposite direction the coast of Antrim and Londonderry appears remarkably close across the sea, even the hills of Donegal are visible in the far distance. In fact the distance across the North Channel to the nearest point of Ireland, Rathlin Island in County Antrim, is but 18 miles as the crow flies.

It follows from the comparatively flat surroundings along most of its course that the Laggan is not a fast-running river, although its shallows and pools are clearly defined. It might be thought that such a small river would only fish well in spate, or during the run-down after one. In the case of the Laggan this is only partly true. The middle and upper reaches do indeed need water if they are to fish well. But the bottom three quarters of a mile above the high tide mark is deeper and has good holding water for most of its length. Here the salmon and grilse gather thickly, and it is easy to spot them and make an estimate of their numbers when the water is in its normal state, i.e. low and clear. There are usually two or three hundred at least in this part of the river, often more. So it is never hopeless to fish there, even in low water, if fine tackle and small flies are used. Naturally a rise in the water helps, but the rainfall is not high in Islay, so spates are not as frequent as one would like. What also helps is a gale of wind, which raises a good wave on the surface. It cannot be too strong, and we found that fish would take well in such a gale without any rise in the water.

I see from my diary that I was lucky enough to catch 7 fish one day in August 1963, all grilse or small salmon up to 8 lb biggest. It was blowing a westerly gale that day, and there was a fine wave on the water. If it had been calm I am certain I would have caught little or nothing.

The coast of Islay is exposed to the open Atlantic to the west, and as there are few trees and no hills on its western seaboard, which could act as a wind-break, strong winds occur fairly frequently. These can be a great asset for the Laggan fisherman.

The rod fishing season lasts from February 25th to October 31st, but fish seldom arrive in any worthwhile number before June at the earliest. July to the end of the season is the best fishing period, though fish are red by October. Salmon are small, averaging 8–9 lb, and from the end of June onwards there are many grilse of 5–6 lb. A 12 lb salmon is a big one, and there are few of over that size.

Fishing is comparatively simple with the river running full after a spate. Incidentally it is restricted to fly only at all times, and to hook, play and land small salmon and grilse is not difficult in a small river of this type, where fish cannot run out any length of line.

It is a different matter, however, when the water is low. Then the middle and upper reaches need exceptionally skilful treatment if they are to be made to yield fish, and an intimate knowledge of lies and likely taking places is required. The lower water is easier, partly because as already pointed out it holds a big stock of fish. But even so, very skilful fishing is necessary if any sort of bag is to be made and fish can become remarkably dour, especially if they are fished over several times a day, when weather and water conditions are unfavourable. To over-fish one's water, especially a small west-coast river when it is out of good fishing order, would seem always to be a bad mistake. It pays far better to restrain oneself, and not make the fish uncatchable through constant 'badgering', until a welcome change for the better in weather and water conditions arrives. Then is the time when one should keep hard at it, and make hay while the sun shines.

The Laggan water is normally perfectly clear, and small flies, a floating line and a light rod are all that is wanted. It is never necessary to throw a long line, and a single handed rod is long enough to cover the water without difficulty, except in the teeth of a gale. Personally I always prefer a rod of not less than 12 feet in length, because it gives better control of the line while the cast is being fished round, but this is purely a matter of personal taste. Thigh waders are all that is needed, and nothing longer—in fact gum-boots are long enough in most places.

As to netting, when I last fished the Laggan no nets were operated until after the end of the rod-fishing season, which seemed a wise and agreeable policy of restraint on the part of the owners—and I hope this arrangement still holds good. And I only hope too that the recent escalation of drift netting off the Irish coast and long-lining off the Faroes has not hit the little Laggan too hard. Its stocks of fish were plentiful enough in days gone by, and could have stood up to a substantially increased toll being imposed on them.

As well as salmon and grilse, the Laggan produces sea-trout, though in no outstanding quantity. There are also several brown trout lochs in various parts of the island, some of which produce quite good catches from time to time, both in size and numbers of fish.

There is also productive sea-fishing to be had in Laggan Bay and elsewhere off the west coast of Islay for those who enjoy it.

The journey to Islay is always entertaining. The best, if not the only route is to motor to West Tarbert in Kintyre, and then to put one's car and oneself on the ferry-boat which sails in about 3 hours to either Port Askaig on the north-west shore of the island, or else to Port Ellen on the south. On a fine sunny day the view in every direction as one sails westwards past the island of Gigha, and across the Sound of Islay, is a magnificent one.

Is there not always a fascination about islands, and the journey to them? One has the same sort of feeling when crossing from Ullapool to Lewis and Harris. It is as though one is entering a small new world, remote and full of exciting possibilities.

For those who look for hotel accommodation in Islay, there is a good hotel at Bridgend, which is fairly small, but quiet and pleasantly situated. There are other adequate hotels at Bowmore and Port Ellen.

The Awe

Formerly a great river for big fish. How did they land 40 and 50 pounders in such fast and broken water?

Any attempt to write about the Awe, that wonderful river in Argyll, is something in the nature of a Highland lament. It is a case largely of past history, and those who can remember this river as it was before 1961 when the Hydro took it over will I feel sure bear me out over this. I am one of the lucky few who fished the Awe in those bygone days, thanks to my great friend Mr. Sebastian Earl. In fact I fished this river, thanks to Seb's hospitality, for a week during three different seasons before 1961 and again in 1961 and 1965. I can therefore well

209

remember the river in its natural state, before the Hydro dam was built and the main flow of water diverted, and so was able to compare it with what one found afterwards. It was a sorry tale. I have not fished the Awe again since 1965, and must admit that I have no great inclination to do so.

For those of my readers who may not know the full story, a brief explanation is necessary. In its natural state the Awe was a short river, barely 4 miles long, linking the 22 mile long Loch Awe with Loch Etive, a sea-loch, the mouth of the river being close to Taynuilt. It was thus very much a counterpart of the Ness and the Lochy, short though sizeable rivers, each of them draining a large loch, fed by headwaters. In the case of Loch Awe the main headwater was the river Orchy, which had a 16 mile course from Loch Tulla on the edge of the Moor of Rannoch lying to the north-east. But there were many other smaller burns which entered Loch Awe throughout its length.

The river Awe had an exceptionally steep downward course, dropping 116 feet in barely 4 miles, and that without any full-scale falls to contribute towards this abrupt descent. It was a comparatively narrow river, in fact, once it had left its outlet from Loch Awe at the Pass of Brander, its width rarely exceeded 25 yards except in one or two of its larger pools such as the Shallows and Fanans. But its current was fierce, and its bed extremely rocky. It was said to resemble one of the smaller types of Norwegian river, so rough was its downward plunge, and indeed this was not an unrealistic comparison. Together with that of the Orchy and the other feeders entering Loch Awe, the Awe's total catchment area amounted to 271 square miles—slightly smaller than that of the Findhorn, and about comparable with that of the North or South Esk, or the Beauly. But it was an infinitely faster and more powerful stream than any of these.

Stories about fishing in the Awe during the old days would provide drama for several volumes. In the early 1900's and up to the 1939 War salmon averaged anything in weight between 16 and 20 lb. 40 pounders were killed almost every season, and I have compiled the following list of as many Awe 50 pounders as I can trace, though no doubt it is not complete:

Weight	Caught By	Date	Where Caught	Remarks
57 lb	Major A. W. Huntington	July 8th 1921	Cassan Dhu	Length 52½ inches Girth 27½ inches Caught on a Mar Lodge 3/0
56 lb	Mr. H. G. Thorton	June 12th 1923	Pol Verie	Caught on a 5/0 Fly.
55 lb	Mrs. Huntington	September 19th 1927	Errochd Pool	Landed in Dalvarde
54 lb	Mr. J. B. Lawes	1877		
54 lb	The Schoolmaster at Taynuilt	1880 (?)	Cassan Dhu	Landed at Crubeg
53 lb	A. McColl (ghillie)	1913		
52 lb	Colonel James Thorpe		Inverawe Cruive	
51 lb	Dr. C. Child	September 1907	Near Taynuilt	Killed on a 'Blue Doctor'
51 lb	Mr. A. Lees Milne	October 1913		In the same month Mr. Lees Milne killed other fish weighing, 47, 44, and 42 lb
51 lb	Major A. W. Huntington	May 22nd 1930	The Stepping Stones	Killed on a Green Highlander 2/0
51 lb	Mr. H. G. Thornton	1934	The Seal	
51 lb	Mr. H. de Pass	1936	Little Verie	

Is this not an amazing record? Maybe the Tay or the Wye could produce a longer one of 50 pounders killed, but it must never be overlooked that the Awe in length is just short of 4 miles! All these enormous fish, as well as 40 and 30 pounders infinitely more numerous, were killed on this astoundingly short extent of water, in contrast to the Tay's or Wye's near 100 miles.

Many of these big Awe fish were caught on fly—a big Green Highlander was a popular choice—though some on bait (sometimes prawn).

It is worthy of note that Major A. W. Huntington, also Mr. H. G. Thornton, caught two 50 pounders here during their fishing career, a feat seldom equalled elsewhere in Britain.

And as to the capture of the 54 pounder by the Schoolmaster of Taynuilt, which he hooked in Cassan Dhu and landed in Crubeg,

Grimble in his *Salmon Rivers of Scotland* (1899) writes as follows:

> I was out that day and met him at the Clay Pool on my way upstream; the fish was still going very strongly. I unluckily did not turn back to see the end of the fight, which eventually finished at Crubeg, the lowest pool on the water, and out of which it is impossible to follow a fish making for the sea.
>
> This was a right good performance, of which anyone might fairly be proud; only a tall active man could have carried it through, as in following from the Otter Pool into the Stepping Stones the water was up to the schoolmaster's chin, and at this part of the fight a man five inches shorter would probably have been beaten.

This was indeed a 'right good performance' seeing that the schoolmaster, and one should take off one's hat to him, followed his fish for the best part of a mile down a broken and turbulent river, but so for that matter would have been the capture of any of the monster fish listed above. Anyone seeing for the first time the Awe's swift and rockstrewn course would wonder how even a 20 pounder could be successfully handled, let alone leviathans in the 40 and 50 lb class. The only hope was apparently to use very strong tackle, and to know beforehand of any particularly dangerous rocks or snags, making every effort from the start to keep a hooked fish clear of them. Even so in the case of fish of 30 lb or over it must have been odds on that a disaster would happen in one form or another, and the fish go free. There is no doubt that the majority of such fish when hooked were lost rather than caught. The hooking and playing of every one of them, whether lost or landed, would have provided a drama unsurpassed on any other river in Britain, such was the turbulence and irregular nature of the Awe's headlong descent.

There is surely no disgrace in losing any fish, big or small, if he beats one in fair fight. Further, it is in fact essential that a proportion of one's hooked fish should escape if it is to be of any fun playing them. Where would be the excitement if every fish hooked was inevitably landed? It is a fish or series of fish lost that makes the landing of the next one all the greater triumph. Only if a loss occurs through some silly and preventable mistake on one's own part is there cause for remorse.

There is a relevant quotation from Isaac Walton's *Compleat Angler*:

Piscator:	'Oh me! he has broken all; there's half a line and a good hook lost.'
Venator:	'Aye, and a good fish too.'
Piscator:	'Nay, the fish is not lost, for take notice, no man can lose what he never had.'

In bygone days there was a spring run, but of Orchy fish rather than Awe fish. Such fish passed quickly through into Loch Awe and then up the Orchy. Few were caught in the Awe, and it was not until June that the latter river began to hold a permanent stock. A similar spring run passed through both the Ness en route for the Garry, and the Lochy for the Spean. In all these cases the spring fish were disinclined to linger in the lower river.

So much for the past, and what is to be found now?

In 1961 the Hydro completed its dam across the Awe at the neck of Pol Verie, about half a mile below the outlet from Loch Awe at the Pass of Brander, and began its operations. Six good pools upstream of the dam were buried deep under the increased head of water, and are a total loss. These were the Brander, the Disputed Pool, the Shallows, the Black Pool, the Seal Pool, and Pol Neugen. This was only the start of the resultant troubles. The water level in the river is now kept more or less permanently low, because a large proportion of the flow is abstracted in order to empower turbines, and is only returned to the main channel three miles downstream and very close to the mouth.

While the course of the Awe from Pol Verie downwards has not changed, and the Orchy and headwaters are still untouched (except that owing to the delay caused by the Hydro dam it is apt to take longer for fish to reach them), rain during the fishing season no longer serves to raise the water level in the Awe. Unless of diluvial proportions it is penned back in Loch Awe to form a head of water for the Hydro. So the river below is greatly changed in character, and not, unfortunately, for the better.

The water flow from October 1st to March 31st is normally very low, though nearly every winter, when at some period or other there is heavy rain, the Hydro Board has to let down a large spate, which may last for several days. But apart from cleansing the river bed this is of no benefit to the fishing.

During the present day fishing season from April 1st to September 30th it is true that the Hydro Board lets down extra water on April 1st, with an increase on May 1st, and again on June 1st. A freshet is also let down on Saturday nights until Sunday. These arrangements are certainly an improvement on what was done when the Hydro first started. Nevertheless they are still far from restoring the Awe to its natural state, and although a weekly artificial freshet is surely better than nothing, it does not take the place of natural spates either in volume of flow or quality of water.

It is also true that in the old pre-Hydro days the Awe was reckoned to fish well in low water, as the fish were then more inclined to stay in the river instead of running through into Loch Awe. But in those days the Awe rose and fell in a natural way with wet or dry weather. That is very different to its running at a permanently lowish level during the fishing season as it does now. In the natural way there would always have been intermittent and sizeable spates from time to time, even in a dry year. They would have drawn new fish into the river, oxygenated the water, enlivened the old stagers already present, and kept the bottom clear of all kinds of fouling.

Little of this happens now. The bottom is apt to become coated with slime, particularly in a warm summer, and the river remains permanently at or near summer level so that fish lack the encouragement to run provided by a rise in water after rain and consequent oxygenization of the water content. What is more their upstream passage is now checked by the high dam at the top of Pol Verie. Admittedly there is a modern fish-pass, I understand of the 'lift' type, at this dam. But there have been many complaints in recent years that fish do not use this pass freely, and that the earlier Orchy fish gather in hundreds in Pol Verie downstream. Surely an advantage to the Awe (if detrimental to the Orchy), one might have thought? And it is true that, when they are fresh in, such fish are caught in larger numbers than ever before in the Awe.

But fish held up by an artificial obstacle very soon become 'potted' and uncatchable. Moreover they are at great risk with regard to U.D.N. when unnaturally concentrated under low water conditions, also with regard to poaching.

The fishing below the road bridge is now said to be of comparitively little use, as fish seldom stay down there. This includes such famous pools as The Oak, Cassan Dhu, The Stepping Stones, and Errochd. And in any case the high water catches anywhere on the river are now virtually out of commission.

The fishing in present days starts at Pol Verie, below the dam. This is a fairly large pool, as Awe pools go, it used to be a good one and still is. It is probably the best on the river in modern times. Below this are found amongst others, the Stone Pool, the Bothy, the Shepherd's Pool, the Meal Pool, Fanans, and the Garravalt—all famous names from long past, and they still all produce fish. This covers the best of the pools in present days.

As to fishing the Awe, there is now no great demand for expertise, coupled with the exceptionally strong tackle needed in former days. Reasonably light tackle, including a rod of 13 to 15 feet is all that is wanted. There is little need to use a fly bigger than size 4, and size 6 would often be better. Most of the pools can now be waded adequately with thigh waders, though just occasionally trouser waders may be needed. The wading fisherman should proceed with caution, especially if he does not already know the water well. It is easy to step off an underwater rock-shelf from knee-depth into six feet or more of water. The mode of fishing is similar to that employed in any other medium/small river, it is seldom necessary to throw a particularly long line, in fact accuracy in casting is often more important than distance.

My own biggest fish from the Awe weighed a mere 27 lb, less than half the weight of some of the monsters listed above. I hooked it wading in the tail of the Shallows on September 21st 1960, on a black Tosh. It was one of those fish whose sole idea seemed to be to get back to the sea as quickly as possible once again. After a short delay in the Shallows it turned its head downstream and fairly bolted! What a run that was, and it was complicated by the fact that the Hydro construction was under weigh at that time. With half my backing out I had to clamber through a lot of wooden scaffolding on the bank, to the entertainment of the construction workers; this was somewhere near the Black pool, and in the end I caught up with this fish close to

Pol Verie, and gaffed it there. It was a cock fish, in good condition, though slightly coloured. What a grand fight! and it made me wonder how on earth they contrived to land those 50 pounders!

The big fish are now of course gone, the present average size being 10–12 lb, with grilse from the end of June onwards, few are caught nowadays of much over 20 lb. This is not the fault of the Hydro (except in so far as a permanently low river does not encourage big fish to enter). The same sort of thing has happened, sad to say, in many other rivers unaffected by Hydros.

Nevertheless one cannot help wondering if sometime in the future, with the development of nuclear power or some other form of energy, Hydros will become redundant. This may well not come to pass during the life-time of the present generation, but it gives one joy, even so, to visualize the possibility of a future happy day when the high peaks of Cruachan will once again look down upon a liberated Awe as it flows unfettered to the sea.

The Lochy

Lovely streamy fly water at Garrybhuie.

Of all the west coast Scottish salmon rivers, the Lochy is without doubt the biggest, and in the opinion of many the best. Mr. Wilson Stephens, writing in the *Field*, refers to the delightful belief of the ancients that rivers have souls. If this is true, the soul of the Lochy must indeed be one of outstanding beauty and purity, shepherding like Arethusa of old its bright fountains, so sparkling and clear, amongst the high hills and precipitous glens of Lochaber. No other Scottish river, not even the majestic Spey, can provide a panorama to

217

outrival that which unfolds itself to the gaze of the angler standing near the Lochy's Falls Pool, or at Loy Mouth, or at Camisky, as he casts his eyes east and southwards towards Ben Nevis' snow-capped peak. All around him stretches an unforgettable display of heather, woodland, and steep hillside, as far as the eye can reach in every direction.

The history of the Lochy as a salmon river is interesting, though there is little space here to touch on it. One hundred years ago, in Victorian times, the great protagonist of most of the fishing in the district, and primarily of the Lochy, was Lord Abinger. There is a fly named after him, described in Kelson's *The Salmon Fly* (1895), and he appeared to own not only the Lochy fishing, but that of the Spean and of the other tributaries also, and the netting rights on all these rivers as well as in Loch Linnhe. Augustus Grimble in his *Salmon Rivers and Lochs of Scotland* (1899) describes Lord Abinger as holding 'a charter granting him all the salmon fishing in the Lochaber district, which right for many years remained unquestioned'. That it was in some places eventually questioned is certain, and in any case the Abinger Estate in due course was broken up. But Lord Abinger was undoubtedly a notable benefactor in his day so far as the Lochy and Spean fishings were concerned. He took off all river nets and cruives, also the nets for several miles along both shores of Loch Linnhe. He did maintain his right to take up to one hundred salmon per annum by net from the river, but W. L. Calderwood writing in 1909 says that this right was never exercised. Lord Abinger also instituted a salmon hatchery beside the Spean, and organized the division of all the Spean and Lochy fishings into well defined beats, with the provision of professional ghillies for each beat. Each beat was let separately. All in all, this was highly advanced procedure for Victorian times, and it set a notable precedent for the future. Calderwood writes in 1909 that Loch Linnhe was still unnetted except for one small fishery opposite Fort William. The estuary and river were still unnetted also, except occasionally to provide ova for the hatchery. The rod-fishing at that date, from his description of it, was obviously still organized in an efficient and workmanlike manner, and indeed the tradition of so doing has survived on the Lochy without a break until present times.

Modern Lochy fishers are perhaps unaware how much they owe to the original foresight of Lord Abinger, and to his wise management and control. There should be a monument to his memory somewhere on the river, or at least a pool named after him, but as far as I know there is neither.

In width and volume of flow the Lochy is about comparable to the Dee at Aboyne, or the Tweed at Boldside. It should be realised that it is only the lowest section, eight miles long, of an entire river system, comprising also the Arkaig and Loch Arkaig (12 miles long), Loch Lochy (10 miles long), the Spean from Loch Laggan and its tributary the Roy, also the Loy which runs in from the west. All these headflows (except the Loy which runs in $2\frac{1}{2}$ miles further downstream) unite below the fall at Mucomir, half a mile from the southern end of Loch Lochy, to form the main Lochy, which has an eight mile course due southwards, except for minor changes of direction, to enter the head of the tidal Loch Linnhe at Inverlochy, one mile from Fort William.

In this respect the Lochy is closely comparable to the Ness or the Awe, being the main and comparatively short outflow from a loch or a series of lochs, fed by a number of sizeable upper headwaters. That both the Lochy and Awe are now deprived of a substantial part of their natural flow is through no accident; in the case of the Lochy it is because the British Aluminium Company, for the last fifty years, has abstracted a high proportion of the Spean's water, close to its outfall from Loch Laggan, as well as the subsidiary flow from Loch Treig, and carries it by tunnel through Ben Nevis to fall into the Lochy only in its tidal reaches at Inverlochy. In times of low water the Hydro at Mucomir is also liable to pen back the natural flow from Loch Lochy. The overall result is that the bed of the Lochy is by nature a wider one than would normally be necessary to accommodate its present artificially reduced flow (although outsized spates do occur from time to time). This wide bed is clearly evident to any angler on the river bank who takes interest enough to look for it; nevertheless the reduced flow does not seem to have exercised any harmful effect on the Lochy fishing, rather the opposite in all probability (though the Spean, Roy, and Arkaig fishings may well have suffered).

In general the Lochy in character is wide, shallow, gravelly, and streamy; in fact it resembles closely the Ness, except that it is only about two thirds of its size. It is in total contrast to its own tributary the Spean, or to the neighbouring Awe, both of which flow in what amounts in places to a gorge, in their respective rocky and constricted channels. The only major rock outcrops on the Lochy, apart from at Mucomir, are at the Falls Pool and below it, at the two Rock Pools, at Rail End (below Camisky), and at the Garden and Cat Pools lower down. Otherwise all the pools are open and of a similar type, with the usual streamy neck, slacker middle section, and a quickening run-out. Sometimes there are long gravelly flats, such as Black Cairn Flat, Garrybhuie, The Drain Pipe, and the Beech Tree, all of which can hold fish in large numbers if the water is not too low, and which fish well with medium or high water, particularly if there is a wind to raise a good ripple.

The bottom in most of the Lochy pools is of small gravel, with few deep holes and few big boulders, though there are enough of the latter to make good lies here and there. The current as a rule is only a moderate one, not nearly so strong as that of the Spey or even of the Dee. Nevertheless the general result of all this is to produce excellent fly water of peculiarly attractive character, which whenever fish are in residence provides first class sport in any height of water, other than dead low.

The clarity of the Lochy water is a notable characteristic. As Loch Ness and Loch Oich are to the Ness, or Loch Awe and Loch Tulla to the Awe, so are Loch Lochy and Loch Arkaig to the Lochy. They form an efficient 'settling tank' for discolouring matter, and thus act as an effective filter. The Spean also, with its attenuated flow brings in little discolouration and only for a short time at its worst, flowing as it does from the dammed back Loch Laggan (9 miles long). Only the smaller tributaries, Roy and Loy, are apt to run coloured after heavy rain, and tarnish the main Lochy; but they clear quickly, and without prolonged rain their spates last for hours rather than days. As elsewhere on the West Coast there is far less peat in Lochaber than in the central Highlands, or in the east of Ross-shire or Sutherland, or in Galloway. Nor is there any extent of agricultural land. The result is strikingly apparent so far as feeder burns and headwaters are concerned. They colour little if at all, and bigger rivers are apt to follow suit. This is an unmixed blessing from the fishing angle.

Nor is there any severe artificial pollution in the Lochy. The main river and its feeders are clear of all major potential sources of this affliction. The disposal of sewage from the village of Spean Bridge at one time long ago, as we read in Grimble, did give cause for anxiety; but this problem has now been efficiently dealt with. Only at Fort William itself, with the British Aluminium Company, or at Corpach on the head of Loch Linnhe, with the Pulp Mill, is there any industrial installation. The British Aluminium Company is scrupulous in maintaining complete purity in any effluent that may issue from its works, while the discharge from the Pulp Mill enters Loch Linnhe three miles west of the mouth of the Lochy, and no ill effects from it have so far been observed. (In any case it is thought that this Pulp Mill may soon cease operations.) There is some minor trace of pollution, it is true, from the village of Caol on the tidal estuary of the Lochy, and there are recurrent instances of minor pollution by silt from gravel workings, and by oil spillages from the railway and garages at Inverlochy. But this is too slight to cause serious harm. Otherwise the main Lochy and its headwaters are free of towns, factories and all other potential sources of pollution. The two distilleries at Inverlochy have little or no effect on the river.

Salmon undoubtedly prefer their river water to be as pure as possible, and ultra-clear water never stopped fish taking. If anybody queries this, let him go fishing in Iceland or Norway, where rivers are often of swimming-bath clarity, yet where fish take lures of all sorts, often large ones, with an avidity seldom exhibited in Britain. I feel sure that, if in contrast river water is coloured or pronouncedly peaty, fish are put off the take, not because they can't see the lure (it needs a complete 'pea-souper' to blind them this far), but nine times out of ten because the impurity in the water sickens them and so distracts their attention.

The Lochy, both banks of it, throughout its length, has been owned these past eighteen years by the River Lochy Association, a syndicate of independent owners, which also owns the Loy and the bottom three miles of the Spean as far as Spean Bridge. Above that point it is the British Aluminium Company which owns the Spean (its tributary, the Roy is separately owned). Control and management of all fishery matters under this ownership is efficient and enterprising, and there is a first class team of ghillies. After mid-June the rule is 'fly only' till the end of the season, and no one would want it otherwise; this applies to all the main Lochy above tidal water. Below this the Fortwilliam Association leases the tidal waters, has its own rules, and allows bait in places.

Hamish Tabor fishing at Loy Mouth, a junction pool.

The main part of the river is divided into four beats, with a maximum of four rods on each beat, and these beats are changed in rotation daily throughout the season—a system which works satisfactorily, and gives all participants as even a chance as possible of good sport. In addition to these four main beats, which extend from Croy Pool at the top, to Foxhunter at the bottom, there is Association Water leased to the local fishing organizations in the tidal reaches. There is also the Loy, together with Mucomir Pool below the fall, and the quarter mile of water below it, which are leased separately; also the lower Spean below Spean Bridge, and the upper Spean above it. These waters are mainly fished by local angling clubs.

The Rock Pool on the Lochy with Ben Nevis in the background.

All these beats can be good at times. The Association water on the lowest part of the river is excellent in a low water year. Fish enter the tidal reaches (which are reinforced by the piped flow of the Spean

water through Ben Nevis); but as long as the water remains
persistently low they are apt to linger down there in large numbers,
while awaiting a spate. This can be a matter of frustration and concern
to the many anglers higher upstream. In summers of persistent low
water the rod catch on the tidal water is often greater than on all the
rest of the river combined. But dry summers in Lochaber, the wettest
district in Britain with an average yearly rainfall of over 100 inches,
are fortunately rare. Usually there is ample water to induce fish to run
well upstream, and to provide a good stock in all the beats from
Mucomir down.

It should be made clear at this juncture that the Lochy by nature is
definitely a 'Summer' river. It is true that there used to be a sizeable
spring run in years long past, but it was never the Lochy which held
any number of springers—always the Spean, or Mucomir Pool at its
entry into the Lochy, for which these fish made post-haste. The Spean
in fact, fifty years ago and more, before the British Aluminium
Company abstraction, was a first class spring river of high repute,
with some big fish. But sad to say those days are long past. Although a
remnant of this spring run does still exist, with some fish creeping in
from time to time (they are not often found below Croy Pool or
Mucomir). Visiting anglers can only expect a modest number of
salmon during the first half of June, and still fewer during May,
though they average 14 lb at this time of year.

As has already been made clear, the spring months are now seldom
worthwhile; but from late June onwards, till the end of the season in
mid-October, the angler will be unlucky if he does not find all the fish
he wants, and have thoroughly enjoyable sport. Thanks to the great
kindness of Major Tabor and Mrs. Stainton, also of Lord Dulverton,
Major David Rasch, and Captain Peter Gibbs, I have been lucky
enough to have fished this splendid river on and off since 1954, and
thus know it reasonably well. Merely to say that I have enjoyed every
minute of my time on it is a gross understatement. There is no river
where one can take more delight in the magnificent surroundings and
more pleasure, whether fishing or not, in the splendid variety and
inspiring character of its (usually) well-stocked pools. It is lovely
fishing. One cannot think of the Lochy as a big river, except when it is

in spate; and it can all be satisfactorily covered by wading or in a few places off the bank. There is only one pool, on the top beat, called the Piles, where the use of a boat for fishing purposes is sometimes an advantage. On the other hand this river is far from small, so it is in fact of a very attractive size for anyone who prefers to do without a boat but who does not want too strenuous wading; who likes to throw a fair length of line, and enjoys having his hooked fish not infrequently run him onto his backing.

The main run of fish does not start to arrive till near the last week of June; and it is not till the second week of July, when the grilse run also arrives in numbers, that the river is likely to become well stocked. So any optimist who goes to fish in April or May should expect to catch nothing, and should not be disappointed if he does.

Any time from about the last ten days of June onwards, however, is another matter. The salmon run fairly heavy to start with, averaging 11–12 lb, though they decrease in weight later. Sometimes there are bigger ones of 15–20 lb. Over 20 lb is now rare, with 30 lb even rarer. Grilse, as usual here as elsewhere, average 6–7 lb. The height of the run is normally between mid-July and mid-August, though as previously explained periodic high water is needed to spread the fish all through the various beats and beyond the tidal reaches.

By mid-August some of the fish are beginning to turn red, and by mid-September the vast majority are coloured. There is no true autumn run in the Lochy, fresh-run silver fish after mid-September being virtually non-existent. What does happen is that a certain number obviously linger in the brackish water of Loch Linnhe, and come in late in the season with tide-lice still on them; but, even so, they are red when they enter the river—quite different from the bright silver and true autumn fish of the Tay, or still more so of the Tweed.

Big fish, as mentioned above, are now scarce. The largest salmon caught during the Lochy Fishing Association's tenure weighed 36 lb from the Boat Pool, on a fly. Another 30 pounder was killed some seven or eight years ago, also one three years ago, and one in 1980. During the 1939–45 War Mrs. S. Pilkington caught a fish of over 40 lb in the Piles Pool. This is the last known 40 pounder to be landed.

W. L. Calderwood mentions a fish of 43 lb caught in the Spean in October 1908, and other 40 pounders are on record in days long past, the biggest being of 47 lb. But as in many other rivers such outstanding specimens seem now to have vanished.

The general stock of fish, however, during the summer months in the Lochy is excellent. This is mainly due to the wise management and good control exercised by the owners and their subordinates. First and foremost there is now no net fishing on this river nor on Loch Linnhe. How many other sizeable rivers in Britain can boast as much? And what a boon to rod fishing and to the survival of Lochy fish! One has often heard it said that without net-fishing rivers would become over-stocked, consequently disease would be rife, spawning grounds would be over-cut, fry would starve, and other disasters ensue. One suspects such arguments emanate in origin from the commercial interests. One cannot help noticing only too clearly that in the few British rivers where no netting or only restricted netting takes place, e.g. in the Lochy, the Ness, the Stinchar, and the Test amongst the former, and the Naver, the Helmsdale, and the South Esk amongst the latter, none of these disasters occur. Fish abound in them, as they do also in the un-netted rivers of Iceland. In other rivers one notices the diminishing return of surviving fish in proportion as the net catches increase. The general inference is obvious.

The spawning grounds for Lochy fish are extensive. They include the Loy, the Arkaig and its headwaters, and these are made more easily accessible by a 'Borland Lift' pass at the falls of Mucomir. This type of modern designed fish-lift has lately given cause for anxiety as being now considered less effective than other types of ladders or passes. Further spawning grounds are afforded by the Spean (to a limited extent only, as gravel is scarce) as far as the falls of Mounessie (some 5 miles above Spean Bridge, and impassable for fish), also by the Roy, and various feeder burns such as the Lundy, which joins the Lochy one mile above tidal water. Fish also spawn in the main Lochy itself, though to a more limited extent in present times than formerly. Widespread gravel banks are of a suitable consistency in most places throughout its length. It seems that such far-flung spawning grounds are ample to produce all that could be wanted in numbers of adult fish.

In addition the Lochy Association in recent years has carried out a considerable amount of artificial stocking with salmon fry, both in the main river and tributaries. How much good may result from this is questionable; but at least it is a step in the right direction.

As is to be expected, this essentially 'summer' fishing is undertaken with fairly light tackle; a 14 ft rod should be long enough, or a light 15 ft carbon graphite rod if you prefer one, together with a floating line and a leader of 10–12 lb breaking strain. If the water is low, even a 13 ft or 12 ft rod may be adequate for those who prefer shorter lengths. Personally in a river of this size I would not be happy with a rod of less than 14 ft, as I find this is quite light enough, can throw a longer line, and enables one to keep better control of the line and fly while the cast is being fished round. But if anyone prefers a shorter length I am certainly not going to argue with him or her. A floating line, or a line with a short sinking tip, spliced to 120 yards of sound backing is what is wanted on the reel. Long trouser waders are essential, even in low water when it may not be necessary to wade deep. It is always a pleasant feeling to have plenty of 'freeboard', and such waders are often useful if one wants to cross the river at some fordable place, in order to fish a pool or pools from the opposite side. There are not, however, many such places, and considerable care should be exercised in attempting this. It is seldom possible to wade across this river except in very low water.

As to flies, all the usual low water patterns do well, provided they are sparsely dressed. Hair-winged flies such as the Stoats Tail, Hairy Mary, Munro's Killer, or the Shrimp Fly are good. There is little to choose between these or others of the same type. At one time there was a vogue during the summer of using ultra-small flies on the Lochy, down to size 10 or even smaller. Presumably this owed its origin to the extreme clarity of the water, and the fact that fish that have been in the river for some time will occasionally take a very small fly when they will look at nothing else. So it is worth having a few flies of this size in one's box as a special card to play when needed. But that is a different thing from using them persistently and the drawback to such small hooks is that either they fail to get a hold when the fish takes, or else that the hold is only a frail one, and that any sizeable fish is liable to come unhooked after a fair time in play. Fly sizes somewhere between 6 to 8 are about right, and these are what are mostly in favour at this present time. It is also, as everywhere else, worth trying much larger sizes of hair-winged flies, up to about $2\frac{1}{4}$ inches long, particularly in strong streams or when the evening light is fading. Such streams as at Croy, Garrybhuie, Fank, and the Garden Pool are appropriate places for this.

Droppers can also be well worth using, if one knows how to manipulate them. The tail fly and dropper should be about 4 feet apart; a wider gap gives too much chance of the tail fly becoming fouled when a fish is hooked on the dropper, and a narrower one reduces the extra catching zone given by two flies. If two flies of different size are used, it is best for the smaller one to be at the tail and the larger one at the dropper. It is also essential to use a really sound knot to attach the dropper leader to the main cast, as great strain is exerted here when a big fish is being played. There are several such knots, which can be learnt from one of the many books or booklets on anglers' knots.

The strength of nylon monofilament for the leader should not be of less than 10 lb breaking strain. This is quite fine enough for use with flies as small as size 8. To go finer is asking for trouble in one way or another; for instance active fish do inevitably run out a long line sooner or later, and if they then thrash and jump, especially if the line is drowned, fine nylon will be broken. Wind knots too *will* creep in, reducing the breaking strain of monofilament by 50 per cent or more. Indeed in the earlier part of the season, when the salmon run larger, and before the arrival of the grilse, it may well be better to use nylon of 12 lb breaking strain, or stronger if a big fly is being used.

There is usually little difficulty in playing and landing fish in the Lochy; there are few boulders or snags, and no violently strong rapids. There is only one really formidable place, and that is at the Falls Pool, one mile below Camisky, where there is a good lie and taking place right on the lip of the fall. When my turn comes to fish this place, I must admit that I feel I am treading on very quakey ground. If a fish is hooked there, and they often are, he has somehow got to be led upstream over some rock formations in the bed of the river, and landed in the big pool above. Usually, with patience and skilful handling, this can be achieved without too much difficulty.

Fishing the neck of Loy Mouth in low water.

But sometimes one comes across an impossibly difficult customer (one suspects it may be a sizeable fish which has only recently run up the falls), which displays a mule-like obstinacy at any attempt to coax him upstream. If he drops back over the lip one knows well that disaster is inevitable. Owing to high trees and undergrowth on top of the bank, and a sheer rock face along the river-side, it is totally impossible to follow down the long torrent below. One may as well hold tight and break at once; otherwise I know from sad experience that the whole line and backing will inexorably be torn off the reel until the bitter end is reached, when there will be a nasty jar, and one will be left to reel up what is left, a sadder and wiser man!

Reverting to landing fish in normal circumstances, one can use a gaff, landing net, or better still beach them. There are many good beaching places all up and down this river, with its abundance of gravel shallows, and it is seldom necessary to land fish in any other fashion.

In other ways there is no special procedure in fishing which is peculiarly applicable to the Lochy. Care should be taken as always not to wade too deep, especially first time down a pool, for fear of frightening the fish lying close in. One can often see them lying in rows in certain pools such as the Falls, the water is so clear; and it is surprising in what shallow water they will lie, especially as the season advances. Polaroid glasses are useful for spotting them. It is always worth fishing the best pools more than once, when they are well stocked with fish, and at different times of the day—also from different sides. A fish which has refused a fly coming from the normal direction will sometimes take it if fished from the opposite side, especially if this has seldom or never been done before. It is a useful gambit to have up one's sleeve.

In summer, as usual, morning and evening are generally the best fishing times. In warm and sunny weather the afternoon is seldom productive; it is often better in such weather to take a siesta then, leaving the water undisturbed for the evening.

It is nothing unusual for a single rod to take five or six fish a day out of the Lochy, or even double figures. The best one day's catch in recent years, so far as I know, was made by Major the Hon. Hew Dalrymple, who caught 15 fish to his own rod off the lower river; but there may have been even larger kills of which I lack knowledge. As to catches on individual beats, 27 fish have been taken in one day off the top beat.

The total catch for the season has been remarkably consistent over the past 10 years. It averages 1150 salmon and grilse for the whole river. The fish caught are usually well spread out through the different beats; but as already mentioned it sometimes happens in an abnormally low water year that the tidal water has a disproportionate share of the bag.

The 1980 season was a peculiar one, with abnormally dry weather until July, and then almost ceaseless rain. The catch has been a poor one, as from July onwards the Lochy has been consistently too high. The grilse run, in addition to that of the salmon, has been well below average. One fears that the recent escalation of long-lining in the summer (1980) off the Faroes may be materially responsible for this, in addition to the abnormal weather. It is significant that almost every west coast Scottish river this season has followed the same pattern. The 1981 season has proved better, but the same anxiety persists.

Sea-trout, curiously enough, have never been of great account in the Lochy, which is unusual in a west-coast river. A fair number of herling are to be found in July, but big sea-trout are scarce. Why this should be so is difficult to say, apart from the recent general scarcity of these fish in most areas. Perhaps it is that the Lochy is so well stocked with salmon and grilse that they overwhelm the earlier-spawning sea-trout on the redds, or that their fry and parr compete successfully with those of the sea-trout for the available food; or there may be some other reason. Nevertheless scarcity of sea-trout only serves to benefit the salmon fry and parr; which have less competition for the available food.

As to brown trout, their number is negligible though they exist in Loch Lochy and Loch Arkaig. Again their absence serves only to benefit the immature salmon. They are rapacious devourers of salmon ova, fry and parr. There are also pike in Loch Lochy, which have no redeeming feature of any sort. Seals occasionally come up the river from Loch Linnhe, where there is a sizeable colony of them. These again from the fishing point of view are nothing but a pest.

As frequent reference has already been made to the Lochy's headwaters and tributaries, perhaps further allusion to them would not be out of place. Its main tributary, the Spean, flows out of Loch

Laggan, 9 miles long, which lies alongside the road from Spean Bridge to Newtonmore. Loch Laggan is 10 miles east of Spean Bridge. 5 miles further downstream the Spean is joined by the Treig from Loch Treig; but the flows of both Spean and Treig are now heavily impounded for industrial purposes, as has already been indicated. In any case salmon do not penetrate so far up the Spean, as they are halted by the steep fall at Mounessie, a further 3 miles downstream, which is impassable for fish.

Two miles below Mounessie lies Roy Bridge, where another tributary enters the Spean from the north, the 12 miles long Roy. This precipitous small river rises in the hills close to Loch Spey. It has no loch upon its course, and therefore rises and falls quickly. Its banks are steep and rocky, and in places thickly wooded. Here and there it descends into what amounts to a gorge, with some deep holding pools; but at intervals it provides good gravelly spawning ground. It is of great importance from this angle for the maintenance of the Lochy stock. Many fish run up it late in the season, and given rain and a fair height of water it provides quite good 'small river' fishing for those who know it well. The fishing on this tributary is separately owned. It seems a pity that bait fishing, including the use of worm, is allowed here! The annual catch on this small river is between 120 and 200 salmon and grilse.

The upper reaches of the Roy, unlike its lower course, are fairly open, with large areas of gravel. It is not going too far to describe them in present times as the main spawning area for the whole of the Lochy system.

Below Spean Bridge the Spean continues on its deeply eroded and rocky course, so different in character to that of the Lochy, until $2\frac{1}{2}$ miles further downstream it merges with the Lochy in the big Mucomir Pool, below Mucomir falls and the Hydro there. That the Spean was once a first class fishing river, and a good spring one into the bargain, is apparent from old records; but now sad to say those days are long past. How can it be otherwise with a river that at normal height has lost the large proportion of its flow? But in high water the Spean can still be well worth fishing, though its banks are rough and its pools difficult of access.

Of Loch Lochy, and the Arkaig that feeds it, there is unfortunately little to be said. A count is made of the salmon and grilse that ascend the fish pass at Mucomir to enter the loch. The number of these has now shrunk to below 200 per annum which means that fishing anywhere above Mucomir, whether in loch or river, is barely worthwhile. The obvious conclusion is that the large majority of fish take the alternative route up the Spean. Do the turbines at Mucomir damage the smolts as they descend during the spring? There is little evidence that they do, but one wonders.

Loch Lochy's main feeder is the Arkaig, a sizeable river but only 2 miles long, which drains the 12 miles long Loch Arkaig to the west, and flows past Achnacarry House, the clan centre of Clan Cameron. Loch Arkaig in turn is fed by a large number of hill burns. It seems regrettable that this large catchment area upstream of Mucomir is so little used by salmon; and the sea-trout too in this area have fallen away. Not many ascend the Mucomir fish pass.

The only other Lochy tributary of consequence is the Loy, which enters the main river from the west $2\frac{1}{2}$ miles below Mucomir. A good junction pool, Loy Mouth, is formed at its entry, which holds fish in any height of water and fishes well from both sides. The Loy is only 6 miles long, and has no loch to feed it, so it is of little significance except as a feeder and a spawning stream. A certain number of fish do ascend it late in the season, but only a few are caught by rod fishing.

To return to the main river, U.D.N although it has appeared spasmodically, has never been so prevalent as to do appreciable damage. This seems to be the same on other west-coast rivers, where there is no early spring run. Is it that the chain of infection is broken during the spring months or is it that the water temperature does not as a rule fall low enough for this predominantly cold-water disease to proliferate? The answer may well be a combination of both.

Finally as can be readily appreciated the Lochy as a salmon river has always received outstandingly beneficial treatment. If you, my reader, are ever lucky enough to fish this lovely river you will undoubtedly experience the advantageous results of such wise administration.

The Gruinard

Rocky and tumbly, with very clear water and a quick rate of fall.

In 1981 Colonel Arthur Gemmell most kindly asked me to stay for a week at Eilean Darag Lodge, near the head of Little Loch Broom, a sea loch on the west coast of Ross-shire, to fish the Big Gruinard. This was a new river for me, although I had previously heard much talk about it and had several times fished the neighbouring Broom. My debut on the Big Gruinard was scheduled for the first week of August, which seemed a likely enough time, and I looked forward to it with high anticipation and gratitude towards my generous host.

234

An hour and a half's drive from Inverness via Garve to the west coast (and what a superb stretch of Highland scenery this road affords!), brought me to Dundonnell at the head of Little Loch Broom, or rather to Eilean Darag Lodge which lies close by. It would be enjoyable to write in detail about the warm welcome and unstinted hospitality which awaited me at this lodge with its attractive walled garden nestling in a deep and wooded valley, amid some of the wildest and steepest hill-country of the west coast.

With this taken for granted however, I will confine myself to matters more closely concerned with the fishing, with a brief mention in passing that the only unharmonious feature of this delightful lodge lay in the presence of an unexpected number of bats which had established themselves in some of the bedrooms, to the dismay of the ladies of the party! How was this problem to be dealt with as the rooms were large and the bats were both tireless and elusive? In the end a swift operation with landing nets (the salmon size was best) provided an effective answer.

There are two separate Gruinard rivers, the Big and Little, the first of which was our target, and I will refer to it in future for brevity's sake simply as 'the Gruinard'. The Little Gruinard river we never approached and I know little of it.

The Gruinard's mouth is at a distance of some ten miles from Eilean Darag Lodge, in a south-westerly direction along the coast, and the drive there in the mornings along the coast road is in itself a delight. The high hills of the mainland rise abruptly on one's left, and to one's right lies the sparkling expanse of Little Loch Broom, leading to the Minch with its myriad small islands along its shores, and with the dim outline of the Harris hills studding the western horizon at 40 miles distance across its grey waters.

On reaching Gruinard Bay the road takes a sharp bend southwards, and one arrives at the only road bridge across the Gruinard. This stone bridge lies at about half a mile above the river's short tidal reach and mouth. It is always a fascinating experience to view for the first time, let alone to fish an entirely new river, and the Gruinard certainly held one's interest from the start. I found an attractive and typical medium-small west-coast stream, rocky and tumbly, with very clear water and a quick rate of fall. It descended rapidly, through a series of small pools of every variety, punctuated by rapids and occasional flats, through an outstandingly rocky and precipitous valley, strikingly reminiscent of Iceland or Norway rather than Britain. Even for the west coast of Scotland it seemed that the Gruinard valley was stark and abrupt to a degree, almost treeless, and with massive outcrops of rock, gouged bare during the last Ice-Age from the jagged hillsides bordering it on either side.

As to the river itself, it was bigger than its neighbour, the Broom, being roughly similar in size to the Borgie in Sutherland or the Luce in Galloway, though smaller than the Helmsdale or Naver. It had the advantage of possessing a sizeable loch at its head, Loch na Sheallach, $4\frac{1}{2}$ miles long by a quarter to three quarters of a mile wide. This loch, so I understand, lies at 279 feet above sea-level; while the river below has a course of only 6 miles to the sea, so its rate of fall is a steep one. Nevertheless salmon and sea-trout have no difficulty in reaching Loch na Sheallach, except perhaps when the water is very low, as there are no serious obstacles in their path. They can spawn in the headwaters above the loch, as well as in the main river below it, or in the side burns, the principal one of these being the Allt Loch Ghiubhsachain to the south. It was thus quickly apparent that the Gruinard was endowed with extensive spawning grounds for a river of its size, and far better so provided than the nearby Broom with its impassable falls. Loch na Sheallach also provides a partial sanctuary for fish.

There was a rough track up the six miles length of the river, as far as the loch; but it was negotiable only at slow speed by a landrover or some similar vehicle, and was too rough for an ordinary car—a blessing in disguise perhaps, as it helped to discourage unwanted intruders.

It further became quickly noticeable after one's arrival that the stock of fish in the river was reasonably plentiful. All the pools with a fair depth of water seemed to hold fish in varying numbers. I say 'with a fair depth of water' because it did not take long to realize that the Gruinard, in spite of the substantial loch at its headwaters, is no different from the vast majority of west-coast Scottish rivers, in that in order to provide reasonable fishing the one outstanding essential is *rain*, heavy enough to raise the water level to a fair fishing height and to maintain it there, the longer the better. When the water in a dry period falls to low summer level only a few Gruinard pools are deep enough consistently to hold fish, which, at the same time, become extremely wary and difficult to catch. Any small river fisherman will know well what I mean, and I am sure there is no need to elaborate. Naturally the Gruinard after heavy rain rises very quickly, with its steeply sloping catchment area, and the loch helps to maintain it at a reasonable fishing level for perhaps three or four days after a fair rise of water, and without the aid of further rain. Nevertheless it cannot accurately be classed anything but a 'spate river' with all the attendant advantages and drawbacks. As on most other west-coast Scottish rivers the Gruinard fisherman prays for heavy and almost continuous rain—there can hardly be too much of it. If there is a dry period and the river falls low, it must be faced that fishing is likely to come pretty well to a standstill, and the lower the water the worse the effect. Now it is a popular supposition that the west-coast of Scotland is about the wettest area in Europe, and that hardly a day goes by without rain. If only this last proviso held good throughout the fishing season how great would be the Gruinard fishermans' delight, and how markedly his catch would improve! But unfortunately it is, as many other suppositions, only a half truth. In fact the summer months from May to August and sometimes September often have substantial periods of brilliantly fine weather, with only showers at best, the bulk of the heavy annual rainfall taking place at other times. Except in exceptionally wet summers, and a cold-blooded assessment shows that these are rare, the fisherman is lucky to experience, on average, a worth-while spate once every three weeks. Showers are of little use; admittedly these may occur fairly frequently, but they are of no help towards raising the river once the water has fallen to a decidely low level. Their only useful function lies in helping to keep the water at a fair fishing level for an extended period after a spate, and in contributing towards a reduced water temperature.

At this stage I should admit that of course the inevitable happened on my only visit, so far, to the Gruinard, in that on arrival I found the river already dead low, and it was destined to fall even lower towards the end of my week there. Every day there were encouraging forecasts of rain on the wireless, and promising looking black clouds appeared on the hill tops, with attendant drizzle from time to time. None of it had the slightest effect on the river which continued relentlessly to shrink in height by an inch or two every day. My only catch for the week was one fish of 14 lb, a good sized one for this river, with one other hooked and lost. Only one single other fish was landed by our party during the week, so it cannot be claimed that we were denuding the river of its stock! Nevertheless enjoyment of fishing is not to be measured by the size of the catch, as one frequently reminds oneself, and this particular week was an outstanding example of this truism.

Why did we not fish more often in the loch, it may be asked, if the river was too low to fish well? The answer was that for some reason difficult to pinpoint this loch no longer fishes well nowadays for salmon, although its sea-trout fishing is still fairly good. In days gone by a fair number of salmon could apparently be caught in it, so the records show. Now one can fish from a boat for long hours without incident—a dull business unless the sea-trout are active. I can offer no explanation, nor so far as I know can anyone else, but it is an inescapable fact. Incidentally, the rule is 'fly only', both on the loch and the whole of the Gruinard river, and trolling on the loch is barred. Perhaps the answer may be that in olden days they used to troll on the loch—one never knows.

I have already mentioned that the stock of fish in the Gruinard appeared to be quite reasonable, especially considering that a fair proportion of it by the time of my arrival must have passed through into the loch, and have no longer been in evidence. And I can only say that this river in general compared favourably with many of the small west or north coast rivers which I have fished. It seemed that one might easily have caught five or six fish in a day to one's own rod, if one had been lucky enough to have hit off a good fishing height of water, and perhaps more. Grimble records a catch of 21 fish to a single rod in a day in 1868, though no doubt conditions in those far-off days were different in many respects from now.

In present times the river is divided into 3 beats, and there is ample fishing water *provided* all the pools or most of them are at a good fishing height.

The fish run small, as might be expected, and many of them in any case are grilse—the average weight running around 7–8 lb. Anything over 12 lb is large.

As to tackle, a rod of 12 to 13 feet is ample, or even a trout rod in very low water. It is seldom necessary to cast anything but a short line in covering these small pools, and it is obvious that fish can usually be beached without the aid of net or gaff. Thigh waders are at all times adequate. 'Dibbing' or 'dapping', as practised on the Naver and Helmsdale, would certainly be a useful method here, though I had little opportunity on my one and only visit to try it, and as far as I know no one else did so.

The main run of salmon and grilse in the Gruinard, so I gather, takes place in June and July, whenever there is a rise in water to bring them in. Few if any fish run before mid-June, and the fishing season ends on October 31st, though by that month the fish are hardly worth taking out.

The sea-trout on this river are worth mention; the best time for them is in June or the first half of July, when they run in good numbers and provide fair sport to anyone interested in this form of fishing. What is more, and unlike the salmon, they can be caught frequently in Loch na Sheallach.

One last word of warning, the midges on the Gruinard are about the most virulent breed which one can find anywhere. No words can adequately describe either their myriads or their persistence on a still summer's day, at any time when there is no wind. Clouds of black tobacco smoke may be the best antidote, but what if one does not smoke? All the usual anti-midge creams and lotions seem to be effective for about five minutes at best, before one is driven almost crazy once again. Mosquito nets or veils may help, but I am told that midges penetrate even these.

I confess I don't know the answer to this problem, beyond praying for a cool breeze or colder wind during fishing hours, when midges disappear as if by magic. If any of my readers can suggest an effective deterrent, I shall be both glad and grateful to hear from him.

The Broom

A good junction pool where the main head waters meet.

Strathmore, as the valley of the Broom is called, leading from the
Braemore Forest to the head of the salt-water Loch Broom on the west
coast of Ross-shire, is without doubt one of the most beautiful valleys
anywhere in Scotland. It nurses the little river Broom, which wends
its rocky way from pool to pool, interspersed with falls, rapids, and
shallows. On either side the hills rise steeply, up to 2000 feet and
sometimes higher; while at the head of the glen the high peak of Sgurr
Mor (3650 ft), with its surrounding heights, dominates the southern

horizon. To the north one glimpses from time to time the silvery expanse of Loch Broom, leading to Ullapool, and eventually to the Summer Isles and the Minch, while near at hand a magnificent display of timber, planted along most of the glen by a former laird of the neighbourhood some hundred years ago, is a delight to the eye.

The Broom is but a small river. It is formed by two headwaters, the Droma stream and the Cuileig stream, which rise in the Forest of Braemore. These two streams both have high falls on their lower course, which fish cannot ascend. Soon after these falls they unite at Braemore to produce the main Broom, which has a fairly direct course, slightly west of due north, to fall into the head of Loch Broom, a sea loch 5 miles downstream.

The catchment area is a small one of only 37 square miles. At the same time it is very steep, with a quick run-off from the precipitous hillsides and the rainfall in this area is high, so that the Broom seldom lacks water for any great length of time. There is a sizeable loch, Loch a Bhraoin, 3 miles long on the headwaters of the Cuileig stream, also Loch Droma, $1\frac{1}{2}$ miles long, on the Droma stream. These lochs are an additional help in maintaining the water level.

The rise and fall of the water level is exceptionally rapid, so the river can be but a diminished streamlet at one moment, and a raging torrent within a matter of hours. It can also fall away quickly once again (though it is to be noted that here as elsewhere that the natural fall of the water is never as quick as the rise). The Broom is therefore a true spate river, so far as salmon fishing goes, with all the attendant advantages and drawbacks. How one longs, when kicking one's heels by a river such as the vast Tay in full flood with the rain beating a devil's tattoo on the roof of the fishing hut, to be installed on some small west-coast river like the Broom, brought into perfect fishing order by that same rain. And, in contrast, what lurid imprecations are hurled at the unrelenting glorious sunshine when one is on that same spate river, perversely shrunk to a trickle, and one hears of, say, the mighty Spey, fishing consistently well with its reduced but steady flow. '*Plus ça change, plus c'est la même chose*,' and how seldom one seems to hit it right!

The course of the Broom, so far as salmon are concerned is only 5 miles long, up to the two falls. And almost all spawning is done in the main river, and in the lowest part of the two headstreams above Braemore and below their respective falls. There are no sizeable side-burns which could provide additional spawning grounds. Breeding space is thus restricted and no doubt if adult fish had access to the 15 or more miles of headwaters, which the falls bar to them, the stock would be at least doubled. But to render these falls passable to fish would be an expensive undertaking and even so would not solve the difficulty, as there are further potential obstacles close upstream.

One must admit that the salmon stocks on the Broom do seem limited, or so it has appeared on the several occasions when I have been invited by kind friends to fish this river. I am told that in years gone by they were considerably more prolific. As the whole stock of fish is to be found in the 5 miles of river below the falls, when the water is low one can make a fair estimate of their numbers. Nowadays one is often left wondering what can have happened to all the fish, have they been poached from the river, illegally netted in the sea, or killed off Greenland or Ireland or more likely the Faroes? There is too a legal net which is operated in Loch Broom near the mouth of the river, but its catch is not thought to be extensive.

Be the cause what it may, the salmon rod catch of present days is not high, in proportion to the number of rods which fish; and even with perfect water conditions (i.e. with the river falling back after a spate) a single rod is not likely to get more than one or two fish in a day.

With the water back at low summer level, salmon are extremely difficult to catch. Incoming fresh fish are unlikely to penetrate far up-river and it is more profitable for the angler to fall back on night fishing for sea-trout, of which more later. The average size of salmon in the Broom is now small, as might be expected—around 8–9 lb. But surprisingly large fish for such a small river, of 15–16 lb, are not infrequently caught. Calderwood, in his *Salmon Rivers of Scotland* (1909), mentions one of 33 lb as well as several of 28 lb, most unexpected monsters. There are also, or should be, plenty of grilse from July onwards.

The legal rod fishing season is from February 11th to October 31st though the middle of June is quite soon enough in actual fact to think of having reasonable sport. From then to the end of the season is the best time to fish, whenever there is rain and a consequent rise in water. By mid-September the fish are becoming red, and bright silver ones from then to the end of October are rare.

One's method of fishing is the normal one for a small river. Thigh waders, or in low water even gum-boots, are all that is wanted for wading. Many pools can be fished off the bank. In high water, if there is some colour (which is likely), a fairly sizeable fly of up to 2–$2\frac{1}{2}$ inches long can be successfully used, as the stream in many pools will be strong. As the water falls and clears there should be an equivalent reduction in the size of fly, down to sea-trout size in low water. In anything other than spate the water is normally of perfect clarity.

Rod length should be of 12 or 13 feet, which is a convenient length for most heights of water. With the river in spate 14 feet may be preferred, but it is never necessary to throw a long line. In low water a single handed rod will be effective, for those who like such instruments, and a floating line, with or without a short sinking tip, in any water height. As an alternative method to the orthodox manner of fishing, the enterprising angler can always fall back on 'dapping' or 'dibbing', in the Naver and Helmsdale fashion (see page 99.). The Broom, being so small a river, readily lends itself to such experiment.

Playing and landing fish usually presents little difficulty. Fish can seldom run out much length of line in the small pools, and it is normally a simple matter to beach them, or else to land them by hand-net. There is no objection to gaffing, if the angler wants to resort to this, but there would seldom seem any necessity for it. So far as grilse and small salmon are concerned it is apt in any case to spoil them, and beaching or netting is far better.

Fishing the Broom when the water is low, in the twilight of a mid-summer night, can be an exciting experience. It is hardly ever quite dark, and fishing is never hopeless at that hour. I remember some years ago my kind host Major David Rasch and I were on the lowest part of the river on such a night, fishing with light tackle for whatever might turn up, whether salmon or sea-trout. Towards the end of the evening I had fished carefully down a good pool of some 30 yards length in the semi-darkness without result. My thoughts were rapidly turning towards a dram or two of Speyside malt whisky in our comfortable lodge before retiring to bed, but at that moment my host turned up, and being obviously dissatisfied with my poor performance, decided to fish the pool himself and see what I had left behind. He was only too right. After not more than a dozen casts, and it was too dark to see the fall of the fly, he hooked something which played wildly and strongly all up and down the pool. Eventually after skilful handling it was beached, and turned out to be a 16 lb fresh run salmon. What a splendid finish to the evening, and I was never more pleased at having my eye well and truly wiped.

On another occasion I was fishing a pool called Glacour, with the river running full and high after rain, with some colour in the water. I had tried the pool down with a fly of about orthodox size, i.e. size 4, and without result. I changed to a three inch long hair-winged tube fly, and quickly hooked something, which also turned out to be a 16 lb salmon. It played strongly in the fast current, but I managed to land it without too much difficulty as my tackle was strong. Both these fish were big ones for the Broom, and it was surprising that so small a river could produce fish of this type.

So much for the Broom as a salmon river, and it is now time to turn to its sea-trout. These should run any time from the end of May onwards, and it is for sea-trout fishing, just as much as for salmon fishing, that the Broom has made its name. Sea-trout can be found at times in the various pools throughout the length of the river, June and July being the best months for them. Bigger fish of up to 4 or 5 lb run first, followed by herling later. Night fishing after dark, when the water is low, is the most effective method; and a warm, moonless night, with little or no wind, and a plentiful run of fresh sea-trout is what is wanted for this. Be sure if you undertake this that you have with you some efficient anti-midge deterrent. West-coast midges are a peculiarly virulent breed, and can ruin your night fishing for you if not discouraged in some way or another.

A week's fishing on the Broom in times gone by used thus to be a good gamble at the right time of year; if the water was low one could fish all night for sea-trout, and if high all day for salmon, and do well with both.

But once again one cannot avoid facing the sad truth that in these present times, like the salmon, the sea-trout have markedly fallen away in numbers. One much hopes that this decrease may only be temporary.

For those who like other diversions besides the quest for salmon and sea-trout, there are plenty of brown trout lochs in the neighbourhood and it is possible to hire a boat in Ullapool and go sea-fishing. Both these pursuits are said to be highly productive, though I have had no first-hand experience of them.

There are three excellent lodges on the Broom, one at Braemore and two at Inverbroom, amid lovely surroundings. For anyone who has to fall back on a hotel, there are plenty of these in the neighbourhood of Ullapool, where there are also shops of all descriptions, including a useful general store known as 'The Captain's Cabin.'

So if you go to fish the Broom it is safe to say that, like me, you are bound to have a pleasant and interesting visit. The size of the catch both for you and your friends is likely these days to be more problematical; but if you are lucky and hit it right you should have no cause for complaint.

The Grimersta

MacCleay's Stream at the head of no. 2 loch.

Lewis, together with Harris, is not a big island. The outermost of the northern Hebrides, it measures at its fullest extent 60 miles in length by 28 in width, with many inlets from the sea penetrating far inland. The result is that there is no space in it for any widespread river system, and certainly its main river the Grimersta (together with its lochs) is by no means large. Lewis presents a curious type of countryside. It is comparatively flat, or rather rolling, with high hills only at one point in the west, few trees, and with large expanses of

246

heather covering endless tracts of thick peat. There are multitudes of freshwater lochs, large and small, scattered indiscriminately over the terrain, and one cannot travel any distance in any direction without quickly meeting salt-water, either in the form of the open sea, or more likely in one of the many sea-lochs which are to be found reaching inland all over the island.

There are few high hills in Lewis, but the southern part of the island, known as Harris, is plentifully endowed with them, rising abruptly from sea level to 2600 feet. These hills are visible from most parts of Lewis also, so they serve to add variety to the scenery, also, more important from the fisherman's angle, to draw the rain. Harris is extremely rough and wild, with its precipitous slopes, endless outcrops of rock, and jagged broken coastline. Its whole ensemble is strikingly reminiscent of Iceland, except that the latter is infinitely larger and its mountains higher and bleaker. (Also it has little heather and no peat, which Lewis at least possesses in profusion.)

It is amid this background that the Grimersta river system and its fishing is to be found. Since the year 1924 this has all belonged to a syndicate of owners, whose ranks are constantly refilled as and when vacancies occur. The first syndicate of Grimersta owners was formed in 1871. In 1918 the whole island, including the fishing, was sold to Lord Leverhulme, and sold again in 1924. The owners, naturally enough, keep most of the best fishing periods in their own hands; but rods from time to time, particularly early and late in the season, are leased to outsiders. The general management of this fishery is first class, there being an elaborate code of rules laid down as regards methods of fishing, beats, number of rods allowed, sharing of rods, and all other matters of consequence. There are sometimes complaints that these rules are too complex; but without a strict code of this sort how is fishing for up to eight rods at a time to be smoothly organised throughout a five month season, with constant changes of rod? To my mind the rules are wholly admirable, and I offer no criticism of any sort.

To return to the river system, the headstreams originate near or just over the border of Harris, and converge to form the large Loch Langabhat (9 miles long), which lies immediately to the north of the high Harris hills, and extends in a north-easterly direction. There is a double outlet at the north-east end of Loch Langabhat, and two separate streams run for not more than half a mile to feed the fourth Grimersta loch, about 2 miles long and extending northwards. There is then a short stretch of river, with a good pool, the Ford Stream, at its outlet into the third loch. This latter loch is a smaller sheet of water, only three quarters of a mile long; it has an outlet stream of about a quarter of a mile, with one or two high water lies in it, leading to MacCleay's Stream, a famous salmon catch. MacCleay was a noted civil engineer, and a member of the original 1871 syndicate. It was he who designed many of the artificial dykes, bulwarks, and piers still to be found in a number of places on the Grimersta. This stream leads into the second loch. Of all the four lower Grimersta lochs this latter is perhaps the least productive. It is narrow, a mile long, and much of its fishing is often let to the Stornoway Angling Association.

There remains the outlet stream from the second loch into the first loch, known simply as 'The Stream', the first loch which is one of the most prolific of all, and the small Grimersta river which drains it.

'The Stream' is short, not more than 60 yards long and about 20 yards wide. But it can be a most productive fishing stretch as long as the water level is not too low. It is not deep, and there is a fair current through it.

The first loch is another one of similar size but wider, i.e. about one mile long by half a mile wide.

The Grimersta river leaves this loch at its north-east corner, and runs northwards for three quarters of a mile into the head of the salt-water Loch Roag—Grimersta fishing lodge is on the west side of this sea-loch (which at this point is only about 200 yards wide at high tide), 500 yards below the mouth of the river.

It will be seen from the above description that the Grimersta fishing consists largely of a chain of lochs rather than a river. These lochs are normally boat-fished, except at their inlet or outlet streams, and sizeable row-boats capable of carrying four people are provided on each of them. The number of boatmen per boat is always two, to cater for any emergency; and this leaves room for either one or two fishermen also in the boat (if in the latter case the rod is being shared).

These Grimersta lochs tend to be shallow, and weedy in places; they undoubtedly form wonderful resting grounds for salmon and grilse, and owing to their lack of depth fish well with the fly (which is the only lure allowed). Loch Langabhat (Icelandic 'Langavatn'—the long lake) is seldom fished. It is remote, and there is better fishing nearer to hand. But the fourth loch is good, particularly an area near the head of it known as 'The Basin'. So is the third loch, perhaps the most prolific of all, with a productive fishing ground alongside a rocky bank on its eastern shore known as 'The Alligator'. The second loch is the least good, but the first loch one of the best. A lot depends on the strength of the wind and its direction. It is essential for good fishing that there should be some sort of wind; flat calm makes loch fishing virtually hopeless. In fact the wind can hardly be too strong, so long as it is still possible to manage a boat. The rougher the wave on the loch surface, the better the fish take. Where is the best fishing area in a loch only experience can tell, but the Grimersta boatmen know well all such likely areas. When a fair wind is blowing it is usually near the downwind shore that the fish gather, though they often tend too to look for the current of an inlet stream, or the quickening draw of an outlet. Such streams seem more inclined to hold the fish steadily, while in the main body of the loch it is likely that they cruise around in shoals.

Fishing a loch is easy. The boatman plays an important part in the proceedings, not only in controlling the boat, but by manoeuvring the angler over the best fishing ground. (It would involve more skill on his part if the angler had to manage his own boat; but on the Grimersta, at any rate, this is not allowed.) The main point which the angler has to bear in mind is the importance of tightening quickly after a rise to the fly has been seen (contrary to the normally accepted rule of fishing). The water is still, or rather without current, and the fish will soon get rid of the fly if no action is taken. The angler should therefore watch the water closely where he reckons his flies to be, and should tighten without delay if he sees a boil or if his line begins to draw. It is normal to use two flies, tail and dropper; not more for fear of tangles. Pattern of fly matters little but hair wings are probably best. In general sizes 4 to 6 are preferred. The bigger fly, if there is a

difference in size, is probably better as the dropper. In recent years
there has grown up a fashion on the Grimersta river and lochs for
using flies winged with Vulturine Guinea Fowl feathers, with their
striking bars of blue and white; and these certainly are effective,
though no more so here than anywhere else. I have caught many fish
on these flies on the Spey, Tay, Tweed, Hampshire Avon, and in
Iceland also. In fact it seems that they will kill anywhere; but not
more so than many other useful patterns. They are supposed to
represent an elver, but I never could see any remote likeness between
these two, apart from a similar length. An elver is a thin, spindly,
silvery and transparent small creature, and a pair of Vulturine guinea
fowl feathers is none of these. However, this is too petty a point to be
worth argument; and what matters is whether or not the fish take these
flies, which they often do.

The usual dressing is as follows and the size can be varied.

Tail: Golden Pheasant topping.   *Ribbing*: Oval silver tinsel.
Tag: Silver tinsel.   *Hackle*: Blue or magenta.
Body: Black silk.   *Wings*: Pair Vulturine Guinea Fowl feathers.

The process of fishing a loch for salmon is very similar to that for
sea-trout or brown trout. Cast a shortish line in a generally downwind
direction, give the flies a moment or two to sink, and then work them
back towards the boat by pulling in line and by raising the rod. Each
successive cast should be made at a different angle, so that as much
water as possible is covered. Fish will sometimes follow and take very
close to the boat. The speed with which the flies are worked should
depend on the size of the ripple or wave—a high wave and they
should be moved quite slowly, but with only a slight ripple a good
deal faster. This method works perfectly well when there are a fair
number of fish present, except as previously mentioned in a flat calm.

Then nothing is much good, though you can try a dry fly if you like—really it is better in these circumstances to forsake the lochs and fish on a section of river, if there is one on your beat, until such time as a breeze arises. It usually does, sooner or later. Lewis is a very windy place, on the edge of the open Atlantic, and there is no shelter provided by trees or nearby hills. There is little difficulty about playing a fish hooked from a boat in a loch. He can always be followed, and should not be allowed to run out too long a line. Provided he is kept clear of weeds, there are likely to be no obstructions which could foul the line or leader, and he can be landed by net into the boat or onto the shore, as preferred.

One requirement is obviously necessary for good sport, and that is the simple one that there should be plenty of fish present in the loch where one is fishing! It hardly needs pointing out that this form of fishing can become monotonous to a degree if fish are scarce. To fish day after day from a boat with never a rise or pull, and hardly ever the sight of a fish jumping, is a dull game at the best, particularly if the weather is foul. One can amuse oneself for some time by trying different types of rod or fly, and by watching the birds, or admiring the scenery; but eventually such activities too will pall, so my advice to the reader if he is going to fish these Grimersta lochs is to make sure that he goes at the right time of year, when they are sure to be holding a good head of fish—that is from the second week of July onwards. Earlier than this is chancy.

On one of the Grimersta lochs one is allowed to troll a fly behind the boat in a certain area on the way to the good fishing ground. If one put on a big hair-winged fly of about $2\frac{1}{2}$ inches length, let out 40 yards of line, and induced the boatman to slow down to half throttle, one could be practically certain of hooking a fish quite quickly. It was interesting that fish could not resist a large fly drawn fairly quickly through dead water, even at a time when they would pay no attention to small flies fished by casting in the orthodox way. But what a despicable procedure this trolling is! One is ashamed to admit having perpetrated such outrages. Such a game fish as the salmon surely deserves a more respectful approach, and no skill of any sort is needed in this method, which amounts to sheer murder.

The river is another matter. It is tiny, smaller even than Broom or Borgie, and can be fished off the bank or by wading ankle deep. Hardly anywhere is it necessary to wear even thigh waders, and gum boots are almost always enough. It is a very pretty tumbling little stream, with a quick series of rocky rapids and pools, some of these latter much improved or even created by the construction of artificial batteries, breakwaters and croys. How many good pools elsewhere, on rivers big or small, are not helped to some degree in this way? Not many, when one considers it closely. It is great fun to fish this stream with small flies and light tackle, and one's day is likely to be full of incident. Fish are to be found in numbers in the river sooner in the year than in the lochs; any time from mid-June onwards until the end of July may be good—after that the lochs became a surer find until mid-September, when fish are apt to appear in numbers in the river once again. It is preferable not to have the water level in the river too low, when fish become reluctant to enter it. Even so there are always one or two pools that will fish; but with medium or high water the fishing is extensive, some eighteen pools coming progressively into order.

The Kelt Pool, the lowest one, is probably the best. It is longer than any of the others, and has good depth. If there are any fish anywhere in the river this pool is certain to hold some. It is only 150 yards from salt-water, and is not too small to hold fish by the hundred when the main run is in progress. It is often possible, with the aid of polaroid glasses, to spot the fish in these little pools when one is fishing them, which only adds to the fun. It is highly entertaining to be able to see the reactions of the fish to one's fly or series of flies, fished in a variety of different ways; and it is also highly instructive. Most of the fish in the Grimersta river are fresh-run, straight from the sea; they do not stay long in the river before passing on into the lochs, but take freely while they are there. Upstream of the Kelt Pool, the best pools are the Bridge Pool, the Long Pool, the Lower Rocky, the Upper Rocky, and the Battery, but there are a number of other ones almost equally productive.

One thing is noticeable about this small river, it is very slow to rise and fall, in marked contrast to the west-coast rivers of the mainland.

The reason is not far to seek. Its total catchment area is a small one, and once the water level of the five lochs has sunk beyond a certain point, rain more heavy and prolonged than normal is needed to raise it to a respectable height once again. And all five lochs have to be so raised in level before extra water can reach the river. This is apt to be a slow process which in a dry year may take days or even weeks to eventuate. In contrast, if once these lochs are well filled with a good head of water, the river will hold its height for long periods at a time without the further aid of rain, also it will never become coloured. So it cuts both ways; but if spring and early summer are unusually dry, it is worth remembering that one may still be short of water in the river, even when a moderate amount of rain does come.

As to the process of fishing the Grimersta river, this is the same as for any other small west-coast stream; but even more care than usual should be taken to keep out of sight of the fish, since this river is so small. When a fish has been played out and landed, its struggles will almost certainly have disturbed the other fish in the pool, even if the angler on the bank has managed to keep out of sight. It is therefore good tactics if the latter leaves the pool in question to fish another one nearby for a short time. If he returns to the original pool after a ten minute or so interval his chances of another fish from it will be much improved.

The average size of fish is small, 7–8 lb or even smaller when the grilse start to arrive, which they do in numbers towards the end of June. The bulk of the Grimersta catch in fact probably consists of grilse. These at least make up in appearance for what they lack in weight. There is a Gaelic proverb which says that but three things in this transitory world are beautiful in death—a young child, a blackcock, and a grilse. In days gone by there was apparently a substantial run of larger spring salmon in April and May, but this run has virtually disappeared nowadays. It seems to be of little use, in present times, fishing before mid-June at the earliest. The best fishing period is undoubtedly between the second week of July and the third week of August. September in some years is quite good, but fish are apt to be getting stale by then. There is no proper autumn run. The record Grimersta fish weighed 29 lb and was caught in April 1927;

but fish of 20 lb or over have always been rare, and there are fewer of them now than at any time in the past. Even a 15 pounder is a big one now, and few in fact are over 12 lb.

The Grimersta has the name of being one of the most prolific fishings in Britain. In the past this description was certainly true. a glance at the record book in Grimersta Lodge will confirm it; or if anyone wants to read a more detailed account, there are two books by Cecil Braithwaite, *Fishing Vignettes* (1925) and *Fishing Here and There* (1935), which are a mine of information and stories. The latter book has an extra two chapters on Grimersta fishing history by John McKay, who was head keeper there until the Great War of 1914–'18, his father having been a ghillie there before him. It is full of interesting recollections. It also has an account of Mr. Naylor's great catch of 54 salmon and grilse on August 28th 1888, when during the current week three rods caught 333 salmon and grilse and 71 sea-trout. Mr. Naylor also had other big individual day catches of salmon and grilse that season, viz. 46. 45. 36. and 27. In the year 1922 the catch of salmon and grilse totalled 1613, which stood as a record until 1925 when the season's yield rose to 2,276 salmon and grilse, and I do not think this figure has since been exceeded.

From 1924 to 1935 the average catch was 1,146 salmon and grilse, the number of rods being seldom more than four on any given day. These figures are certainly outstanding, and it is doubtful if for numbers alone they could be surpassed, anywhere in Britain; one would have to look to some of the Icelandic salmon fisheries for that.

Cecil Braithwaite also relates an amusing occurrence when in July 1923 the Hon. Lucy Holland, fishing the fourth loch, caught 2 salmon, on dropper and tail fly respectively, hooked and landed at the same time. They weighed 6 lb and 5 lb. He also recounts that he himself had performed a similar feat. No doubt other Grimersta fishers have done likewise.

But, sad to say, here as in many places elsewhere this is a story of the past. For whatever reason it may be, Grimersta catches and stocks have declined disappointingly in these recent years. If a cause is sought for this, one might well look to the escalation of drift netting off the Irish coast, or of long-lining off the Faroes only 200 miles from

Lewis, or possibly to the Greenland fishery, and last but not least to the increase in local illegal fishing. So if today you are going to this fishing, don't expect to do even half as well as Messrs. Naylor or Braithwaite, as if you do you are in for certain disillusionment. In my own case I must admit that two of my five visits there have resulted in a totally blank week, or as near so as makes little difference. On the other hand, if you hit it right, you may still find little difficulty in killing double figures in the day; and for anglers who do not want to wade to any depth, nor to have too strenuous fishing, and who are satisfied to catch numbers of small salmon and grilse, often from a boat and probably all under 12 lb, there could hardly be a better rendezvous than here.

As to tackle, nothing elaborate is wanted. There is a fashion for using single handed rods of 10 feet or so. These may be adequate on the lochs, but on the river something longer will be needed if the wind happens to be adverse. Personally I would settle for 12 feet if not 13 feet, whether on river or lochs, because modern rods are so light, and the longer length gives better control of line and fly while the cast is being fished, as well as greater casting capacity. But it is largely a matter of personal taste.

Besides the salmon and grilse there are also plenty of sea-trout, the Kelt Pool late in the evening is a good place for these; but they are seldom deliberately fished for, with the salmon and grilse so much in the limelight.

All Grimersta fishermen automatically stay at Grimersta Lodge, mentioned above, which is close to the mouth of the river and 18 miles from Stornoway. It is a Victorian fishing lodge, overlooking the sea loch, partly rebuilt since its original foundation or at least added to from time to time. It possesses all that could be desired in the way of comfort and amenity, both management and staff being first rate.

Behind the lodge there is a small clump of trees, the only trees which I have seen in the island, except at Stornoway. Curiously enough these trees form a much sought-after haven for cuckoos, which every year seem to gather there in numbers, and utter their call at all hours of the day and night. It seems an odd place to find these birds; perhaps some expert can explain?

There is always an excellent team of boatmen and ghillies who arrive each morning at the lodge for the assistance of anglers; and there is also a subsidiary team of watchers, under the direction of a headkeeper, whose main task is the prevention of poaching. This at times is a serious problem involving much hard work, and a constant watch has to be kept all round the clock. There is danger of poaching both in the river and lochs, also in the sea loch and around the coast, but the management deals with this in an efficient manner.

The journey to Lewis (or Harris) is an amusing one. One can go by sea from Ullapool in Ross-shire, there are two sailings in each direction every day except sundays during summer, and the car-ferry ship takes about $3\frac{1}{2}$ hours to reach Stornoway. On a fine day the views from the Minch, looking towards the coast from Sutherland right down to Skye, are magnificent. There is an alternative sea route from Uig in Skye to Tarbert in Harris, the crossing is shorter but the ship smaller. One can take a car with one on either passage. The Minch can be rough, but in summer seldom seems to be so. An alternative method is to fly to Stornoway from Glasgow, which makes the journey quicker. The management at Grimersta lodge can provide motor transport.

So in many ways the Grimersta fishing has great attractions, not least in its surroundings and wild remoteness. But it is an entirely different type of fishing to what one experiences even on a medium—small river, such as the Naver or Helmsdale; whereas to fish a large river such as the Spey or Tay involves a totally different procedure. It is as well to bear this clearly in mind.

The many interesting visits I have made to the Grimersta have been entirely owing to the great kindness of Colonel George Kidston-Montgomerie, and I shall always be grateful to him. We have fished together in so many different places in Scotland, England, Ireland, and Iceland, and there could be no better fishing companion.

SCOTLAND

Rivers of the North Coast

Borgie—Naver—Thurso

The Naver, Thurso, and Borgie, naming them in order of merit, all have an undeniable distinctiveness, though the Naver might be considered close in character to the Helmsdale.

All three rivers have a spring run, that of the Naver being substantial, but in general their best fishing is now to be had in July or soon after, when the grilse run has arrived. Rain on all of them is an asset, though less essential in the case of the Naver, which holds its level better than the others.

The surroundings here are wild and unspoilt, being attractive to an outstanding degree.

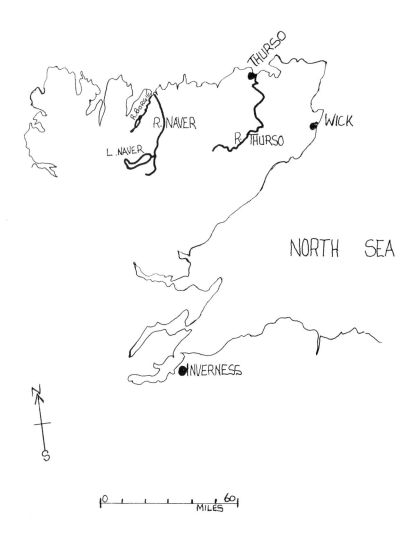

THURSO

R.Bogair

R.NAVER

L.NAVER

R.THURSO

WICK

NORTH SEA

INVERNESS

N

S

0   60
MILES

The Borgie

The Borgie runs through wild and unspoilt surroundings.

This small but pretty river rises 6 miles north of Altnaharra, close to the head of Loch Naver, in the north of the county of Sutherland. It drains an area of approximately 62 square miles, and has a course of 21 miles in length, near due north in direction, to fall into Torrisdale Bay on the north coast of Sutherland, close to the village of Skerray. There are four lochs on its upper course, namely the Loch of Coulside followed by Lochs Loyal, Craggie, and Slam, the latter three being contiguous. Below Loch Slam the Borgie has a $9\frac{1}{2}$ mile course to its mouth in Torrisdale Bay, with a fall of around 10 feet half way en route. Fish can ascend this fall, but seldom do so before mid-April.

The countryside upstream of Borgie Bridge, which lies about $2\frac{1}{2}$ miles above the mouth of the river, is wild in the extreme, rolling, and heathery, and uninhabited, with the craggy outline of Ben Loyal (2504 feet) dominating the south-western horizon. Except for the secondary motor-road from Borgie Bridge via Tongue to Altnaharra, there is no evidence in this area of the hand of man, apart from some forestry plantations, one suspension bridge at the falls, and numerous artificial croys and batteries in the river. For anyone who delights in wild places, and likes to commune alone with Nature, there could be few more attractive riversides than that of the Borgie. How grateful one should be in these present days for remote surroundings of this sort, even if one has to permeate to the northernmost areas of Britain to find them.

All the best fishing on the Borgie is from the falls downstream to about one mile below Borgie Bridge, some 4 miles of river. Everywhere this river is of the normal type of small highland flow, with a quick succession of rapid and pool, but one notices that most of the pools are markedly artificial, in that some owner in the past has made remarkably good use of dykes, croys, and batteries to create man-made pools, where in nature there would be little but a thin rush of shallow water.

The water is normally transparent and clear; even after rain it colours little, thanks to the filtering effect of the four lochs mentioned above. The result is that it is frequently easy to spot any fish that may be present in the pools, and equally easy to discover when a pool is empty. Also in a small river of this type one has to take extra care to keep out of sight of the fish. It is easy to frighten them, if one does not take a good deal of trouble.

The Borgie has a spring run of small salmon of an average weight of 8–9 lb. Anything over 12 lb is a big one and the early fish are apt to be the largest. There are also grilse and sea-trout from June onwards, as well as summer salmon.

The rod fishing season is from January 12th to September 30th but few fish appear before April. July is probably the best month in present times, provided there is rain and some high water. This is one thing which the Borgie does need at frequent intervals; and during any period of continuous dry weather and low water it seems that the run of fish dwindles. Unfortunately the rainfall in this part of Sutherland is not high—in complete contrast to what happens on the west coast, so Borgie spates are not as frequent as one would like. In low water the Borgie does not fish well, unlike its bigger neighbour the Naver, which in anything but drought can still produce a fair number of fish. But if one is lucky and gets a wet July, one can have fair sport on the Borgie.

I must admit that on the occasions when I have fished this river I have found a disappointing lack of fish, even at good periods in the season. And I gather the same drawback is often experienced by others. It seems to be nothing unusual to find the whole river from the falls down holding no more than an odd fish or two at best. How is the fisherman profitably to employ his time during such periods both on the Borgie and other rivers, when fishing is written off as hopeless? This is an old and frustrating problem, which it is up to each individual to solve in the way best suited to his temperament. There are other alternative occupations, maybe, such as trout fishing, sea-fishing, visits of inspection to other rivers, photography, tackle repairs, fly-tying, and so on. But on a salmon fishing expedition these are only stop-gaps. Personally I prefer not to leave the river on such occasions, even if I don't attempt to fish. There is usually something to be learnt about the river's bed or its flow, particularly in time of very low water; but it is a maddening business trying to kill time while awaiting the longed-for rain.

On the other hand one hears of friends or acquaintances sometimes doing quite well with their fishing on the Borgie, given enough rain.

The average yearly catch in the past has been between 200–300 fish, not a lot for the amount of fishing done and for a nine month season. And a good proportion of these fish used to be caught on worm, a method which to the mind of many anglers is not acceptable. One wonders why it is that the Borgie is not more prolific. Everything would seem to be in its favour. There is no netting anywhere on it, and its mouth is only one mile crow flight from that of the Naver, which has an excellent stock of fish. One would imagine there are good spawning grounds in the many small headwaters. Nevertheless I know that a river in Iceland of similar size and (apparent) character as the Borgie would probably produce 1000 fish in a season, if not more, in spite of inferior spawning conditions. Perhaps this comparison is unfair and out of context, but even in Scotland, a river of similar type, and unnetted as the Borgie is, could be expected to produce a much bigger catch. Is it that the fish once in the river run through too quickly? One would not have imagined so, as the falls alone should check them. Or is it that many Borgie fish are apt to link up with the shoals of the more numerous Naver fish, and enter the wrong river? One would not have thought so, as this is contrary to the salmon's accepted behaviour. There are plenty of seals off the coast (and they badly need to be reduced in number); these could exercise a deterrent effect; but on the other hand they do not stop a good head of fish entering the nearby Naver. Is there bad poaching? One hasn't heard of anything unduly detrimental. Or is it simply that one expects too much, and that this small river is too hard fished? In this connection one could say that the Borgie would provide very pleasant fishing if one lived on it, and simply fished it at intervals only, whenever it was in first class order. But it does not lend itself to continuous fishing throughout the season for six days each week. Such a process is bound to lead to much disappointment; and this small river simply does not possess the necessary capacity for such treatment. Nevertheless one is still left without an explanation why the stock of fish is not greater. It is hard to find a convincing reason for this; and without further and much closer and more detailed study I would not attempt to produce one.

For fishing a little river of this type nothing ambitious in the way of tackle is needed. To throw a long line is never necessary, though accuracy in casting is important. A rod of 13 feet should at any time be long enough, and in low water one could drop to 12 feet, or even to a single handed rod of 9 or 10 feet. All the usual types of thinly dressed summer flies are adequate, together with a floating line and a leader of 10 lb breaking strain of best type monofilament. With the river in spate it may often be worth trying, here as elsewhere, a much larger hair winged fly, of up to say two inches length. And in lower water 'dapping' or 'dibbing', as practised on the Naver, can also be effective here.

A certain number of sea-trout ascend the Borgie in summer, and there are many brown trout lochs in the neighbourhood. Both provide extra diversion if the salmon-fishing fails.

There is an adequate hotel near Borgie Bridge, which is the obvious lodging place for a visiting angler. It has the merit of being close to the river, and within easy reach of all parts of it, though a car is needed for transport to the upper beats. A good deal of walking is also involved.

It may simply be that I have been unlucky in the timing of my visits to this river, and for that reason am unfairly prejudiced. But, from what I have gathered from others, I do not think so. I must admit that I have never fished the Borgie in July, which has the reputation nowadays of being the most prolific month. This may well be the case, with the arrival of the grilse. Given rain at that time, no doubt the fishing at times can be rewarding. My final verdict, however, about this river is that while its character, its surroundings, the accommodation, and the general atmosphere are all very pleasant, there is definite need for a bigger head of fish.

The Naver

In the lowest water conditions fish will still enter the river.

The Naver could well be classed, together with the Helmsdale which it so closely resembles, as the best of the smaller Scottish salmon rivers. It is the largest river in Sutherland, draining the sizeable Loch Naver (6 miles long and half a mile wide), which lies on the north side of Ben Klibreck (3154 ft), about 15 miles crow flight inland from the north coast. From the eastern end of Loch Naver to its estuary into Torrisdale Bay at Bettyhill, the Naver has a fairly direct northerly course of approximately 18 miles.

264

The main headwater of the Naver is called by a different name, i.e. the Mudale, which in turn is fed by several parent streams rising in the high hills towards the west, uniting to give the Mudale a total length of some 10 miles before it enters the western end of Loch Naver near the small village of Altnaharra.

There is also a substantial tributary, the Mallart, which rises to the south of Ben Klibreck, and then skirts its eastern face to join the main Naver after a 6 mile course, half a mile below the latter's outlet from Loch Naver.

The whole of this river system, together with its feeder burns, gives the Naver a catchment area of 186 square miles, slightly larger than that of both the Thurso and the Helmsdale. The surroundings of this river are wholly delightful. The valley is a fairly wide one, without steep hills to close it in, although one often has the view of Ben Klibreck's lofty blue outline on the southern horizon.

Habitation is sparse, just a few crofts or cottages from time to time, and here and there a larger house, such as the attractive fishing lodge at Syre. A lovely bright sparkling river, with green or heather-covered slopes on either side, climbing quickly back to peaty and rock studded moorland! Tree growth by nature is scarce in all this neighbourhood, though there is a good deal of birch along the river bank below Syre, with occasional rowan trees or firs. The Forestry Commission, however, has been active in recent years alongside the upper part of the river, and there are large plantations of evergreens in the area south of Syre Lodge. These only serve to enhance the view and to give shelter for the fisherman on windy days.

The wild and rough coastline in the neighbourhood of Bettyhill also offers a splendid panorama both to east and west, varying from golden sandy beaches to stark jutting headlands and rocky islets or skerries—a dangerous coast in the days of sail.

Above all the outstanding attraction of Strath Naver is surely its peaceful remoteness; there are no towns here (or anywhere within 40 miles, for that matter). Its only village is Bettyhill on Torrisdale Bay, which has less than 1000 inhabitants. Nor are there railways or main roads. The nearest railway is either at Thurso, 32 miles from Bettyhill, at Kinbrace, or at Lairg, 46 miles away to the south; and the only sizeable road, which runs parallel with the course of the river, is a single track for the 24 miles from Altnaharra to Bettyhill, with passing places for cars at intervals. Nor are there any airfields, nuclear installations, oil refineries, hydros, or other similar afflictions of the modern age, to mar the serenity of such idyllic surroundings. One lives in hope that they may long be preserved from 'development' and 'progress'.

Thanks to the kindness of various good friends, I have fished the Naver at intervals since 1969. There are without doubt many Naver fishermen who have fished it much longer than I have, and who know it far better than me, with my limited experience of it. To them I apologise for any inaccuracies which may creep in to my description of this river or its fishings. I can only say that I wish that I had had the opportunity to fish this lovely river far more often and for longer periods, and so be more familiar with its fishing and all that goes with it.

The rod fishing season lasts from January 12th to September 30th, and the net fishing season from February 11th to August 26th; but in fact the nets, which belong to the river owners, have not for many years been operated before June 1st, in order to encourage the entry of spring fish. Nor for that matter are they worked to anything approaching full capacity afterwards. This is a sound policy, which must surely pay an excellent dividend.

There are six beats on the Naver which belong to a syndicate of owners, together with various lodges along the river. There is also a short stretch of private water, not far above the tidal estuary, which belongs to Lord Roborough; and below that is Association water.

The fishing on Loch Naver, whether for salmon, sea-trout or brown trout, is leased by the Altnaharra Hotel, as is the fishing on the Mudale. The Mallart fishing also is leased separately.

Management of the Naver fishings is exceptionally well exercised and deserves the highest commendation. Here is one river, for a change, which is certainly not over-fished. The main Naver is divided into 6 beats, excluding the private water and the Association water, and one rod only is allowed on each beat, *except* that a lady may be allowed to fish as a second rod in company with the original incumbent. The idea is, of course, that members of the 'weaker sex' are not expected to fish as keenly or for such long hours as their male counterparts. In most cases we all know that, broadly speaking, this is what happens; but we equally know that in certain other cases the exact opposite prevails, and not too infrequently!

Ribald humourists for a long time have made good capital out of this rule, which has been the butt of many witticisms, not difficult to imagine. We find that the Prince of Victorian anglers, Thomas Tod Stoddart, long ago gives the following emphatic advice with regard to lady companions: 'never fall in love with one you meet by the waterside; there are some situations where every woman looks an angel'. However, the overall principle of a single male angler is an excellent one. It gives plenty of room for the keen fisherman, even when seconded by a lady companion, and even in the lowest water; and it will be a sad day if ever this rule is lifted. The tendency nowadays on almost all fishings, owing to financial pressure, is for the number of rods to be continually increased until all the fun is spoilt. One has seen it happen, and deplored it, in so many places time and time again. Once a rule of this nature has been lifted it is difficult to re-impose it; and one can only hope that the Naver owners will be strong-minded and stand fast by this first class rule.

Beats are changed in rotation every day, so that in the course of a six day fishing week a rod will fish the whole length of the main river, (apart from the private water). This is an excellent system, which works well, and gives everyone a frequent change of scene, and as even a chance as possible of good sport. The beats do vary in results from time to time, according to time of year, water height, and water temperature, so that daily changes are no bad thing, though they do mean that a newcomer may take a long time to get to know the whole river in detail. A similar system of beat distribution applies on the Helmsdale.

The Naver is another 'Fly Only' river all through the season, like all other rivers north of Inverness; and for such excellent fly water this can be regarded only as an unmixed blessing. One knows only too well what would happen if indiscriminate bait fishing were allowed on these small rivers with their plentiful stocks of fish, concentrated in a number of easily covered pools. The idea is abhorrent.

In character the Naver is a medium–small river, with a fair stream throughout its length, and with pools of every type. The fall from Loch Naver to the sea is 247 feet over 18 miles, an average of 13 feet per mile. This is a steep descent, especially considering that there are no falls or sudden drops in level, which gives an ample current for good fishing throughout the whole length of the river. The water is normally clear, the bulk of it flowing as it does through Loch Naver, which acts as an efficient filter. Only after heavy local rain does it become peat-stained, to any degree, very seldom badly enough to put fish off the take. It has sometimes been said that all the rivers north of the Beauly Firth can be classed as 'spate rivers', but in the case of the Naver and the Helmsdale this is definitely not true. Without doubt its fishing is at its best after rain and a rise in water, but its low water fishing can be quite productive for those who know the river well. This is one of the Naver's great merits, that even in the lowest water conditions fresh fish will still enter the river, and can still be caught. This is in marked contrast to what happens on a number of other small highland rivers. Fishing on the Naver never comes completely to a standstill, and the visiting angler need never despair. No doubt both the presence of Loch Naver as a headwater reservoir, and the absence of falls or any other obstructions to the passage of fish, are a valuable asset in favour of low water fishing.

In high water also, after snow melts or heavy rain, this river practically never goes out of fishing order; though its appearance changes, and it temporarily assumes the guise of a river of some magnitude.

In fact it is fair to say that the Naver is one of those few rivers which still provide that unmixed advantage for its fishers of usually running at a reasonable fishing height—no small consideration if one is making a journey of several hundred miles to fish it.

The pools on the Naver are of many different types, offering a pleasing and wide variety. One finds every different sort, narrow and rocky, wide and gravelly, fast and slow, big and small, straight or on bends, high water or low water pools, everything in fact that the most discriminating fisherman could desire. What is more there are good pools on all the six beats, so that no-one is left out of the running at any time. If the author was pressed he might, like most Naver fishermen, cite a preference for Dal Mallart, Dal Harrald, and perhaps Syre Pool, but how difficult a choice when so many are good.

A typical pool which can be fished off the bank when there's sufficient water.

There are excellent and widespread spawning grounds, both in the main river itself and up the tributaries and headwaters—much gravel of the right size and consistency, spreading a long way back into the hill burns. It is this expanse of suitable breeding space which goes far towards providing the Naver with its prolific stock of salmon and grilse. Predators there are, of course, the usual consortium of brown trout, herons, gulls, mergansers, goosanders and eels; but no worse than anywhere else, and at least there are no pike, either in the river or in Loch Naver. In the sea, off the north coast, however, there are far too many seals. These have increased out of all reason since 1945, and do a vast amount of damage. There is a crying need for their numbers to be steeply reduced. They are capable of catching salmon either in river or sea whenever they want to, and often tear pieces out of the wretched fish, simply for amusement. Their mere presence will scatter fish in all directions. It is not surprising that the seal is the fisherman's *bête noire*.

Further information about seals may be of interest. The total seal population off British coasts at present is estimated by the International Council for the Exploration of the Seas as 15,000 grey seals and 10,000 common seals. The majority of this seal population is to be found off Scotland.

Grey seals are estimated to eat 15 lb of fish per day, and common seals 11 lb.

This brings the total weight of British fish eaten by seals to an estimated 50,000 tons of fish per year.

What proportion of this immense total consists of Scottish salmon and grilse on the way to their native river is difficult to assess. But even if it is as low as 2 per cent (and one would have thought this a conservative estimate) it means that a total weight of 1000 tons of salmon and grilse or over 280,000 fish in number (at a theoretical average weight of 8 lb per fish) is eaten by seals every year. In addition many more are injured, suffering from seal bites.

Such figures may well be thought alarming; but there are plenty of ignorant people who object to reasonable measures to control the expanding population of seals, voracious and merciless predators as they are. It is to be hoped such people never complain about the rising cost of fish!

The type of tackle you will need for the Naver, will as on any other river depend largely on the time of year when it is your good fortune to fish it. In early spring and up to about mid-April you will want a rod of not less than 14 feet, possibly longer in order to cover a river running free and full with the likelihood of your having to contend with difficult winds. There is little shelter from wind coming from any direction, and gales from north-east or north-west are not infrequent, direct from the ice-bound fjords of Norway and Iceland. It can be bitterly cold and you should be clothed accordingly. Your line should be a sinking one, of a weight to suit your rod, or else a floating one with a sinking tip. Your leader should be strong, there is little point in using monofilament of less than 14 lb breaking strain and 16 lb is often better. Do not forget that there are kelts to be dealt with at this time of year, as well as fresh fish. Your fly should be large, up to $2\frac{1}{2}$ or even 3 inches long, and a hair winged tube is probably best. You can land your fish by gaff or net, or by beaching. There are plenty of suitable beaches if you prefer this latter method. Your waders need only be of thigh length, though you should be prepared to throw a long line in places en lieu of wading far in. Such wading as there is is not difficult, there is no need to wade deep, and many pools can be fished off the bank.

As spring becomes warmer and April gives way to May, your tackle can be changed to the normal floating line summer outfit—a light rod of somewhere from 12 to 14 feet, floating line, leader of 10 lb or 12 lb breaking strain and small flies of sizes 6 to 8. Occasionally, as in other rivers, it may be worth trying a bigger fly, perhaps even 2 inches long, in the strong streams or at dusk.

There is no particularly advantageous method of fishing the Naver. This river resembles many others of similar size and the procedure of fishing all of them is much the same and hardly varies. The main requisites, apart from appropriate and sound tackle, are good and accurate casting, complete control of the water speed and depth of the fly as it fishes round, absolute steadiness of nerves if a fish is seen to rise at the fly, and a cool hand while the fish is being played.

With the water in good fishing order and running at a fair height, a skilful angler who knows the water well should be able consistently to catch a good number of fish during any good period of the season, running even into double figures for the day from time to time. Naver fish when fresh run are good takers, and most of the pools are easily covered. The two top beats are usually the most fruitful, but all of them are good at times. The bottom two beats are best in lowish water, when the fish are inclined to stop down there in greater numbers. It is when the water falls low and fishing becomes progressively more difficult that skill and knowledge of the water really bring their reward. It is then that the really good fisherman can still catch fish, while more mediocre performers cannot (see p. 94 on the Helmsdale).

It is seldom that one has any very desperate battles with hooked fish. The Naver salmon are not nowadays big enough, nor is the river itself large enough for them to run out a great length of line and backing. It is usually easy enough to follow a hooked fish along the bank. This is the one drawback which goes with the smaller sized rivers. To hook a fish of 30 or 40 lb and have a desperate and prolonged struggle with it in the fast current of a mighty river such as the Spey or the Tay, or in Norway the Sundal or Rauma, is an experience which these days cannot be expected on the likes of the Naver, Thurso, or Helmsdale. I say 'these days' because big fish in the past have been caught on all these three latter rivers, yet there would have been hardly room for them, one would imagine, in such comparatively small waters to show their full mettle.

One tactic often successfully employed on the Naver in warm water should be mentioned, and that is the method of 'dibbling' or 'dapping' the fly (as described in the Helmsdale chapter, p 100). A fairly large hair-winged fly is best, or else something similar to the 'Elverine' fly, tied with a vulturine guinea-fowl wing; and the angler should use a short line and 'dib' this fly along the surface, preferably at the edge or in the middle of a strong stream. Fish will come at a fly so fished when they will look at nothing else, and an expert performer can achieve startling success in this way. The only drawback entailed is that for every one fish landed three or four may be risen and pricked, which will probably make them chary of taking again, anyhow for the time being.

There is one outstanding desirability on the Naver, as on all other salmon rivers big or small, and that is that the angler should know the river and its pools like the back of his hand. Obviously such knowledge can only be gained through experience, and by listening carefully to what other fishermen, both skilled and unskilled, have to say. It cannot be emphasised too strongly that local knowledge in the case of any river is more than half the battle e.g. knowledge of the exact lies of the fish at any time of year and in any height of water, of which pools fish best and at any given height, of the precise location of the best taking places in every pool, and how best to cover them, of where are good places to hook fish on a rising river, or where there are any bad snags that can lose one a hooked fish. A store of such wisdom and its like is worth its weight in gold. It will pay you many times over to grasp any chance of acquiring it.

PLATE 6

Lord Thurso at Westerdale. A rocky and tumbly stretch of the Thurso.

The author fishing MaNaire Pool on the lower Naver.

PLATE 7

"Little Ivar", one of the ghillies on the Sundal river at Elverhoi, Norway.

Landslide, the outlet from the lake Flod on the Vatnsdalsa, north Iceland. This water needed a ripple, or better still a wave, and then the fishing could be meteoric.

A good ghillie will help you greatly, especially in the early stages of your apprenticeship. There are few permanent ghillies on the Naver, and the incoming rod often has to find his own assistant if he wants one. This can usually be achieved, and there will be no difficulty in recalling his name—almost certainly it will be McKay, the predominant patronymic of this neighbourhood, and he will be distinguished only by his forename. Apart from ghillies, there are water bailiffs who watch the river closely, and are effective guardians against any sort of poaching. The only form of poaching which continues to give anxiety is illegal drift netting out at sea, which is far harder to combat than river poaching.

Regarding the size and types of Naver fish, the pattern of their runs resembles closely that of the Thurso or Helmsdale or other neighbouring rivers. The spring salmon, averaging 10–11 lb have diminished in numbers over these recent years; nevertheless there are still a fair number of them, thanks no doubt to the wise restraint on netting; and a competent rod in late March or after may well average up to two fish or more per day. As is usual elsewhere, the Naver in bygone days produced bigger fish than it does now. Grimble, writing in 1902, mentions one of $35\frac{1}{2}$ lb caught on the 6th April 1891 by Percy H. Wormald. There may have been bigger ones than this, but nowadays anything over 20 lb is rare.

The best of the spring run is likely to take place, as might be expected, between late April and the third week in May; but much depends on the water height. Fish continue to run in reduced numbers throughout June until they are reinforced by the arrival of the grilse towards the end of that month. July is now as a rule the most productive month of the season, and one can be almost sure of good sport then. August can sometimes be good, given rain, but many of the fish are becoming 'potted' by then, and the run of grilse dwindles. By September almost all the fish are red, or fast becoming so, and are capricious takers. The river will be full of them, but the bag uncertain. In any case it is just as well that valuable potential spawners should not be subjected to too high a toll. The average total bag for the season on the Naver is a high one, and without disclosing any secrets it can be put at around 1200 fish or more. Double figures to a single rod in a day during the height of the season are nothing unusual, though a fair proportion of the bag is likely to be of grilse.

As to the different beats, as has already been said they all hold good pools. It is generally accepted that Dal Mallart on the top beat is about the best pool on the river, the two top beats being perhaps the most prolific, except in time of very low water when incoming fish are more likely to stop lower down.

The season of 1980 was a curious one. It was an extremely dry spring, with little snow left over from the previous winter. During April, May and June the river shrank to unprecedented drought conditions, and fishing suffered badly. It became a hard task for fish to move from pool to pool, an almost unheard of state of affairs on this river. Moreover, U.D.N. unfortunately came into evidence. In July, however, the welcome rain arrived and continued to fall repeatedly during the rest of the season, in greater quantity than normal. The predictable result was that July, August and September all produced excellent fishing. The stock of fish in these later months was all that could be expected, in spite of the great toll of salmon and grilse taken by long-line off the Faroes this summer, a new adverse development (it seems that it was the west coast rivers which were chiefly hit by this).

1981 again produced a low water spring, owing largely to lack of snow during the winter as much as to general lack of rain. There was one appreciable rise of water towards the end of April, which yielded good fishing for a few days; but at other times, with the river fallen right in, very little was caught. How surprising however the quirks of Fortune can be! My friends and I were due this year to stay at that lovely Syre Lodge and fish the Naver during the second and third weeks of June, a thoroughly unpropitious prospect it seemed after a spring drought, with June normally a dry summer month. But not at all. . . . During our first week there the heavens opened, and for a day or two the rain was little short of tropical. Far from being too low the river became too high, an almost unheard of event in June. Most of the pools were too big and strong to fish for several days, and no doubt many incoming fish ran straight through into Loch Naver. But during our second week the water settled down to a reasonable height, as the rain had ceased; we did well every day, killing some 45 fish for two rods without the assistance of ladies! The following week apparently produced even better fishing, but sadly we had left by then. After that I gather the river steadily subsided again to an unwelcome low level until the autumn.

Apart from the fishing in the main river, Loch Naver produces good boat fishing throughout the season. Its average depth is about 12 feet. Salmon and grilse are caught in it in numbers, together with some sea-trout. They take the fly well, and there are few better fishing lochs anywhere in Scotland. Incoming fish have no great distance to cover in order to reach this loch, and there are no falls or obstructions in their path. Late in the season fish can also be caught up the Mudale. Both this river and the loch are normally fished from the Altnaharra Hotel.

The Naver's main tributary is the Mallart, already mentioned, which holds a fair number of salmon and grilse for several miles upstream. There are falls near its entry into the Naver, but these have long ago been rendered passable for fish, by blasting. The Mallart is a small but precipitous stream which flows out of Loch Coir' an Fhearna, on the south-east side of Ben Klibreck, and descends about 325 feet over its short course of $6\frac{1}{2}$ miles. Other tributaries of the Naver are numerous throughout its course, but none of them is more than a good sized burn.

Sea-trout, as well as salmon and grilse, enter the Naver in fair numbers from June onwards. Good catches of herling are sometimes made in the tidal reaches; but elsewhere they are seldom deliberately sought after, salmon and grilse not unexpectedly taking pride of place. There are also quantities of brown trout to be found in the numerous remote lochs and lochans of the neighbourhood, many of which are seldom fished. There is all the fishing here, to be had for the asking, that any keen trout fisherman could desire. Some of these lochs also hold char.

There are several lodges on the Naver which belong to the various owners of the fishings. Of these perhaps Syre lodge is the pleasantest. It lies on the left bank of the river about $3\frac{1}{2}$ miles below Loch Naver, and in situation and interior comfort leaves nothing to be desired.

This lodge also has the fishing rights on two different beats simultaneously, an advantage by no means to be despised.

If they are not fortunate enough to be staying in one of these lodges, visiting fishermen have to fall back upon a hotel. Of these there are two within comparatively easy reach of the fishings: one is at Bettyhill on the mouth of the river, fairly large, and possessing a fine view out to sea; and the other a smaller hotel near Borgie Bridge. Both are about 10 minutes drive from the bottom beats of the Naver and about 35 minutes from the upper beats. There are also hotels at Altnaharra and at Tongue, which are popular with fishermen; but their distance from the Naver beats is greater.

One word of warning to those who do not already realize it, the heather covered slopes which border the Naver are a prolific breeding ground for adders. Adders are dangerous to humans, let alone to dogs or other small animals. In the summer of 1980 a certain young lady, seated near the river bank, had the misfortune to be bitten by one, and had to be taken quickly to Thurso hospital in considerable distress—a thoroughly unpleasant experience.

There is little I can add about Strathnaver except that there could be no better small river fishing anywhere in Britain than here. Whether in the cold though invigorating climate of spring, or in the sparkling and radiant atmosphere of summer, the pleasure of fishing this delightful river, with its extensive beats, its constant array of fish, and enchanting variety of pools, never wanes. Long may such fishing endure!

The Thurso

Lord Thurso with his ghillie on the upper river which is more rocky and streamy.

The Thurso is the biggest and most prolific salmon river in Caithness. It rises in the hills on the Sutherland border, and has a course of some 34 miles, its general direction being due north. It falls into the Pentland Firth, with the sizeable town of Thurso (pop. 9,100) at its mouth. In size it is a medium–small river, of an average width in its lower reaches of perhaps 25 yards, about the same size in fact as its neighbours, the Naver and Helmsdale, which in many ways it resembles. It has a catchment area of around 160 square miles, all of it in Caithness.

Some 10 miles from its source it flows through Loch More, a sizeable sheet of water about one mile long and half a mile wide. There are hatches at the outlet from this loch, which can be used to control the flow of water into the river below and there is also a salmon ladder here, which allows fish to enter the loch and to use the headwaters for spawning.

Although fish are occasionally caught in Loch More, the main Thurso fishing lies on the river between this loch and the sea. There is some 24 miles of it, varying widely in character. The newly arrived fisherman who emerges for the first time from the hospitable Ulbster Arms in the main street of Halkirk, this hotel being conveniently situated midway down the bottom half of the river, will find a wide variety of different types of pool depending on which part of the Thurso he is to fish. There are twelve different beats on the main river, all of which have fishing on both banks; and a maximum of two rods is allowed on each beat. These beats are changed daily in rotation, and there is a sizeable stretch of Association water near the mouth. 'Fly only' is the rule at all times on this river, with no bait of any sort allowed.

The newcomer fisherman may have been told that there is much slack water on the Thurso, which needs either a spate or at least a strong wind from the right direction in order to fish well, such a wind as will produce a pronounced ripple of the surface. He may also have gathered that 'backing up' may be necessary—that peculiar form of fishing whereby the angler starts at the tail of a pool and works upstream taking two or three steps backwards or upstream during the fishing round of each cast, in order to keep the fly on the move through dead water. (I far prefer to pull in or 'strip' line when fishing such water, and keep the fly moving thus, while standing still myself.) All this, though partly true, is to a considerable extent exaggerated. Only three or four of the middle beats lack streamy water and are totally dependent on a wind or on a high river to be effective. The other beats all have good streams, and well defined pools. After all the Thurso has an average fall of 12 feet per mile between Loch More and the sea, so inevitably a good deal of its course is speedy. In high spate it develops as strong a downstream rush as most other northern rivers, which anyone who has seen it in this state will readily confirm. But the average rainfall in this part of Scotland is not high, so that spates during the fishing season, especially in summer, are unfortunately infrequent except in abnormally wet years. I say 'unfortunately', as high water at reasonable intervals is always an advantage in the smaller north country rivers, as we all well know. Do we not all experience that heady taste of anticipation when we sally forth to fish on the first occasion after a Highland river has fallen back from high spate into good fishing order? The slate has been wiped clean, and who knows what is now lurking in our pools and awaiting our flies, in the shape of unlooked-for monsters or myriad fresh fish? But the catchment area of the Thurso, except in its highest headwaters, tends to be flat, and there is little high ground sufficient to hold the snow in early spring or to draw the rain later.

It is true that in periods of prolonged low water the Thurso does not fish well. Not many fish enter the river then, and the nets take the majority of those that do. Fish already in the river become 'potted' and disinclined to move from pool to pool. They take badly or not at all, and can become more or less uncatchable. This is a risk inevitable on most small Highland rivers and the mid-summer period is the worst. We all get caught out by drought both on the Thurso and elsewhere from time to time.

There is plenty of trout fishing available in most areas in the north, both in loch and river. Should one therefore not include trout tackle amongst one's kit, to give one an alternative to the salmon if the worst comes to the worst? This has often been suggested, and it may well make sense in some cases—but, I don't know . . . to a confirmed salmon fisherman trout *do* seem trivial. Perhaps one is better off getting right away from it all, and going on a boat trip to, say, the Orkneys, or taking temporarily to golf at a time when 'even St. Peter could not catch fish'. During such periods one can take the firm resolve not to waste energy and keenness in fruitless effort. Far better to husband both of them in patience until the weather changes, as in due course it must. Or else one can experiment in the hope of bringing off the occasional miracle, gratifying without doubt if one succeeds. In any case the hardened salmon fisher needs a mental armoury impervious to disappointments caused by factors outside his control; and where, one might ask, would be the fun in fishing if catching fish was always a certainty? though the misfortune of bad fishing weather naturally falls hardest upon anglers whose fishing time is limited, perhaps to only one or two hard earned weeks holiday during the season.

To return to the Thurso and its pools, one finds all types of these, as has already been said. In the upper reaches near Loch More the river is smaller, and the pools are apt to be rockier and more tumbly. The water is normally as clear as one could want, flowing as it does through a sizeable loch. There is also a second smaller loch, Loch Beg, on the course of the Thurso immediately below Loch More. Salmon like to gather in Loch Beg, and they are often caught where the river enters it, a likely cast.

The surroundings of the upper river are heathery and peaty to a degree, but only after heavy rain does the water become peat-stained. Peat water is not a common hazard here as it is in some other rivers. Lower down, the Thurso flows through agricultural land; but as this is 90% grass, it causes little discolouration of the river at any time. The pools here become bigger and deeper, but even in the lowest reaches near the mouth the river is never more than of medium size, and always provides good fly fishing.

The rod season on the Thurso lasts from January 11th to October 5th (inc.) and the net season from February 11th to August 26th. In years gone by the spring fishing was excellent, and the river could be classed as a very early one. W. L. Calderwood in his *Rivers and Lochs of Scotland* (1909) records 21 salmon taken by a single rod in a day, and 19 salmon on two different occasions. He does not mention the month in which these great catches were made, but almost certainly they were during the spring, when in the early years of this century and up to the 1939–45 war spring fish abounded.

Of late years, as in most rivers, the pattern in the Thurso has

The river at Halkirk.

changed. Spring fish have become ever scarcer, and now form a minority of the stock. Grilse and small summer salmon which enter the river from mid-June onwards constitute the bulk of the catch, the average weight of the former being 5 to 6 lb, and of the latter 8 to 9 lb. Big fish are now scarce, anything of over 20 lb being a rarity. The two biggest fish caught in the Thurso during the 1980 season weighed 23 lb (in September) and 22 lb (in March).

One outstanding fish was caught on April 16th 1922 by William Miller, a ghillie, and his fly (appropriately) was a Dusty Miller. It weighed 44 lb. There is a model of this fish in the Ulbster Arms. Most of the big fish of the past, like this one, were springers. 'Jock Scott' in *Game Fish Records* (1936) lists an even larger one of 47 lb, caught in 1923, but disappointingly gives no further details. The average total bag for the season is now around 800 salmon and grilse, varying from 1211 in 1974 to 236 in 1976, when the exceptionally hot, dry summer meant a correspondingly long period of low warm water. There is also a fair run of sea-trout.

July to the end of the season is now without doubt the best fishing period; July and August being pleasant months to fish, given enough water (though they can be dry). September on average produces more fish, though they are getting red by then, as they are in early October, when a lot are sometimes caught during the first few days of the month. This is usually the wettest part of the season.

The tackle which you will need if you go to fish the Thurso will be the same as for any other northern river of similar size e.g. the Oykel, Naver, or Helmsdale. In early spring you will need big flies of 2 or 3 inches length, with a sunk line, though not too heavy, as the Thurso is seldom deep; perhaps a sinking tip only is best. Later you will graduate to a normal summer outfit of lighter rod and floating line, which will see you out till the end of the season, except that a big fly up to $2\frac{1}{2}$ inches long may always be worth trying in a strong stream or when the river is running high after a spate. 13 feet will be about the right length for your rod, 14 feet if the river is high and the wind strong, or only 12 feet or perhaps less for low water. I found that in low and warm water on the Thurso 'dibbing' with dropper and tail fly, as practised on the Helmsdale and Naver, was effective, as might have been expected. Indeed I think this method would do well on any of the smaller Scottish rivers under such conditions.

Thigh waders are normally adequate everywhere. You can take long trouser waders with you if you like, to cater for the possibility of high water and the need to wade deep in a few places; but you are unlikely to want them, except as added protection on a foully wet day, or to wade across the river.

Netting is carried on at the mouth of the river in Thurso harbour till August 26th, and it is perhaps not entirely a coincidence that the best fishing is normally obtained after the netting season is over. One wonders if from the owners' point of view, in rivers such as the Thurso, it might not be a better financial proposition to let more fish enter fresh water, through working the nets less hard, and to charge a higher rent for the rod fishing.

That the Thurso was in by-gone days a more prolific salmon river than it is now is beyond doubt. W. L. Calderwood records that on July 23rd 1743 no less than 2560 salmon were caught in one haul of the net in the Cruive Pool immediately upstream of Thurso town. This catch was vouched for in a written statement made by three eye-witnesses, George Paterson, Baillie of Thurso; George Swanson, shoemaker there; and Duncan Finlayson, senior fisher there. Some haul, some net!

The general atmosphere and surroundings on the Thurso are delightful. The country near the coast is fairly flat farmland, though rolling and with stone walls. The higher hills of the Orkneys can be seen towards the north. Further inland one reaches a peat country, wild and heather-covered, though still flattish. The high hills of Morven and Scaraben can be seen on the southern horizon, towards the Sutherland county boundary; and there are many small lochs scattered over these moors. Further westward still, beyond Loch More, one finds a wild and uninhabited hinterland, rough and hilly in places, with only the single-line Inverness-Wick railway disturbing the solitude. There is something fascinating about all this. No doubt the wildness and remoteness of Caithness contribute to the general attraction, and the fact that one is as far north on the British mainland as one can penetrate. Incidentally, if you happen to be a Sinclair or related to that distinguished family or clan, you would be unwise to pass through the Ord of Caithness, a pass on the road between Sutherland and Caithness (en route perhaps to or from the Thurso) on a monday. This is said to be unlucky, ever since that long-past monday in the summer of 1513, when the Sinclairs passed that way southwards to Flodden Field, whence only one of them returned. Often there is a distinct touch of the Scandinavian in this area, sometimes exemplified in the features of the local population and more often in the names of both people and places. What for instance

Two nice fish on the bank, and a discussion on tactics.

is Wick but 'Vik', so common a Norse place name, Thurso but 'Thorsa' or 'Thor's river,' Halladale but 'Halladal' or 'Halla's dale' (Halla being a common personal name in Norway and Iceland)? Indeed, looking at the map one finds that 90% of the Caithness place names have a Scandinavian origin. This is readily recognisable to anyone who has fished for long years in Norway or Iceland. There is something familiar here, which gives much pleasure. Caithness is a part of Scotland unique in character and of delightful distinctiveness.

On the odd occasions when I have fished the Thurso I have

thoroughly enjoyed both fishing and surroundings. The Naver and
Helmsdale may produce more fish with fewer rods, it is true—but
they are netted considerably less hard.

I found that with careful tactics and with due regard to one's
ghillie's advice, very welcome if one did not know the water well, it
was not unduly difficult to average one fish per day. If one was lucky
and had the water falling back into good fishing order after a spate, it
would obviously have been possible to have achieved a considerably
higher bag, though personally I have never caught more than three fish
in one day on this river.

If I had any constructive criticism to offer about the Thurso, it
would be that both netting and the number of rods should be
reduced. Nevertheless the rod-catch of the Thurso, as it is, is
substantial; and the fishing demands considerable skill if success
under anything but the easiest of conditions is to be obtained. In
simpler language, the fishing is seldom easy, but the river great fun to
fish. Need one look for more?

IRELAND

Some of my happiest and most rewarding fishing experiences have been over a long period in Ireland, in particular on that magnificent river in County Cork, the Blackwater.

Even if Irish rod fishing has now fallen on evil days, it is very enjoyable to recall the great times of the past, and to try to convey to readers some sense of the peculiar light-heartedness as well as of the outstanding success which my companions and myself formerly experienced on this river.

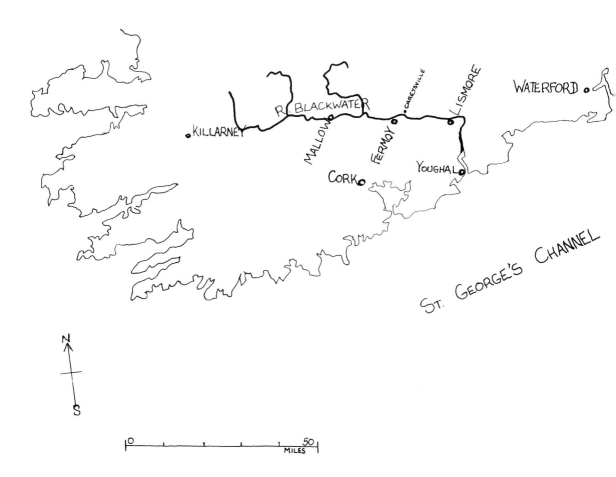

The Blackwater (Co. Cork)

Landing a fish in the Cabin at Careysville. This was a very good pool about 100 yards downstream of the weir. It is early in the season and there is still snow on the bank of the Quay Wall opposite.

The Blackwater is often cited as being Ireland's best salmon river. Whether this is true or not I would not like to say, as my fishing experience elsewhere in that Country has been limited to a few odd days on the Lennon (Donegal) and the Boyne (Meath). But on the Blackwater I was lucky enough to be a tenant on the Duke of Devonshire's water at Careysville for at least a fortnight and often a month every year from 1952 to 1971.

I cannot write about Careysville without feeling extremely

287

nostalgic. When I first arrived there in my younger years it seemed like a salmon fisherman's Xanadu! One arrived up a narrow gravel drive between rhododendrons to the front door of a solid looking squarely built house of typical Irish Georgian character, with apparently little out of the ordinary to distinguish it from many other such houses in the neighbourhood. But what a staggering panorama met the eyes as one stepped through the front hall and into the sitting room or dining room, and looked out of the windows at the Blackwater 150 feet below, together with its valley spreading to right and left for miles into the blue distance; with the outline of the snow-flecked Galtee Mountains rising to 3000 feet on the northern horizon, some 15 miles away. Immediately below the windows, one could look down and watch the salmon jumping one after another, and often three in the air at a time, in a famous pool called the Sand Hole. What a sight to greet one's eyes before breakfast, or out of the bathroom window during one's early morning shave! Further upstream towards the Weir a series of equally fine pools displayed themselves to one's gaze, with fish showing in all of them.

There are possibilities of endless digression writing about the fascinations of this place: the sea of daffodils in March; the incredible lush greenery during April and May; the vast skull and antlers of the ancient Irish elk, dug out of a nearby bog and now gracing the Careysville front hall; the old water mill at Clondulane, 300 yards upstream of Careysville House, which was still working in the early 1950's; the little tackle shop on the river front in Fermoy where according to Billy Flynn (of whom more later) the salmon had once tried to break through the windows in order to get at the display of flies, on an occasion when floods had raised the water level to the first floor storey!

I will do my best to confine myself more closely to fishery matters. The Blackwater is a river of roughly the same size as the Tweed or the Wye. It rises near Ballydesmond, on the borders of Cork and Kerry, and has an easterly course of 120 miles (including 19 miles of tidal estuary) via Mallow, Fermoy, Ballyduff and Lismore; from Lismore downstream it is tidal, and at Cappoquin just below this point it takes a sharp bend southward to fall into the open sea at Youghal.

In some ways the Blackwater resembles the Tweed, but its flow (except at Careysville) is less strong, and its bed less gravelly or rocky. In character it is more like an English river, the lower Wye for example, and it has a copious weed growth in summer. Its banks too are luxuriant with sally bushes and meadowland or 'inches' (they would be 'haughs' in Scotland), lush and fertile. All this is easily explicable climatically, as County Cork has a mean temperature and rainfall approaching that of Cornwall.

The main feature of the Careysville water has always been the large weir (it would be a 'cauld' on the Tweed) from bank to bank at its head. This was built in mediaeval times to provide a head of water for Clondulane Mill.

The weir is amply provided with efficient fish-passes, and fish can ascend the face of the weir itself at certain heights of water. But it has always served temporarily to check a proportion of the incoming fish on their upstream path, particularly in early spring when the water is cold. This in the past used to guarantee a good stock of fish in the Careysville water, at least till mid-April. On my first arrival there on February 1st 1952, I remember sitting on a riverside bench and counting the fish as I saw them jump. Believe it or not I saw 92 fresh fish jump in one minute, timed on my watch. These were fresh fish not kelts, and as any fisherman knows February is a month when, with cold water, fish are said to show little. Perhaps this will give some sort of idea of the stock of fish which Careysville in the spring of the 1950's or early 1960's was liable to hold. Nowhere, not even at Delfur on the Spey or Islamouth on the Tay, have I ever seen such a massive concentration of salmon. In those days the yearly bag at Careysville was anything between 400 and 1000 fish, or more, almost all caught in the first three months of the season.

In the peak year of 1927 this beat produced over 1700 fish up to the end of April, averaging $16\frac{1}{2}$ lb. Admittedly nothing like it has ever been seen again, but has any other beat in Britain ever been able to show a comparable catch of such heavy fish in such a short period of the season? I doubt it. By the 1950's the average weight had dropped to around 11 lb and it has dropped further since then.

The Careysville water is only 2 miles long. It has both banks all the way, except for the bottom half mile where Kilmurry has the left bank. The best pools are the Top Flat (below the weir), the Cabin, the Quay Wall, the Sand Hole, the Castle, the Lane Stream, the Flats, the Lickannan and the Coraneen—but there are other good places too. In fact at different heights of water there is fishing over the whole stretch. All parts of the beat are within walking distance of the House, and the fisherman has no real need for a car—another rare advantage in these present days.

In high water the fishing is nearly all from the bank, though with some boating in places. The Blackwater fishing boat is of a curious type, known elsewhere in Ireland as a 'cot'. Rather like a canoe, it has a flat bottom and a pointed prow and stern; and is propelled either by a paddle from the stern, or else by a pole. In medium or low water there was a good deal of wading with long trouser waders. The bed of the river as a rule was not rough and the current not strong, so wading presented little difficulty. But if the current was not strong in regard to wading, the 10 foot fall over the weir at the top of the Careysville beat ensured good streamy water for fishing purposes at least to the bottom of the Lane Stream, half a mile downstream. In this respect the Careysville water was fortunate; it was much streamier than the general run of Blackwater beats, and for that reason was better fly water. The local supposition was that fish did not come onto the fly until St. Patrick's Day (March 17th), but I remember catching 11 fish on fly in 1965 on the opening day of the season, early in February, so not all the fish were aware of this rule! In high water however, and with the cold temperatures of early spring, it must be admitted that it was far easier to catch fish on bait than on fly. Wooden devons were about the best bait. Indeed the Blackwater as a whole could not be classed as a first class fly river. Fish as a rule took freely only when the river was at a fair height, and it was then often too coloured for a fly to do well. When it was low and clear, in fact in good fly order, fish usually ceased to run, as the vast majority of them were caught in the estuary nets. The residents were then apt to become 'potted', and refuse both fly and bait.

Incidentally it was during my Blackwater days that I learnt about the full effect of peat content in the water in discouraging fish from taking. It is sometimes maintained that peat water does not put fish off. Those who maintain this should have fished at Careysville when the stock of fish was plentiful, for their eyes to be widely opened.

What happened was this. After heavy rain the river would rise by anything from 3 to 6 feet or more, and would colour. For the first 24 hours the colour would be derived from the normal run-off from agricultural land, not too drumly or too thick, and a few fish would still take. But then invariably the Kerry bog-water from high up the river would in due course arrive. It was bright brownish yellow in colour, thick with peat deposit, and no doubt acid to a degree. Fish might be present in hundreds or even thousands, but not one would then look at any sort of lure. It was quite futile to try to tempt them. This situation might last for a couple of days; after this if there was no more rain a few fish might be caught on bait during the third or fourth day, and many more as soon as the water became reasonably clear. But they always were willing to take bait a day or two sooner than fly.

This sort of thing happened time and time again over the 21 years I fished at Careysville and there was no ignoring it. I came to the firm conclusion that as regards peat in the water it is only a question of degree. A little peat, and no harm is done, even with a moderate amount fish will still take; but a full dose of it will put fish right off until such time as the water becomes reasonably clear again. No doubt the Blackwater bears the name it does for good reason, but the same principle must apply, one would have thought, in all British rivers that flow from or through a peat foundation (e.g. The Spey).

Apart from peat, the Blackwater in the days when I fished it was apt to suffer from artificial pollution. All the sewage of Fermoy and Mallow, both towns of considerable size, went untreated into the river, together with effluents from installations such as beet-factories, gravel pits and creameries. It was not a happy state of affairs. I don't know whether things are better now, but I hope so.

Nevertheless, in those days the start of an expedition to Careysville in February or March, right at the beginning of the fishing season, was nothing short of hilarious, coupled with the sure anticipation of finding abundant stocks of fish. The only uncertainty would concern the state of the water, too high and one could be flooded out, too low and frozen out.

My fishing companions were usually Major Anthony Tabor, Mrs. Stainton, Captain Patrick Hazlehurst and Mrs. Hazlehurst. What fun we all had! The fishing was extremely light-hearted, and our four ghillies contributed immensely to the enjoyment. Billy Flynn was the oldest of them. He could be unbelievably funny, was a splendid raconteur and had an immense fund of humorous stories which never failed in their appeal.

Of all Billy's almost endless fund of stories, the two most memorable were perhaps the one already mentioned concerning the salmon and the flies in the tackle shop window in Fermoy, also another where the owner or tenant of the fishing had on one occasion instructed his ghillie to pass the verbal message across the river and have it relayed to the cook at Careysville House: 'Five for dinner, and not three.' This eventually reached the kitchen in the guise of: 'Pie for dinner and not tea.' . . . the cook's reaction being left unrecorded! But of course it was Billy's inimitable style of narration rather than the substance of his stories which brought the house down. He would have made a fortune on the stage.

Apart from his story-telling, Billy would make profound remarks from time to time. For instance, when the rooks were cavorting in a high March wind Billy would observe that 'when the crows are doing a four-in-hand reel it is a sure sign of treacherous weather.' Curiously enough he was usually accurate in such forecasts! Alas! Billy died in 1964; and the three remaining ghillies, experts all of them in everything to do with fishing and boat management, were drowned in a tragic boating accident in the autumn of that year. They are all very sadly missed. It was a catastrophic disaster.

To get to Careysville from England one could either fly to Dublin or Cork and motor on, or else put one's car on a ferry boat at Fishguard, Holyhead or Swansea, and go by sea, a journey which never lacked entertainment. I have already described the natural attractions of the surroundings at Careysville, so will add little here except to say that the countryside upstream of Fermoy and around Mallow was hillier and even more enchanting. It provided a fitting background to Spenser's *Faerie Queen*, much of which, the reader may be surprised to learn, was written in this neighbourhood, at Kilcolman Castle close to Mallow.

One noticeable feature of the Irish countryside is the astonishing number of ruined castles, and what on the Borders would be known as 'peal towers', which crop up everywhere. There is no lack of them in County Cork, a legacy, one imagines, from a troubled past, and they all add to the attractiveness of the general scene. Another striking feature is the inordinate number of public houses (Guinness being the most popular drink, or Jameson's whiskey). There seem to be whole villages consisting of little else, together with an excessive number of ass-carts in the streets, presumably used for the transport of the necessary liquor!

To return to the Blackwater and its fishing, it may have struck the reader that this chapter so far has consisted largely of a panegyric about Careysville rather than a survey of the whole river. I'm afraid this is partly true, because except for one day at Ballyhooly I never fished anywhere else on the Blackwater except at Careysville during all those years. Naturally one saw other parts of the river and heard plenty of talk about them, but the Careysville fishing was so far in a class by itself that one had little inclination to fish elsewhere, even if one had the opportunity.

A complete and detailed record of the fishing, and of all the fish caught since the early years of the century, has been kept at Careysville House. It made interesting reading and ensured that everything was correctly recorded instead of being left to the uncertainties of memory or hearsay.

I see from my own fishing diary that our two best fortnights at Careysville were in March 1954, when four of us caught 256 salmon, and March 1955 with 194 fish. On the opening day of the season in 1965 four of us caught 53 fish, 19 of them on fly—with a total of 140 for the week.

Salmon were so plentiful in 1954 that I remember on several occasions, when fishing the Flats, losing a fish unhooked in mid-river, and yet hooking a second one while retrieving my minnow back towards my own bank. One hardly noticed the loss!

Of course it was not always like this, but even when things were bad it was seldom due to lack of fish and almost certainly to floods or very low water. Once our score dropped to 90 for the fortnight, but this was unusually disappointing.

I should emphasise at once that all this was before the arrival of that dreaded scourage U.D.N., which originated in Kerry and reached the Blackwater in the autumn of 1965. Whether due to its disastrous effects, or to other causes as well, things have never been the same on the Blackwater since that date.

The first impact of U.D.N. on the spring fish of 1966 was a calamity, and no one who saw it is ever likely to forget it. The effects seemed to be all the more catastrophic owing to the concentration of fish at Careysville. There is no point in dwelling on this, and it is past history now, but fishing for the next year or two suffered drastically.

Naturally there were many other beats on this long river— Ballyhooly, 6 miles upstream of Fermoy, was the best of them; Kilmurry and Kilbarry, immediately downstream of Careysville were also fairly good at times, but the rest were apparently indifferent. There was a long stretch of Association water, immediately downstream of Fermoy, which used to produce 200–300 salmon in the season, mostly caught on prawn; but it was dull slack water.

Apart from Ballyhooly, it was safe to say that all the best fishing on the river lay downstream of Fermoy.

After the arrival of U.D.N. in the autumn of 1965 I continued to fish at Careysville for a further six years; and returned there for a week at the end of February in 1975. It was not encouraging, and by degrees one sadly renounced hope for the immediate future.

The big fish of course are all gone now. In the 1920s and 1930s one can see from the records that 30 pounders were quite common and it was seldom that a week went by in the spring without one or two of them being caught.

The record fish for the Blackwater weighed 52 lb and was caught in March 1930 by Brigadier-General E. C. Walthall. The next biggest was one of $51\frac{1}{2}$ lb caught by Mr. O'Mahony in 1926, and another of 50 lb was taken on February 6th 1930 by Mr. J. Latham. Billy Flynn claimed to have killed one of 51 lb, having foul-hooked it in the Top Flat at Careysville and landed it in Paddy's Stream. Those who know the Careysville water will realize what an epic contest this must have been. Billy had no gaff with him, and claimed to have 'dug his grave' in the bank. What he meant was not clear, but presumably some sort of beaching place was extemporized for a maltreated fish.

It was not as a result of U.D.N. that the big fish disappeared. The process had started many years earlier, and a similar development has taken place on many other former 'big-fish' rivers, as we all know. Nowadays a 20 pounder from the Blackwater is a big one, and not many are caught of that size.

Besides salmon and grilse there were also vast pike at Careysville. No doubt they failed to run the weir, and so congregated downstream. I remember looking over the bank into deep water at a pool called Haddon's Hole one day, and there was an enormous pike lying close to the side at my feet . . . so big that it took one's breath away. It must have been well over 40 lb, judging by its length, and it looked like a shark. Unfortunately I had only a fly-rod with me, and by the time I returned with a bait-rod it had vanished. There was unlimited food for pike in the Blackwater in the way of dace and other coarse fish, and no one, so it seemed, bothered to fish for them. The record rod-caught Blackwater pike weighed $42\frac{1}{2}$ lb and was caught some years ago near Fermoy, but no doubt there were bigger ones.

My description of the Blackwater employs mainly the past tense. This is for the good reason that except for one week in 1975 I have not fished it since 1971. But from what I have heard there has been little change for the better since I was last there. Spring fishing does not even approach what it used to be. The average size of fish is now only 8–9 lb, and their numbers are comparatively insignificant. Only February is now a likely month, except that more grilse in present times manage to get past the nets in June and July.

The cause of this? I have no doubt that one has to look no further than to the prohibitive netting, legal and illegal, round the coasts and in the estuary. Unfortunately the tidal estuary of the Blackwater is a long one, all of the 19 miles from Lismore to Youghal, and it is netted the whole way. We have all heard, too, of the excessive drift netting everywhere along the west and south-west coast of Ireland, from Donegal to Cork. In addition we know of the toll taken by Greenland over these past ten years, and now also by the Faroes.

True there is an extensive hatchery on the Blackwater, but of what use is it to turn out parr or smolts if the adult fish are to be caught elsewhere?

Sad to say it seems that the general outlook is bleak. Is the Blackwater destined to go the same disastrous way as those formerly magnificent salmon rivers, the Shannon, Suir, Barrow, Nore, Lee, Erne, and Boyne amongst others? One profoundly hopes not, yet one cannot but be anxious.

Of all the European Atlantic salmon countries, Ireland should surely be the most prolific in fish. It has wonderful rivers, fine spawning grounds, magnificent feeding for fry, parr, and smolts, and an exceptionally favourable climate. Yet without resolute and effective protection this Aladdin's cave of piscatorial treasure is plundered and squandered. Dare one hope that the downward drift will ever be arrested? So far as the Blackwater in particular is concerned we know from the past the magnificent potential which awaits firm and wise control.

'Hope deferred maketh the heart sick'; nevertheless what alternative have we but to live in hope?

NORWAY

Bjora—Stjordal—Rauma
—Gloppen—Sundal

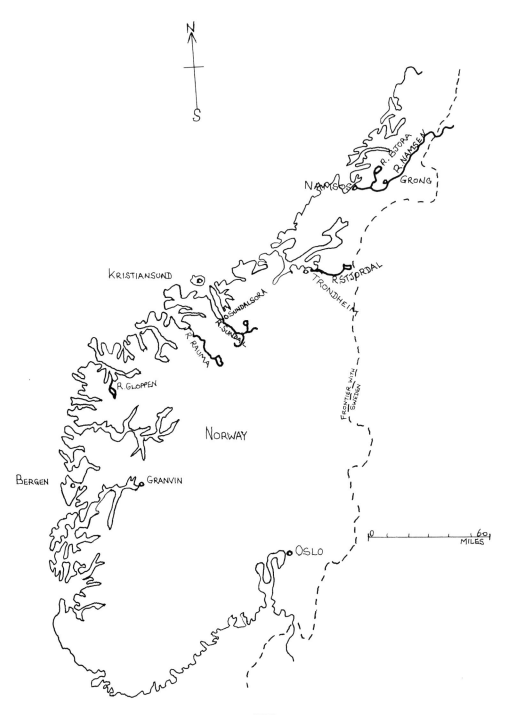

N

S

NAMSOS

R. BJØRA
R. NAMSEN
GRONG

KRISTIANSUND

TRONDHEIM
R. STJØRDAL

O.SUNDALSØRA
R. SUNDAL

R. RAUMA

R. GLOPPEN

NORWAY

FRONTIER WITH SWEDEN

BERGEN

GRANVIN

OSLO

0   60
|___|___|___|___|___|___|
            MILES

298

Norway

The rapids below Piba Pool on the river Sundal. No fish was ever successfully taken down these.

I am sorry to say that any account of my fishing experiences in this wonderful country with its superlative rivers is purely in the nature of reminiscence, and for that reason is unlikely, so far as the present state of rivers and fishing is concerned, to be of practical value to today's would-be Norwegian fisherman. The last time I fished in Norway was in July 1967, and too many changes have taken place since then to allow me to offer any worthwhile advice about Norwegian rivers as they are now. However I am sure that the appropriate methods of fishing have changed little; so perhaps after all my recollections may in some way be of use, or perhaps of entertainment to those who are already Norwegian *habitués*; I hope therefore that the reader will pardon their inclusion here.

I first went to Norway at the end of June 1935 during my Oxford days, in company with two close friends Mike Wills and Allen Parker. Our excitement prior to leaving rose high, and I do not think any of us had been abroad before, let alone to Norway. Our destination was a river called the Bjora, about 60 miles north of Trondheim. It was a tributary of the famous Namsen, and was said to provide good fishing—otherwise we knew nothing about it, except the rent, which amounted to £50 for our Fuglaar and Rottesmo beats for the whole of July!

We travelled to Newcastle by train, and then to Tynemouth, where we boarded a steamship called the *Jupiter*. (I think she was later sunk during the 1939 War, and this would not in any case have been a great loss!) She was not a particularly comfortable vessel, and on the crossing to Stavanger I remember she rolled excessively—it is surprising how rough the North Sea can be, and this was before the days of anti-seasick pills. We all felt pretty ill in spite of, or perhaps due to the excellence of the ship's table d'hôte. Norwegian food as a rule was delicious, particularly the sea-fish and the incomparable smoked salmon. By contrast however there was a particularly foul brand of goat's milk cheese, brown in colour and nauseous in taste, never to be forgotten. Eventually the mountainous outline of the Norwegian coast showed up on the north-eastern horizon, it was visible from far out to sea, and we were thankful to put in to the shelter of Stavanger harbour. One's first close view of the Norwegian coast was never to be forgotten, the high mountains plunging abruptly into the sea, the rocky skerries, and precipitous fjords infiltrating so far inland (the Sogne fjord, for one, penetrates for over 100 miles inland from the open sea). The west coast of Scotland off Inverness-shire or Ross-shire has something of the same appearance; but everything in Norway is on twice the scale, the hills are twice as high, the rivers twice as big (or larger), their falls twice as high, the sea twice as rough (or so it seems), and so on. Also Norway has permanent snow and glaciers, which Scotland lacks.

We did not go ashore at Stavanger, nor at the next port of call, Haugesund, a small town about 50 miles further north. Only when we got to Bergen, a city of splendid appearance and great antiquity, did we disembark. Bergen is built largely on hillsides, its houses mainly of wood with the roofs painted in a variety of different colours, all adding to the gaiety of the summer scene. Its buildings descend sharply to the quayside and docks, on the edge of the fjord. One of the principal sights of this city, the third largest in Norway after Oslo and Trondheim, was the fish-market. Here all sorts of sea-fish were kept alive and active in tanks or troughs of salt water, so as to ensure that the dinner-tables of the citizens of Bergen were supplied with a product of indisputable freshness, as well as providing an incidental and rudimentary aquarium for sightseers.

At Bergen we transhipped into a small coastal steamer of about 800 tons, which rejoiced in the name of the *Kong Harald*. She and her sister ship the *Sigurd Jarl* used to ply up and down the Norwegian coast, calling in at the various ports. The *Kong Harald* was no paragon of comfort either, and for two or three days we wended our way northwards up the coast, calling in at such places as Aalesund, Aandalsnes, and Molde. When visiting Norway one is apt to forget how far to the north one's travels are taking one. Bergen itself is on the same latitude as the Shetland Islands, and only 200 miles crow flight to the east of them. Yet the Norwegian coastline up to the North Cape extends for a further 900 miles north-east of Bergen, to a point 340 miles inside the Arctic Circle. And thanks to the Gulf Stream, all harbours on this coast, so widely extended into northern latitudes, are ice-free throughout the winter.

The arrival of the *Kong Harald* was obviously an event of importance in the weekly routine of these coastal towns, and most of the local population seemed to gather on the quayside as we berthed. The scenery was wonderful all the way up this broken and mountainous coast. In a way it was similar to that seen from the Minch, except that as mentioned already the hills were much higher and steeper, also there was a good deal of snow on the high tops. It was noticeable on our voyage northwards that our passage lay always inside the outer perimeter of islands, the equivalent of Mull, Skye, and the Outer Hebrides. Only once did we emerge into the open sea, and then only for an hour or two. We were glad it was not for longer. Also one noticed that the spectacular impression created by one's first sight of fjords after a day or two began to pall. It could not be denied that one fjord was very like another.

Eventually we fetched up at Trondheim, the second largest city after Oslo, and another very ancient one, where the Kings of Norway

are crowned. Here we transferred to a train, destined for Namsos, a further hundred miles to the north. This train was a slow runner, perhaps wisely so; and after an hour or so we made a leisurely stop at a junction which bore the surprising name 'Hell'. As soon as I saw this, I jumped out quickly and ran to the booking office to buy a return ticket for this destination, quite forgetting of course that this was the one station on the whole Norwegian railway system where such a ticket would be unobtainable, seeing that one had already arrived! However I remedied this at the next stop, and still today have two of these intriguing tickets in my wallet.

North of Trondheim the country was not so mountainous, but much more thickly forested. Hills rose only to a thousand or two thousand feet, but everywhere thick forests of spruce, larch, and fir trees of all sorts proliferated. The soil was sandy, and seemed fairly arid. It was too far north for any corn crop, though the weather was hot and sunny, and of course it was light all night.

The train took us in due course to a junction called Grong. We had crossed several interesting looking rivers en route, fast and tumbling as is normal in Norway, and at Grong we had our first sight of the mighty Namsen, about which so much has been written, and which looked overpowering to our inexperienced eyes. The railway now turned westwards, and followed the course of the Namsen towards Namsos at its mouth. After 20 more miles we alighted at a small country station called Overhalla, where a hired car awaited us, and we drove on a dust road for about 6 miles through thick forest to reach our final destination, Fuglaar farmhouse, on the banks of the Bjora. So in all this journey from London took the best part of a week. Nowadays, I suppose, having flown to Oslo and thence to Trondheim or Namsos one could be there in almost one day. Another divergence from the present-day set-up was the then astonishingly high value of the pound. Anything one could buy seemed dirt-cheap. Now I understand a cup of Norwegian coffee costs nearly a pound. We live in stirring times! But one feature about such a journey, or one like it, which must always remain the same was the vivid contrast between the last sight of our native land, shrouded in the smoke, dirt, and general pollution of the industrial Tyneside, and our arrival within a short time, as though by magic, at the superb Norwegian coast with its harbours, sparkling with clear air, cleanliness, and freshness. One was apt to feel humiliated that one's own country afforded such a shabby comparison.

Turning again to our Odyssey we found Fuglaar farmhouse quite tolerable, a wooden building, clean and comfortable, though without any modern sanitation; and we were looked after by an elderly incumbent called Karl Morkved, who together with his wife were the soul of hospitality and kindness—nothing was too much trouble, and in the twilight of the evening Karl would regale us with Norwegian folk-songs, played by lamplight on his fiddle.

Now for the Bjora itself—at first sight we were shocked and bemused. We had expected a foaming rapid rocky river, tumbling down from high mountains, of the kind one had so often heard of or seen depicted in Norway. Instead we found a solid slow-running flow, with few streams, and they of only very modest speed, running over a sandy bottom in a winding course through vast fir forests. It could not have been more unlike one's usual conception of a Norwegian river, and one could hardly believe one's eyes when in shocked amazement one first regarded it. The general impression it initially gave was to remind one, so far as its flow was concerned, of one of the slacker and least productive-looking sections of the lower Wye. One's first horrified reaction was to organise a return journey home without delay; but the wrongness of such an impromptu decision was only revealed by stages.

The first reassurance presented itself when Karl Morkved, in an impressively nonchalant manner, let slip the information that, of the 30 and more fish killed on the beat during the previous month of June, no less than 5 had been of over 40 lb. This sounded more like what we had been looking for though as yet we were hard pushed to take it in! The next encouragement was when we hurried down on the evening of our arrival to look at the river, and arrived at a pool called Runningen, on a bend at the bottom of our beat. A tenant from the previous party of British fishers was operating there. She had not fished for more than three minutes in front of our eyes before she hooked a fish, played it, and landed it. It weighed 38 lb, and was in prime condition, covered with sea-lice. This did not seem to occasion great jubilation on the part of the captor, indeed there was a certain disappointment that a sixth forty pounder had not been added to the month's tally! Somewhat awed we returned to our farm. Further enquiry elicited the news that in June Bjora fish *averaged* 30 lb and that our predecessors during that month had caught over 30 of them. On checking up later we found that both these items of information were strictly correct. There were at least two other rivers in Norway where fish averaged as high a weight at that time, the Aaro, and the Evanger (also known as the Vossa or Bolstad), and for all I know there may have been more. The Namsen fish averaged 24 lb. In July the Bjora average sank to about 25 lb, due to the influx of a certain number of grilse weighing around 7 lb. The record Bjora fish was one of 57 lb, though bigger ones were said to have been lost. This was quite likely. The forests, through which this river flowed, in most places came right down to its banks, and the river bed was studded with both branches and tree roots, fatal snags if a fish got round them in play. The only hope was to use ultra-strong tackle and hang on like blazes, as we soon found out. Very strong tackle was necessary on every river I fished in Norway. What was more, it was important to have one's backing of a stronger breaking strain than one's leader, even if this meant having a reel of outsized capacity to hold it. If a fish had run onto the backing and then was snagged so that something had to break, it was better that the leader and fly alone should go, rather than the whole line as well, and some of the backing in addition.

Well, as can be imagined, we soon got down to it. It was mostly boat fishing, casting not harling, with either fly or spoon—large sized ones, and the strongest possible gut. No doubt we were inexperienced fishermen—at the age of 19 one would hardly expect otherwise; and it would take too long to relate all our adventures. Nevertheless at the end of the month we finished up with 19 fish, averaging 25 lb, amongst which were one 42 pounder and several 30s. It was quite enough to whet our youthful appetites for Norwegian fishing, though it may seem a modest total now.

I remember losing two huge fish. One was very exciting. He lay in a pool called Nokel Nes, and everytime anyone covered him with a fly he would boil at it, or show an immense length of back. Our boatmen, Kristian and Johann, got very worked up about this fish. 'Stor lax, meget stor lax!' they would exclaim, shaking their head. This went on for a day or two, till it came to my turn again to fish the pool. This I did in the normal way, and sure enough when I reached his lie, up came the monster as usual, but retired to his lair without touching my fly, leaving me in a state of shock and incredulity at his size. I sat down in the boat for a minute or two to collect myself and think things over. My tackle was alright, the strongest gut and a 6/0 Spey fly, I think it was a Dallas; and I had a 16 foot greenheart rod. Then my boatman Kristian made a brilliant suggestion; he had no English, but indicated by gesture that we should row over and cover the fish from the opposite side. This we did at once, and of course it worked 100 per cent. At the first cast over him the fish took as though he had been waiting a fortnight for my fly. But oh dear! one might as well have tried to hold a mustang. There was about ten seconds lull before the storm, and then a mighty surging rush for 60 yards downstream and out of the pool. All might yet have gone well, but the line at once went fast, and rowing up to it we found it firmly enmeshed in a huge sunken tree root, with the strong cast snapped to pieces—so that was that. Very sad. This fish was estimated at well over 50 lb. Another day I hooked one that pulled like a porpoise. I had him on for 10 minutes, but never saw him. He too smashed me round a tree root. Five minutes later I hooked another one in the same pool, called Snag Pool, and landed him—42 lb—but the first one felt a good deal heavier!

There were few days that went past without one having a drama of one sort or another. I remember one day I was casting from a boat and had not yet got out my full length of line. It was a bright sunny morning, and I could see my 2/0 Black Doctor (I still have this fly) coursing through the stream, near to the surface and close to the boat. Suddenly a large salmon appeared, as from nowhere, and I saw him chasing through the water after the fly, with every spot visible. He followed it for several yards, and then both fly and fish disappeared into a patch of shaded water where they could no longer be seen. There was a moment of breath-taking suspense, and then the line tightened . . . he had caught it! and in due course I landed him, so I know his exact weight, 29 lb—by no means enormous for Norway, but what a sight for a young aspirant! I still remember this episode clearly, even after 40 years interval.

The Bjora was used for floating timber. Tree trunks looking like telegraph poles were floated downriver from saw-mills higher upstream and collected below. Some of these trunks would get jammed in backwaters, and sometimes while one was fishing a raft of them would come floating down on top of one. The only thing to do was to stop fishing until they had passed. I often wondered what would happen if one was playing a fish at the crucial moment, but soon found out. One day, just when I had got a good 25 pounder about half way under control, a glance upstream revealed the horror that about 50 tree trunks were approaching fast—I did the only thing I could; that was to put the rod top three or four feet under the surface, and hold the fish to the best of my ability with a completely submerged line, until the menace had floated over. This plan worked well. There was no crisis, and I duly landed my fish without further trouble.

We were told there were bears, wolves, lynx, and elk in the forest, but they never disclosed themselves. We did however see plenty of capercailzie and woodcock on most occasions as we walked down to the river. We also found plenty of clegs, mosquitoes, and bluebottles, all of which could be tiresome.

One day I went to fish on the nearby Namsen, near Overhalla. This was an enormous river, half as big again as the Tay at Perth. Its

The author in 1935 with two fish from the Bjora—42 lb and 29 lb.

Michael Wills with a Bjora fish.

current was strong, and its pools upwards of half a mile long, before they redissolved into fierce rapids. The method of fishing was by 'harling', in a sizeable boat propelled by two boatmen, each with a pair of oars. One put out two or three rods at the stern, and towed spoons or large flies indefinitely to and fro across the width of the river. On the day I fished it had been raining, and the water was rising all day. I neither hooked nor saw anything. This seemed to me an excessively dull method of fishing; but it is apparently practised on many of the larger Norwegian rivers besides the Namsen, e.g. the Vefsen, Mals, Tana, and others; and many of the biggest salmon are caught in this way. To my mind it is not worth bothering with, and I would warn any prospective Norwegian fisherman to ascertain beforehand whether or not his proposed river is a 'harling' one—and to avoid it if it is. (The only British river which is often 'harled', so far as I know, is the Tay.) I left the Namsen without regret at the end of my day on it, and returned thankfully to the Bjora to resume more orthodox activities. Such was my first experience of Norwegian fishing. It gave me an ever memorable thrill that has lasted to the present day.

The record Namsen fish weighed $70\frac{1}{2}$ lb and was caught by Svein Kjolstad in 1924 at Jorum. It was surely caught by harling. The biggest fish of all weighed $79\frac{1}{2}$ lb, and was caught on July 28th 1928 at Storfoss on the Tana river in the Finmark, by the Postmaster H. Henriksen. This too was caught by harling. One wonders what happened to the mail that day!

The next time I went to Norway was two years later in July 1937. I went again with Mike Wills, also with his brother David, and their cousin Tony Wills. We were bound for a river called the Stjordal, which lay to the north-east of Trondheim and ran into Trondheim's fjord. We made a similar voyage from Tynemouth, but direct to Bergen this time, and then on in an efficient and comfortable Humber van. Later on we over-turned twice in this van, without doing much damage either to ourselves or the vehicle.

It was a long and circuitous route to Trondheim and took 3 days. The scenery as usual was magnificent, especially in the coastal areas. I remember we stopped to view from its summit a most spectacular waterfall, called Voringsfoss. Quite a large river, about the size of the Aberdeenshire Dee at Ballater, tumbled over a cliff face and seemed to drop endlessly in perpendicular fall. We could not see the bottom, it was shrouded in mist and spray with a rainbow—all most impressive. Later we stopped to ask the way at a lonely croft beside the road in a forest. (Our Norwegian was limited.) The owner could not have much liked the look of us, as he peered out of the window armed with a nasty looking hammer gun at full cock. We went on.

At last we arrived at Flornes, our final destination, about 30 miles beyond Trondheim towards the Swedish frontier. We lodged in the usual type of Norwegian farm, very clean and pleasant, but with no sanitary system, and the hot water supply for the bath was provided by what looked like a donkey-engine. One had to light a fire at its base and wait hopefully amid smoke and smuts. One of the farmers was called Bjorn. He was an enormous man and a Goliath in strength. He could lift the forequarters of a pony into the air, and sometimes did this to show off, somewhat to the pony's surprise. Norwegian ponies were heavily built, strong and tough—what would be termed in Scotland 'garrons'.

The Stjordal river was delightful in appearance, and much closer to one's idea of what an ideal salmon river should be. It was fairly fast and rocky, without being spectacularly so, and had plenty of rapids and pools which provided good fly fishing. Its water was very clear, like that of most Norwegian rivers. Altogether it resembled closely the middle part of the Aberdeenshire Dee in size and character.

But if the river looked promising, the fish stocks were not. Possibly we were too late in the season, and June would no doubt have been a better month. As it was we did not find many fish, and did not catch many. I suspect that by that time the many nets in Trondheim's fjord and at the bottom of the river were taking a prohibitive toll. However we caught enough fish to make our fishing interesting, the biggest of them being 24 lb, and the whole expedition was a delightful one. How splendid and carefree those days were—so soon to be smothered for ever under the black cloud of the 1939 War. On the return journey we flew back to Croydon from Oslo, landing at Göteborg, Copenhagen, and Hamburg en route. We left Oslo at 8 a.m. and were at Croydon by

5. p.m. which seemed miraculous. Flying was almost unheard of in those days. So ended a very happy party.

It was not until June 1957 that I found myself in Norway again, this time as the guest of Major Anthony Tabor and Mrs. Tabor, who have my everlasting thanks for a wonderful experience.

On this occasion we flew to Oslo, and went on to Aandalsnes by night train, and after a 20 year interval travelling was much easier and quicker. We left the train at Aandalsnes to motor 6 miles up the Romsdal, as the river valley was called, the river being the famous Rauma, which flowed into the Molde fjord about 100 miles to the south-west of Trondheim. The scenery was stupendous, even for Norway. Behind Fiva lodge, the 150 year old white wooden house that was to provide our living quarters, towered the 5000 feet sheer face of the Troll-tindern (the Troll's fingers), from which every so often an avalanche of snow descended with a noise that rivalled thunder. Snow on the high mountains lasted right through the Norwegian summer, and there were many glaciers. If the sun was hot, rivers that originated in the Dovre-fjell or other high ground could rise four or five feet with melting snow. On the other side of the Rauma, the majestic Romsdalhorn, said to be unclimbable, dominated the valley. This peak displayed over 4500 feet of sheer and solid rock, rising abruptly from the river side. Legend has it that near the top of this mountain there is a lake on which floats a golden bowl. Needless to say neither lake nor bowl has ever been found; but one could well understand how the sight of the Romsdalhorn peak, glowing bright in the light of the setting sun, when all the lower slopes of the valley were shrouded in the late evening twilight, could give rise to this or any other similar type of legend.

Every now and then a boulder would detach itself from near the summit of the Romsdalhorn, and its fall downwards could be followed by puffs of smoke (or dust) whenever it hit the side of the mountain face. Each contact would produce a reverberation like a cannot shot, but by the time the sound of this concussion had reached our ears, the boulder (which could be as big as a small house) would be long past the point of impact, and would have fallen perhaps another 500 feet. Alongside the Rauma the valley was a quarter to half a mile wide, luxuriant and with a haycrop, wild flowers, and birch trees. On the sea, during midsummer, this far north, the sun hardly sets at night, only for an hour or two. In Romsdal however it did not show above the Romsdalhorn till nearly 10 a.m. and it was down behind the Troll-tindern by 4.30 p.m., even though it never became dark at night. This may give some idea of the extraordinary topography of this valley. Anyone who is interested in a more detailed description of it should not fail to read the chapter on 'Salmon Fishing' in that wonderful book *Sport* (1888) by W. Bromley-Davenport. Fiva, together with its fishing on the Rauma, has belonged to the Bromley-Davenport family since before that date, and the above chapter is in my humble opinion the most vivid and enthralling description of episodes in salmon fishing that has ever been written. Bromley-Davenport likened the Romsdal to 'the happy valley of Rasselas'. It was indeed an apt description.

The Rauma fulfilled all one's wildest expectations of what a perfect Norwegian river should be like. Its bed was about the same width as that of the lower Spey, or perhaps a little wider in places. But its current was twice as powerful and its pools twice as deep, if that can be visualized. Near the top of the Fiva water there was a formidable foss, or fall. It was not impassable for fish; there was no sheer drop; but the river descended I suppose nearly 150 feet over about 200 yards, in a tremendous foaming cascade. If the water was high fish could not ascend this foss, the current was too powerful, and they had to wait until the water level fell. A similar situation arises on many rivers in Norway, where there is a large and powerful foss or series of fosses. The Sand River near Stavanger is a good example. I understand that in a high water year, fish are brought to a complete halt by the weight of water coming over its fosses, and they have to wait until the river drops before they can ascend. The foss pool, downstream of this fall on the Rauma, was therefore a good one, the best on the whole river, and it was called Aarnehol.

There was a second foss at Nedre Fiva, about a mile downstream. This was not such a formidable obstacle to fish ascending, but it involved certain and total disaster if a hooked fish went down over it. Nedre Fiva pool, below it, was also a sure holding place, like Aarnehol.

Fish on the Rauma then averaged 23 lb, but much bigger ones were frequent. Bärd, the head-ghillie, said that he had never caught a really big one on fly, only of 53 lb! Bu Tabor, a year or two after our visit, caught one of 52 lb. He landed it by himself, which was a sterling performance—40 pounders were common, a number being landed every year. An odd 50 pounder was often caught. The biggest one I can trace scaled $60\frac{1}{2}$ lb, and was caught in 1926 by Lord Davenport. And in 1949 Mr. J. Oates Kent had 10 salmon of 19 to 33 lb in one morning, while a friend of his landed one of $57\frac{1}{2}$ lb. At the time of our visit three or four 30 pounders were caught almost every week, and anything under 16 lb was contemptuously dismissed as a 'litel lax', a small fish, hardly worth notice. And so it went on; but for size of fish in the Norway of this time this was nothing unusual. What was unusual however, even for Norway, was the mighty strength of the Rauma current. Often one was carried down half a mile of river, or more, by a fish of any size; and many a big fish was lost because slowly but inexorably he drew the struggling angler downstream, till in spite of every effort the curtain fell on his final exit into the waiting jaws of Nedre Foss.

Very strong tackle was the only answer. A leader or trace of at least 30 lb breaking strain (it did not stop the fish taking), big and sturdy hooks, and an unlimited supply of strong backing on one's reel. After that, when a fish was once hooked, one could do no more than hold on like blazes, and hope for the best. Fishing was all done by casting, either from a boat, or when wading. There was no harling on this river. The wading was rough and the current strong. One could not go in far, and had to be careful.

What a grand sporting river this was! and how one enjoyed it. Scarcely a day went by without some outstanding drama of one sort or another; and the fish, as usual in Norway were magnificent. They were not present in huge numbers, not at any rate while I was there; we fished from June 11th to June 20th which was rather too early in the season, and caught 20 between four of us. But there were several 30 pounders amongst them, and quality certainly made up for any lack of quantity.

I have already mentioned the head ghillie at Fiva, whose name was

Bärd. He was an excellent type, reliable, capable, and knowledgeable about everything to do with salmon. We were lucky to have him, and he had the merit of being able to talk English fairly fluently. The second ghillie was called Nils. He too was a benevolent type, but getting on in years, and his English was a bit sketchy. When fishing was bad Nils would sometimes disappear without warning for a day or two. It was said that he used to get blind drunk on 'bay rum', whatever that may have been. He said he could not help it when the fishing was bad. One afternoon when I had failed to catch anything, Nils offered to take me to the salmon trap and let me catch some fish out of the trap with a landing net, by way of making up for a bad day's sport. He said it was quite easy like that. No doubt he was right.

My next visit to Norway took place in 1961, when I had a few days fishing on the river Gloppen which runs into the Nordfjord, 50 miles south of Romsdal. There is not a lot to be said about this river. Again it was one of fair size, about as big as the Spey, and a boat was necessary if one was to cover the pools properly. Its main drawback seemed to be that only the bottom one mile before it entered the fjord was accessible to fish. Above that there was an impassable obstacle over which the water thundered and tumbled. Also it seemed that the fjord below, even at that date, was hopelessly over-netted. I only hooked one fish during four days fishing, and landed it. It weighed 25 lb. The scenery and surroundings were as magnificent as ever, nevertheless I do not recommend this river to any would-be Norwegian fisher, unless it has much altered for the better in recent years, which I strongly doubt.

In 1967 Captain and Mrs Charles Burrell most kindly took me to the Sundal (or Driva) at Elverhoi. We fished for 10 days from mid-June onwards. The Sundal like the Rauma provided an unforgettable experience, and I think the fishing at Elverhoi was as good as any in Norway at that time. This river was of about the same size as the Rauma, but its current was even faster. One fished it either by wading, or else from a very small and insecure looking boat, just big enough for angler and boatman, but with no room to spare. The stock of fish was more plentiful than that of the Rauma; two of us caught 23 in 10 days, all on fly, and averaging 22 lb. We used flies of size 6/0 to

8/0, (it needed a powerful rod of 16 feet or longer to drive home these big hooks beyond the barb), and monofilament of not less than 30 lb breaking strain. Even then one sometimes failed to hold fish, and got broken around rocks or other obstructions. Big fish of 40 lb and over were not so common as in the Rauma; nevertheless the late Lord Stair caught one of 61 lb soon after the end of the 1939–45 War. He caught it on a fly in Piba Pool, and landed it, believe it or not, in 20 minutes. Piba Pool (the Pipe Pool) was christened after a pipe lost by the Lord Leicester of the day in Victorian times on the banks of this pool. His Lordship was apparently a great sportsman and a very keen Sundal fisherman. There is a photograph of him in Elverhoi lodge. He was a small man with an immensely thick and bushy black beard. He is photographed alongside a small bear, which he had shot. Unkind critics said that there was a close resemblance between the hunter and his prey.

Piba Pool has an immense and torrential rapid below it. No hooked fish has ever been successfully taken through it, so that any fish hooked in this pool had to be landed there, without any deployment downstream.

A boat-load of German troops, during the 1940–45 occupation of Norway, was drowned in this rapid.

During our 10 days fishing in 1967 we caught no fish of 30 lb or over, though several close to it; and we may have lost some of that weight or heavier.

I think that of all my limited Norwegian fishing experiences, the Sundal provided both the best fishing and the greatest excitement. Alas, I have never returned to Norway since 1967, good fishing there being so difficult and expensive to obtain; also I have been fully occupied elsewhere. But my general impression of Norwegian salmon fishing was that potentially it was the best of all, in any country anywhere. The rivers were quite magnificent, and the greatest fun to fish; and the fish both as to size and quality were unsurpassable. In addition the wild and spectacular nature of the countryside was an added and continual source of delight.

But, sad to say, there is a reverse side of this medal, and I gather that during recent years things have greatly deteriorated. The main bugbear of Norwegian fishing has always been the problem of over-netting. Norway is a land of what we would call small-holders. Any farmer whose land runs down to a fjord or to a river bank seems normally to have the right to put out a net, or (in the river) a trap; and many of them do so. With the present high price of salmon this is a

Piba Pool on the Sundal.

valuable financial asset to the income from a small farm. No Norwegian Government seems to have been able to take the bull by the horns and curtail this right, even if it has wanted to. Admittedly there is an extensive 'slap' on nets and traps at weekends. But enforcement is difficult, and not always effective. The result is that far too high a proportion of the stock of fish has for a long time been caught by other means than by angling.

In addition, of recent years, there has been the extra and extensive toll of salmon taken by long-lining in international waters off the Lofoten Islands to the north-west of Norway, of which we have read and heard so much. When added to the depredations of the normal netting system, this for a long time effectively ensured a dire scarcity of adult fish in the rivers. The situation may be better now, since the Norwegian Government has obtained a 50 mile fishing limit out to sea, and thus can stop the activities of foreign fishing boats in this area, and exercise greater control. I only hope it is so.

One effect of over-netting apparently has been that the large three and four sea-winter fish, which used to be such an outstanding feature of Norwegian fishing, have now become a great deal scarcer—Grilse on the other hand have increased, but it is doubtful whether it is worth making a long and involved journey to the Arctic Circle, or near it, simply to catch grilse. One can do this more easily at home.

Part of the trouble is of course the present high value of salmon in the market, which applies as much in Norway as anywhere else. I remember well on the Bjora and Stjordal, before 1939, that there was no market for the fish one caught, and they could not be kept for any length of time. We ate a few of them, but gave all the rest to our boatmen, who liked to hang them up in their chimneys and smoke them for the winter. Now, with the introduction of deep-freeze since 1945, salmon from even the remotest rivers in Norway command as high a selling-price as anywhere else in Europe. There is little need to elaborate on the consequent escalation of fishing rents, and of the general demand for fishing.

Modern air-travel, so speedy and (comparatively) comfortable, has also done much to revolutionize the background of fishing in Norway, as elsewhere. From London to Oslo is now a matter of two or three hours, likewise from Luxemburg, and of little more for that matter from New York, or Chicago. From Oslo on to Narvik is again only a matter of hours. So all of Norway is within comparatively quick reach of anywhere in either Europe or North America. This again has done much to make good Norwegian fishing almost unobtainable. The demand for it far exceeds the supply. Really first class fishing in Norway is not only scarce, but even if it can be obtained the expense of the combined rent, journey, and accommodation is extremely high; the total cost for one rod for a week is likely to be a minimum of £1500, and probably a good deal more. Even bad fishing is expensive, as well as desperately disappointing for anyone who is foolish enough to rent it. There is no lack of it. It is easy enough to journey around 1500 miles to a remote district in Norway, and find a comfortable and picturesque fishing lodge, some marvellous scenery, and a wonderful rocky and tumbling river, which in every way looks perfect, except for the distressing fact that it is totally devoid of salmon!

I am confident that you, my reader, will be sufficiently wide-awake not to be caught in such a trap. In addition to the hazards already listed above, there are other possible drawbacks in the way of Hydro-electric works recently erected, which can ruin a river through diverting its main stream or flooding its best fishing stretches, or saw mills which fill a river with saw dust and suffocate its fish. The drawbacks of harling have already been described, so I will say no more here.

Taking an all round view therefore, I would be very chary of recommending any friend to embark on fishing in Norway nowadays, unless he was going at the right time of year, i.e. mid-June to mid-July in most places, to a good beat on a first class river, free of Hydro works, and which could show a truthful record of consistently reliable catches over a period of several years. He would be very lucky to have the chance of fishing such a beat on such a river, also he would have to be prepared to put his hand deeply into his pocket to pay for it. But if he was granted all this, I could find it in my mind to be profoundly envious of his good fortune.

One last word on the character of the Norwegian people. They always seemed most friendly and generously disposed towards British sportsmen; and one found them hospitable to a degree. They were extremely honest, clean, hard-working, and conscientious. One could find few faults in their character; possibly sobriety was not one of their strong points, but who could blame them for this in view of the long drawn-out winter and its dark days, which it falls to their lot to face? It is to be hoped that the country's newly found wealth from the North Sea oilfields will not in any way cause any deterioration in these beneficent traits.

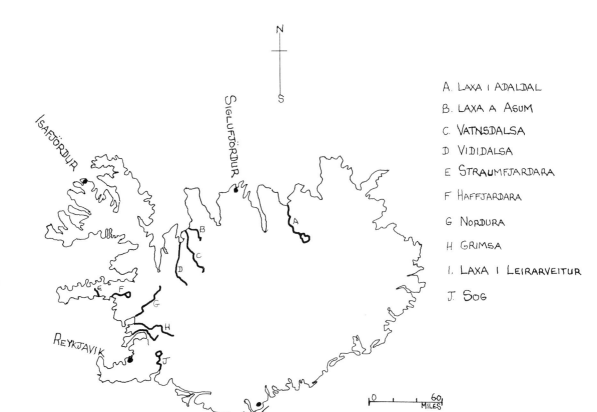

A. LAXA I ADALDAL

B. LAXA A ASUM

C. VATNSDALSA

D. VIDIDALSA

E. STRAUMFJARDARA

F. HAFFJARDARA

G. NORDURA

H. GRIMSA

I. LAXA I LEIRARVEITUR

J. SOG

318

ICELAND

Laxa i Adaldal—Laxa a Asum—Vatnsdalsa
—Vididalsa—Straumfjardara—Haffjardara
—Nordura—Grimsa—Laxa i Leirarveitur—Sog

Iceland

The rivers provide excellent fly water. They have plenty of falls, a fair stream, and well-defined rapids and pools.

I had the good fortune to fish in Iceland for a fortnight to a month every year from 1960 to 1977, on ten different rivers altogether, though on two in particular more than on the eight others. This was a fairly widespread experience over 18 years, and I hope that this account will be of some interest and help to anyone contemplating fishing in that island. First a few comments on topics of general interest, and then more on fishery matters.

Iceland is a larger island than one might expect. It is appreciably larger than Ireland and nearly twice as big as Scotland, but its population is negligible by comparison, being only of 200,000 inhabitants, of which two thirds live within 35 miles crow flight of Reykjavik. It follows that most of the country is deserted, or is only very sparsely populated with scattered farms. Reykjavik (pop. 100,000) is the only large town, and it lies on the south-west coast. Akureyri on the north coast is the next largest with 16,000 inhabitants. There are a few other small towns with a population of up to around 4,000, otherwise only scattered farms along the coastal area or up the river valleys. Inland the country is virtually uninhabited.

Climatically Iceland is remarkable. Although so far north (its northernmost extremity just touches the Arctic circle), Iceland in summer can be quite warm. I have known the temperature on the north coast rise to the surprising height of 85° in the shade. On the other hand it can also be fiendishly cold, with frost and snow even in August. It is a most unsettled and quickly changing climate, never the same for more than three or four days on end—at the most. Much depends on the direction of the wind. A north wind is invariably cold and can be bitter (the permanent ice-cap is only 45 miles from the north coast), but a south or south-west wind is warm. It seldom seems to blow from any other direction. Rain is not frequent, though there is more of it on the south and west coast than on the north and east. It follows that anyone who fishes in Iceland should be prepared for any sort of weather, with appropriate clothing, and it is quite unpredictable what he will meet during the fishing season, which basically is from the last week in June to mid-August.

There is little need for more than a brief description of Reykjavik and other Icelandic towns. Reykjavik is a large and modern city, of typical Scandinavian type and has all the usual amenities. One thing it does lack, the visiting angler should be warned, is a first class fishing tackle shop. Only rather crude and elementary tackle was available. The angler should therefore bring everything with him that he reckons he will need, particularly spare fly rods, in case of accidents. It will be impossible to replace such rods at short notice, and in the case of other items such as fly-lines or waders it will be difficult also.

There are a few tackle shops in country towns, such as Akureyri, Blonduos, or Borgarnes; but only rudimentary items are available.

As to topography, Iceland presents the most extraordinary mixture of different kinds of country. Much of it is very bleak and volcanic, particularly the south-west peninsula near Keflavik (the main airport). Inland it is quite rough, steep, and mountainous, with enormous snow-covered glaciers in many areas. It is rocky, bleak, and barren to a degree, and often volcanic in appearance. Mountains rise frequently to 4000 feet or higher. The highest one, Oraefajokull on the south-east coast, is 7000 feet high, rising abruptly from the sea. There are four active volcanoes, Hekla, Askja, Surtsey, and the Vestman-naeyar, still liable to erupt, though the first three at any rate are far from human habitation. When an eruption does take place volcanic ash is apt to be blown with the wind all over Iceland; it has also been known to reach Sutherland and other parts of northern Scotland under the influence of a north-west wind, without anyone there realizing at first what it was.

There are a large number of hot springs all over Iceland, where water emerges all through the year slightly below boiling point. This hot water is of great value in many directions. From the fishery angle it has two merits, it keeps some rivers from too severe freezing in winter, and it provides water of an equable temperature throughout the winter for fish farms and hatcheries. But in other ways too it has valuable uses, for instance it forms a hot water supply for any house, village, or town within reasonable distance of a spring. For example all Reykjavik's hot water supply, for all purposes, comes from nearby hot springs. Also it is widely used to heat greenhouses, which produce flowers and all sorts of fruit in profusion (even bananas are not unknown).

The Icelandic countryside is by nature tree-less, except for diminutive birch and mountain ash in places. But there is a prolific haycrop along the coastal areas and for some distance up the river valleys, grass seems to grow luxuriantly on the low ground, which is rather surprising; also in the river valley where I did most of my fishing there was an abundant growth of mushrooms—excellent ones; and one could fill a basket with them on any day in the intervals between fishing—very welcome for next morning's breakfast, though the Icelanders considered them poisonous and were surprised when one did not drop dead after eating them!

Wild flowers were present in fair profusion, above all the purple wild thyme, which from a distance looked much like heather, also wild pansies, cotton grass, hawkweed, campions, and occasionally dark blue gentians. Heather occurred infrequently, and only in certain districts of the south and east. It was sparse and spindly, and did not grow thickly as here at home. Surprisingly enough we also found shamrock on the north coast, which may perplex those who consider it exclusive to Ireland. Perhaps it was introduced by the Irish monks, who were the original colonizers of this country!

Turning to matters more closely connected with fishing, there are some 64 rivers in Iceland where salmon can be found, but of these only about 20 can be considered first class for fishing. The best fishing areas are on the west and north coast. There are one or two good rivers on the east coast, though not many, and the same goes for the south coast. There are also a number of large glacier rivers, which are of little use for fishing. Such big rivers, of the size of the Spey or Dee, inevitably rise far back inland, and have their origin in snow covered glaciers. Their water, as a result is thick and milky all through the spring and summer, and salmon will not use them, unless they have a clear water tributary up which they can run to spawn. A number of magnificent looking rivers are thus useless for fishing, owing to their perpetual snow water.

It follows that a good Icelandic salmon river must be either spring-fed or lake-fed, and fortunately there are plenty of these. It follows also that most of them are of medium or small size by our standards; in fact there are only two of what we would call large salmon rivers in the whole country, the Laxa i Adaldal in the north and the Sog in the south, both approximately equivalent to the Spey in size. Most salmon rivers are of similar dimensions to our Naver or Helmsdale, and many are still smaller. They are invariably streamy, rocky, and gravelly, and with a quick descent. They all have falls at some point in their course, most probably in their upper reaches, and sooner or later one of these is likely to be an impassable obstacle to the passage of fish. Their water is almost always of extreme clarity. They maintain a remarkably level height, owing mainly to the absence of artificial drainage in the hills. In places, inland, these are vast bogs. Also, as mentioned above, there is seldom heavy rain; and even when there is, these rivers are apt to rise very slowly over a period of two days or so, and fall equally slowly.

By comparison in Scotland anglers have been deploring the quick rise and fall of rivers, owing to artificial drainage, ever since Scrope's time. Iceland affords an example of what in some cases may have happened in Scotland too, before the hand of man changed it. From the fishing point of view there is one important advantage resulting from this feature, which is that an Icelandic river is practically never out of good fishing order through the water level being either too high or too low, or the water being too dirty, or rising. One can travel the necessary 1400 or so miles to one's river in Iceland with a quiet mind so far as the above hazards to fishing are concerned. In fact one is practically certain to have good fishing conditions throughout one's visit; the only possible drawbacks, provided one is there at the right time of year, are violent winds, the weather and consequently the water temperature becoming too warm (though this is not likely to last for more than two or three days at the most), or on one or two rivers, particularly the big Laxa i Adaldal, floating flannel weed (of which more later). Otherwise one can be sure of one's water being in good order, which is more than one can say for most rivers in Britain. ('Laxa' in Icelandic simply means 'Salmon River'. There are a number of different 'Laxas' in Iceland, distinguished from each other by a suffix of one sort or another).

The birds are a wonderful side-interest—most types of duck (and in August geese), waders of all sorts, golden plover, terns, ringed plover, ravens, wagtails, buntings, Icelandic falcons, merlins, occasional white-tailed sea eagles, divers, gulls of all sorts, ptarmigan, and many other species. Their presence blends so happily with one's fishing activities, and is a constant source of interest. Four legged wild creatures are scarce, except for arctic foxes and now mink. Polar bears arrive occasionally on the ice bergs or floes from Greenland, but they are very savage, and have to be destroyed at once. Seals round the coast there are in plenty, but the Icelanders have no misplaced inhibitions about keeping their numbers under control, and they are not protected. There are too many of them all the same. Icelandic ponies have handsome lines; they seem to be of much finer strain than their Norwegian counterparts, and each farm seems to have a varying number of them. Sometimes they are useful for fishing purposes, the angler holding his rod riding one, and his attendant another, with a third on a leading rein carrying panniers for waders, lunch, fish, and anything else that may be wanted. They move at a smart trot where the going will allow, and are a useful substitute for a land-rover where there is no road.

One tiresomeness which I have forgotten to mention is the presence, whenever the weather is warm, of innumerable small black flies, like miniature houseflies. These follow one in a cloud everywhere one goes, though they disappear like magic the minute a cold wind arises. They seldom bite, and merely cause irritation; but one decidedly needs some sort of anti-midge ointment to discourage them. There are also bluebottles, which appear in numbers in warm weather. One has to keep them away from one's fish, or they will soon render them fly-blown. I have never seen a mosquito in Iceland, nor a wasp, nor any midges or clegs, so far as I can remember. I don't think any of them exist. When one catches a fish, it is fatal to leave it unattended and lying in the open on the bank. A raven, gull, or mink will discover it within a matter of minutes, and start to dismember it as soon as one's back is turned.

Icelandic salmon are normally of fairly small size, two sea-winter fish averaging 8 to 12 lb in weight. In the rivers of the north and east coast three sea-winter fish of anything from 16 lb to 25 lb are also to be found. But the only river where there seems a possibility of a 30 pounder is the big Laxa i Adaldal; and even so the chance of such a fish is remote. There is one Icelandic 40 pounder on record, but it was netted. It is in numbers of fish caught rather than in size where the Icelandic salmon make their mark. There are also a large number of grilse in all rivers, usually more numerous than the salmon, and these run at any time from early July onwards. I should have said that the salmon run on the west and south coasts starts about the middle of

June, and continues till the second week of August. On the north coast it is about ten days later, and on the east coast a week later still— these dates naturally being subject to slight variations in an early or late year.

There are also plenty of sea-trout in Iceland, but the best runs and the biggest fish are always on the north coast. Curiously enough they start to enter the rivers well ahead of the salmon, and the beginning of June or even May can see a good number of them coming in. They continue to run at intervals until August. These north-coast sea-trout I know from my own experience can be large. On the Vatnsdalsa, the river which I knew best, the biggest we killed weighed 14 lb, and we had double-figure fish most years, as well as plenty of smaller ones. For anyone who cared to fish in the tidal part of that river there were sea-trout and arctic char to be caught in hundreds, but it was not a particularly interesting form of fishing; and as we were pre-occupied with salmon and grilse, we rarely attempted it.

Brown trout were fairly common, and also reached a large size, if the feed was good. In salmon rivers they were often ignored. Inland lakes were said to hold many large ones. Some of these lakes were only accessible with difficulty, with the aid of ponies and a tent. If they were really inaccessible I have no doubt that the stories about their large trout were true, and by large I mean up to 10 or 12 lb or more in weight. But it was noticeable that any lake which Icelanders could reach by car held none of any size. Fishing in them was too intensive.

The only other fish of note was the char. There were, broadly speaking, two varieties, the sea-going char, also known as the arctic char, and the fresh-water char. The former was a handsome fish. He had a bluey green back and pinkish sides spotted with white, but he lost his brilliant colour scheme soon after capture and consequent exposure to the atmosphere. Char are members of the 'Salmo' genus; and the arctic char had similar habits to the sea-trout, that is he descended to the sea at an early age, grew mightily on sea-food, and then returned to fresh water to breed. He was plentiful on the north and east coast, and averaged about 2 lb in weight. Specimens of 5 or 6 lb were fairly common, and the record weight was 13 lb. Arctic char foregathered in shoals. They were voracious takers, and a nuisance if they collected in a salmon pool. One could not keep them off the hook, and by kicking and splashing they ruined one's chances of a salmon for the time being. If one went out with the deliberate object of catching them, armed with the appropriate tackle (either fly or fly-spoon), it was not difficult to catch 50 on a good day. This was fun for a day or two, but it soon palled. These fish made excellent eating. They cut pink inside, just like sea-trout, and were nearly as good.

There were also fresh-water char all over Iceland, which like brown trout never went to sea, and fed and bred in lakes or rivers. They were plentiful, though indifferent fish from a sporting angle, not difficult to catch, and not appetising to eat. They were however considerably larger and more numerous than the char sometimes encountered in Britain.

To return to the salmon and grilse, their residence in fresh water did not last long. There was nowhere a spring run before June except possibly some odd fish in the last days of May, and spawning took place in October or early November before the winter freeze-up. Kelts went back to the sea in the autumn, unless they got trapped by the winter ice (all rivers froze semi-solid every winter). If they did get so caught they were unlikely to survive. Spawning gravel was usually plentiful and of good consistency, but salmon did not often penetrate into headwaters to spawn. These were usually at too high an altitude, and would be frozen solid in winter. As it was, when the break-up of ice came in spring, the loss in ova buried by gravel must have been large. It was worst if one or two false thaws came before the main one.

One or two small points were noticeable about Icelandic salmon. In most respects they exactly resembled our own fish in Britain, but they cut rather paler as a rule when on the table, instead of having that deep rosy pink of good conditioned British fish. Also the fresh-run fish had many sharp teeth, like kelts, though they soon lost them in fresh water. This seemed to indicate that they had only recently left their feeding grounds, a supposition which was supported by the unusually keen manner in which they took.

They carried sea-lice in just the same way as our British fish, and sea-trout and arctic char carried them also. Some of the grilse were very small. As a rule they averaged between 4 and 6 lb., but there were small ones too. My own record was $1\frac{1}{2}$ lb.

Now a few words about the process of fishing. Icelandic rivers without exception are excellent fly water. They have plenty of falls, a fair stream, and well defined rapids and pools. They are not usually deep, and their water is extremely clear. It needs rain of the heaviest description to put any colour into it. In addition the water temperature seldom rises much over 60°F, it is more likely to be in the upper 40°s or low 50°s. These conditions it need hardly be pointed out are ideal for fly fishing, either with a large or smallish fly; except in the smallest rivers there is seldom any need to go smaller than size 6, always with a floating line, with or without a sinking tip as preferred. Size of fly seems to make little difference. Often large hair-winged flies of up to $2\frac{1}{4}$ inches length are eminently successful.

What makes Icelandic angling so outstandingly rewarding is without doubt the absence of netting. Except in the estuary of the Hvita (the White River) on the west coast, and of the Olfusa on the south coast, there is no netting anywhere in Iceland, either in the rivers or fjords or sea. It is this unique factor rather than a natural super-abundance of fish that results in the superb Icelandic angling— in fact Iceland is not a great salmon producing country compared to Norway, Scotland, or even Ireland. Its annual salmon catch by both net and rod is around 75,000 fish a year. Compare this to Norway's 400–500 thousand, and the similar figure for Scotland and Ireland— the contrast of course being that in the latter three countries the vast majority of fish are caught by net, while in Iceland the majority are by rod.

The history of salmon netting in Iceland is interesting. Early in the present century when there was no restriction on netting, and when salmon first realized a value in the market, albeit a small one, Icelandic farmers and fishermen quickly brought salmon stocks down to a point of well-nigh extinction by excessive netting. The Icelanders are very wise about fishery matters; and they then went to the opposite extreme in banning all net-fishing for salmon (except in a very few places) and relying principally on rod-fishing. This policy in subsequent years has repaid them many times over. The rod-fishing in the past 25 years has been of far greater value than net fishing ever could have been, and the salmon and grilse abound.

Owing to the absence of netting new fish come into a river on every tide, so long as the run lasts, and can be expected every new fishing day. Very few rivers become too low for fish to run, and this is one of the great contrasts between Icelandic streams of medium or small size and similar rivers in Britain. Moreover the Icelandic salmon and grilse run is very concentrated; it only lasts for seven weeks or so, which at first sight may seem a drawback compared to the lengthy season of some Scottish rivers. But it does mean that an angler who has travelled say 1400 miles for a fortnight's fishing provided he goes at the right time is bound to find the main run of fish, or part of it, taking place during his visit. Without fail this happens year after year. Is this not an advantage of some significance?

Mention has already been made of the favourable water temperatures normally to be expected during an Icelandic summer, also of the voracity with which fresh salmon take. This last is most

Playing a fish amid a typical Icelandic landscape.

noticeable. One gets the impression that a fresh fish in a pool will chase avidly after a fly with the deliberate intention of eating it, or at least killing it, with something of the same keeness shown by a terrier after a rat or a pike after a trout. If there are four fresh fish in a small pool, there is nothing to stop the angler, if he plays his cards well, capturing at least three of them. Twice I have had it happen in Iceland that a fish has been so excited at being fished over that he has done a porpoise jump into the air to seize my fly as he re-entered the water again. This was a fascinating sight resulting on both occasions in a fish well and firmly hooked; and it must show acute keeness on the fish's part to make sure of thus mastering his prey! As fish become staler, with a lengthening stay in the river, they do by degrees take less well, as one might expect. Nevertheless it is again noticeable that, for some unexplained reason, stale fish in Iceland will take far more keenly and frequently than their counterparts in Britain.

What is more, both fresh fish and stale fish will take, as already mentioned, when the air is colder than the water—and freely. I have caught them often with the air ten degrees (F) colder, on a big fly; this is no unusual achievement, but with similar conditions in Scotland one can shut up shop. The explanation behind such free taking? I would hazard a guess that fresh Icelandic salmon are only a day or two's journey or less from their sea-feeding grounds, and the memory of luscious sea-feed is still with them, while British salmon are perhaps a month or longer away from their dining room, especially if this happens to lie to the west of Greenland. There is no other apparent explanation, apart from the generally more favourable weather and water conditions in Iceland, as already indicated.

An interesting feature of Icelandic fishing is that one can often see plainly in the water the salmon one is fishing for; the water is so clear, and one is often fishing from a rocky ledge or cliff top from where one can look down on all the fish in the pool. This leads to a fascinating process of observation and experiment in the trial of different sizes and patterns of fly, of different speeds and methods of fishing, and of watching the reactions of the fish. Some fish would show immediate interest, and would take at once. These were presumably new arrivals. Others would show a milder interest and would rise to the fly

Lord Lansdowne hooks a fish in the Green Banks Pool on the Vatnsdalsa.

or follow it without taking it. With careful and not too persistent handling such customers could often be persuaded to take in the end. Others would show absolutely no interest whatever; and after a cast or two they were better left undisturbed. But what was interesting above all was to see the different ways in which fish would take. There was no stereotyped method whatever, and no limit to the different types of take. Some fish, small salmon or grilse, would rise like lightning to the fly the moment it landed in the water, and would seize it with avidity, just like sea trout or brown trout sometimes do. Others, particularly larger fish, would adopt a more deliberate attitude, and rise comparatively slowly from their lie, and yet would take without hesitation rather in the assured manner of a club habitué with a glass of favoured vintage port. Others would be more hesitant, and would follow the fly round for a yard or two, or even right to the end of its lateral course, before finally taking it. Nor was there any guarantee of which way a fish would turn after taking. Usually he turned back directly towards his lie, but not infrequently he would turn the other way with his head towards the angler's bank, and make a full circle of 360° before seeking his lie once again. And of course fish frequently reacted to the fly, or followed close behind it, without breaking the surface of the water. This would have been invisible to a fisherman in normal circumstances. It was in fact not going too far to say that the majority of fish reacted in one way or another, even if they did not take. Let this be of encouragement to an angler fishing an apparently unresponsive river when so far as he is aware the fish are sternly ignoring him.

Krubba Pool. A sure holding pool on the upper Vatnsdalsa.

As to playing and landing fish, there was usually little difficulty. Fish certainly played well, they were lively and often fresh in from the sea. Sometimes the larger ones of 15 lb or over put up a prolonged battle. But neither fish nor river was outsized, and it must be admitted that one never had or could have had any of the classic encounters with heavy fish such as those one has experienced or heard of in the Spey, Awe, or Tay, still less in the Rauma, Sundal, or Alta. To this extent Icelandic fishing lacked drama. So it was normally easy to land Icelandic fish. Beaching was by far the best method, if a suitable beach was available, which it usually was; or failing that netting with a light portable landing net.

The going along the riversides was rough. Usually one could get a car or better still a land-rover fairly close to one's pool; but not always, and there could sometimes be a mile or more of rough walking. It was not the walking so much as getting the fish back which could be the main problem. It was no joke to be faced at 10 p.m. with 15 or 20 fish to be transported a mile back to one's vehicle when one was single handed and the arctic wind was blowing cold. A pony or an assistant was invaluable in such circumstances, but they were not always available. If one left some of the fish on the bank overnight, it was likely that the mink would have made a bean-feast of them by the next morning. The best plan, if one's return journey lay in a downstream direction, was to float as many fish as possible down the river, tied up in a sack or two sacks, and at the end of a long cord held in one's hand. It was a slow and laborious process, but it saved much effort.

The question of tackle for Icelandic fishing is straight-forward, but as already said you would be well advised to bring all that you are likely to want with you. On the small rivers a 12 foot rod will be long enough; on the larger ones a 14 foot will be best, or even a light 15 foot. It is not that you will need to throw a long line, but you will almost certainly have to contend with adverse winds of full gale force on occasions. On such days I have noticed that those who fish with single handed rods are apt to go home, saying it is unfishable, those with rods of 12 or 13 feet do continue to fish but with great difficulty and painfully. But those with 14 or 15 foot rods, although they may have a rough time, often come home loaded with fish. The moral is obvious.

Fly fishing to my mind is the only method worth pursuing. Icelanders are usually keen worm fishermen, but this is a brutal though killing method. For fly-fishing purposes only a floating line or floating line with sinking tip will be needed, even on the coldest days, and nylon monofilament need seldom be stronger than of 12 lb breaking strain. Polaroid glasses are a valuable asset, both for lessening the sun's glare and for aiding the spotting of fish. Do not leave behind mittens for the hands, and warm pullovers, for cold days—though you may often not need them. As to waders, thigh length ones will normally be enough, but if you are fishing one of the bigger rivers it will be advisable to include trouser length ones in your kit. You may well find them useful, not only for normal wading, but to cross the river from time to time. Bridges are few and very far between. Flies for fishing have been mentioned already. When fish are fresh-run size of fly seems to matter little, and all the usual patterns are effective.

My Icelandic fishing experiences carried me to many different rivers, as I have said. The first river I fished in 1960 was the Straumfjardara, a small west coast river, about the size of the Borgie in Sutherland, or the Broom in Ross-shire. It was very pretty, rocky, and tumbly, with three falls in its course. Without knowing the water or ever having been to Iceland before I see from my diary that I caught 51 fish between July 20th and August 3rd. Their average was only 8 lb but the biggest was 18 lb, and I thought this was promising enough to warrant a second visit in 1961. This time I went to the Haffjardara, another west-coast river but larger, as the guest of Mr. Sebastian Earl, and later went again for a fortnight to the Straumfjardara. On both rivers we had a large bag, and most entertaining fishing. It really opened one's eyes as to what Icelandic fishing could be like. In 1962 Pat Hazlehurst, Tommy St. Aubyn, and myself went to the Vatnsdalsa on the north coast. During the fortnight we were there we had a huge catch, mostly of large salmon. Pat Hazlehurst caught 17 good fish one day before lunch. Tommy St. Aubyn, although a skilful trout fisherman, had hardly ever caught a salmon before, one or two at most; but nevertheless he accounted for over 50 in that memorable fortnight. Out total bag was 256 fish. We did not know the water, and had no local help, otherwise we might have caught nearly twice as many. From then on I fished the Vatnsdalsa with friends every year until 1977. We had magnificent fishing. The salmon averaged 11 lb, our biggest ever being 26 lb, and the grilse 7 lb. Things were never quite as good again as they were in 1962, but sometimes they came pretty near to it.

Mrs. Hazlehurst with two fish amongst many others which she caught on the Laxa a Asum.

I used also to have frequent days on another neighbouring small river, the Laxa a Asum. This was the most prolific river in Iceland, and if one didn't catch double figures in the day one was doing poorly. The fish were small, mainly grilse averaging 5–6 lb. Occasionally one got a sizeable salmon—the biggest I ever killed there weighed 18 lb. This was an enchanting small river almost exactly the same size as the Borgie in Sutherland, or the Dart in Devonshire, but it produced consistently good fishing day after day with little variation, as soon as one knew its good places. It was never out of good fishing order. It had two falls, but fish could ascend both of them, and there were two large lakes on its headwaters. All the same after a few days on it one had had enough. When one starts to bemoan one's ill-fortune if one hasn't killed double figures in the day, it is time to look elsewhere! This river used to produce between 1500–1800 rod-caught fish in a 10 week season. Only two rods were allowed to fish at a time. What about that? you Grimersta, Naver, and Helmsdale fishers!

I also fished the Nordura, another larger west-coast river, and one of the best in Iceland. It was magnificent fishing, the river being about the size of the upper Dee; but now I hear it is greatly over-fished, another result of the lure of the dollar.

Other rivers which we fished intermittently were the Grimsa, and the Laxa i Leirarveitur on the west coast, the Vididalsa and the Svarta on the north coast, and the Sog on the south coast. Of these, the first two were excellent rivers, though we were not on them at the right time. The Vididalsa too was a very good river, and had plenty of larger fish, like many of the north coast rivers. The Svarta was indifferent and lacked fish. The Sog on the south coast was a large river by any standard, but it was slower running and seemed to me to provide rather duller fishing than most Icelandic rivers, though it held a reasonable stock of fish. Other rivers in Iceland I know only by hearsay, but they are all delightful in appearance, and the best of them should without fail provide good fishing with the all-important proviso that one goes to them, and to the right part of them, at the right period of the season.

There are some general regulations governing the conduct of fishermen in Iceland, of which it is as well to have fore-knowledge. The first and most important is that everywhere in the country it is strictly illegal to fish after 10 p.m. or before 7 a.m. In addition not more than 12 hours fishing out of the 24 are allowed on any river. The usual fishing times are from 7 a.m. to 12 noon, or from 8 a.m. to 1 p.m.

and then from 3 p.m. to 10 p.m. To start with this seems a tiresome arrangement to British fishermen, who are used to fishing without restriction at whatever time they choose. But in fact this regulation has its merits. If Icelandic fisherman were not thus restricted they would undoubtedly fish in relays all around the clock, (it is light all night till mid-August), and rivers would become badly over-fished. Also the number of rods on any given river is strictly controlled by the Ministry of Fisheries. This again is no bad thing, as it is another safeguard against over-fishing. The number of rods allowed is in proportion to the river's yearly catch; and the result is that, compared to what we normally see here in Britain, most Icelandic rivers are not heavily fished.

In conclusion my general finding on Icelandic fishing is that for numbers of fish caught, or likely to be caught, by rod fishing it is still the best in the world, in spite of being 'opened up' in the modern era of exploitation.

It is also a most attractive and interesting country, still upspoilt, with wild scenic surroundings unique in character, and with a most healthy and invigorating climate.

So far I have elaborated the many merits of Icelandic fishing, but as usual anywhere there are two sides to the picture, and it seems only fair to mention some of the accompanying difficulties or drawbacks that are liable to occur.

Gales I have already mentioned; they are almost certain to occur at intervals, and possibly for days on end. One should be prepared for them. Floating flannel weed in some rivers can be troublesome. It is caused either by hot sun on a lake or headwaters, causing this weed to rise off the bottom and float down-river in quantities, or else by a rise in water. It does not often occur and many rivers are entirely free of it, though one in particular is badly affected from late July onwards, the big Laxa i Adaldal. Such weed makes fly fishing extremely difficult, as one seems to catch a lump of it on one's fly with every cast. On the other hand the Icelandic worm fishers are not much bothered by it.

A bigger drawback to the whole process of Icelandic fishing is now the high cost, not only of the fishing itself, but of living accommodation, food and drink, journey, car hire, and other incidentals. Inflation in Iceland is rampant, and costs seem to rise every year. If you employ a cook or an amateur ghillie (there are no professionals), the scale of wages is likely to shock you—perhaps £160 for a week, or more.

In addition to the general cost it is extremely difficult to obtain good fishing. The demand is high, particularly amongst American and Continental fishermen, and modern air travel has made the journey so quick. Iceland by now has been thoroughly 'discovered' and advertised, more's the pity. There is a daily jet service from New York in 5 hours, from Chicago in $5\frac{1}{2}$ hours, from Luxemburg in $2\frac{3}{4}$ hours, from London in $2\frac{1}{2}$ hours, and from Glasgow in under 2 hours. This takes one as far as Reykjavik with ease, and it is only subsequently that transport difficulties are likely to arise. One usually needs a car when fishing, and in this case one can hire a self-drive Volkswagen of uncertain running capacity in Reykjavik or Akureyri, and hope for the best. It is a matter of luck what quality of model one obtains. To reach the east or north-east coast one can fly from Reykjavik on a local plane, whereas to motor there takes two days, with a night's stop on the way. Roads are of gravel, except close to Reykjavik, and their surface rough with pot-holes. By-roads are often better than the main-road, which has a good deal of traffic on it. There is one main road only, which circumvolves the whole island, except that on the south east coast it is liable to be washed away by floods from time to time. Laws against alcohol for car-drivers are very strict. It is illegal to have taken any drink within 8 hours of driving, or to have an opened bottle of drink in one's car. Penalties are severe, and the police are watchful.

If you lease fishing you should make quite sure that your lease is reliable, and that you are dealing with reputable characters whom you can trust. You will have to pay your rent well in advance, and matters do not always develop in a clockwork manner after you have done this. Iceland is a country where almost anything, favourable or unfavourable, can happen. I say no more, but you have been warned!

If you want to sell the fish you catch, or some of them, to help defray expenses, this may be possible, though it is not always easy. You will somehow have to get them to Reykjavik, or to a local town, and sell them to a dealer there. Your dealer may be reluctant to pay you for them until the following spring, when he has sold them abroad—also by then the Icelandic Kronur, following its usual path, will probably have been heavily de-valued, so you will get a poor bargain. In any case you will be paid in Kronur, which are of no value anywhere outside Iceland (no country will pay for them), so unless you are returning to Iceland the following year, or can dispose of them in some special way, they will be of no use to you. The whole process is thus fraught with uncertainty.

One final hazard as regards Icelandic fishing should be noted and borne in mind. It is this. I have already indicated that as a general rule the run of fish in Iceland is very reliable both as to numbers and time of entry. This is no doubt in part due to the absence of netting, coupled with the Ministry of Fisheries' wise regulations to prevent over-fishing by rod. However, and in spite of all this, just occasionally rivers here and there go through a bad patch as regards their stock, such a patch lasting for as long as perhaps two or three years. In the past this has been the result of some natural disaster; it could be the result of a spawning season being badly affected by freezing and ice, or of the water temperature of the sea being unduly cold at the particular time when the smolts descended, with consequent lack of food, followed by starvation. Alternatively there might be an excessive number of cod all round the coast for a year or two, as no doubt cod have their up and downs as do other fish; and they are voracious devourers of salmon smolts, so the salmon stocks would suffer. These are only some of the many factors which could, any or all of them, have an unforeseen and detrimental effect on fish stocks from time to time. Occasionally too, in spite of the Ministry's regulations, greedy rod-fishermen succeed in causing the stock of a river to dwindle.

But, in addition to all this, a recent and possibly much worse danger is in the limelight; it is the newly developed long-lining off the Faroes. If the Faroese now kill several hundred thousand salmon and grilse every year, when formerly they only caught a handful, and when they have no salmon rivers of their own, how many Icelandic fish are they killing? The south-east coast of Iceland is only 200 miles crow-flight from the Faroes; and it seems a curious coincidence that in

1980 some Icelandic rivers were seriously short of fish, while this year (1981) many rivers were even more badly affected, for reasons so far unknown. Undoubtedly there is cause for concern.

How does Iceland compare with that other famous Scandinavian venue for fishing, Norway? Those who have read the preceding chapter will realize that the types of fishing provided by these two countries are poles apart. Comparisons are odious—but one cannot help being aware that while Iceland produces for the rod an almost unlimited number of small fish and a large number of smallish rivers where they abound, Norway has a larger number of far more exciting and impressive rivers, where there are (or should be) fish of markedly greater weight. The drawback to Norway at present is, of course, the comparative scarcity of fish, though one may still hook a monster and have an epic struggle with him.

Which type of fishing is preferable? The choice is up to the individual; he may find it hard to come to a firm decision, and perhaps this is not necessary? If he is lucky perhaps he may be able to enjoy both alternatives.

Conclusion

This brings to an end the conclusions drawn from my fishing experiences on different rivers up to the present, though I live in hope that the future will still be generous in further provision. A lifetime is not long enough for this game, as in course of time one realizes only too well. It has been rightly said that there are no experts in fishing; no one lives long enough! The trouble is that, as soon as with increasing experience one begins to think one has really attained a fair understanding of the whole matter, one begins to realise that whole new vistas are continually opening in front of one, and that one is only stumbling on the mere verges of knowledge and proficiency. Never in a lifetime will one be able fully to master the full intricacies of the art. As in chess, the gambits are beyond calculation. Nor does one live long enough to fish in all those many splendid waters about which one has heard so much, such as, speaking for myself, the Alta, Evanger, Aaro, and Sand River, to name but a few in Norway, and the Moisie, Cascapedia, Restigonche, or George River in Canada, the Thera, Hofsa, and Laxa i Dolum in Iceland, and many others in Britain. One cannot do everything and fish everywhere. Nevertheless I do realise that in my own case I have been very fortunate in what I have had, and can never be grateful enough to the kind friends who have been so generous in their invitations and in their company. In France they say: *La vie sans amis, le jardin sans fleurs*. This applies as much or more to fishing as to any other sport or occupation. More than half the fun is lost if after catching or losing an exceptionally large fish, or after an outstanding day, or even a blank one, one has no one to whom to relate one's triumph or disaster, as the case may be. How empty too can be a series of fishing days spent entirely by oneself instead of amidst the camaraderie of friends and companions.

In addition to the rivers already mentioned, I have had odd days on the Torridge and Taw in Devonshire, the Coquet in Northumberland, the Welsh Dee, the Etive and Carron in Scotland, and the Boyne and Lennon in Ireland. But my experience of these has been too limited to justify any description of them or advice about them. So I leave this to others.

One often wonders about the future of this wonderful sport. Since the 1930s when I first started fishing there have been big changes in many ways. Where will it all end? The most noticeable change lies perhaps in the ever increasing number of anglers and would-be anglers, both British and foreign, while neither the available fishing nor the stocks of fish have correspondingly increased. I feel sure that this latter statement is beyond dispute. Maybe on certain waters more fish than formerly are now caught, this statement is frequently put forward to show that the fishing in question has undoubtedly 'improved', or at least is no worse than it used to be. But this argument does not carry weight unless the number of rods fishing is also taken into account. If this latter number has trebled in recent years, or thereabouts, which seems normally to be the case, is not a total catch three times as large as in the old days now required to maintain the fishing at its former standard? From the angler's point of view this surely is the only rational basis of calculation. But how often in fact has this requirement been fulfilled? It would be hard to cite any factual examples.

Commercialisation of fishing has unfortunately increased. Landlords, harassed by taxation and inflation, are sometimes apt to look upon the letting of their fishing purely as a commercial asset, with the sporting aspect disregarded. This leads to such drawbacks as rents assessed at an unreasonably high level, constant change of tenants with some unsatisfactory individuals amongst them, too many rods fishing at a time, and no restriction on the use of unwelcome lures such as prawns and worms. Equally tenant fishermen are sometimes apt to look upon their lease simply as an opportunity to kill as many fish as possible in a given time by any or all legal means (as well as by some not so legal). Such attitudes on either side if pursued far enough must inevitably lead to everyone's disadvantage, if not to disaster, and a noble sport is thus prostituted. The general increase in the number of rods, already mentioned, is partly due to financial reasons, for it is obvious that the more rods there are, the higher the rent that can be demanded. It is also partly due to the growing pressure exerted by a continually increasing number of would-be fishers. A wise proprietor or manager of a fishery will spare no pains in taking a firm stand against this detrimental trend. There is no surer or quicker way to ruin even the best fishery than to put too many rods on it. Sporting agencies, responsible for letting arrangements, are often not blameless in this matter.

There are many other changes. For instance dramatic improvements in the manner and methods of transport have since 1945 enabled anglers from all parts of the world to travel quickly to areas formerly denied to them. In these modern days an American angler from as far afield as say Texas or California can for instance be on a river in Norway or Iceland almost within a matter of hours. To our grandfathers such possibilities now afforded by air travel would have outrivalled the most far-fetched fantasies of H. G. Wells. And to a more limited degree the use of the motor-car, which is now on the road in millions in this small country alone, has put the most remote fishing within easy range of anyone who is minded to reach it.

The increased value of fish in the market is another harmful factor. It leads to more ruthless poaching, as well as to increased commercialism and increased disregard of the sporting aspect both by landlord and tenant.

Fish are now being caught in the sea in great numbers where formerly few or none were killed, e.g. off Greenland, the Faroes, the Lofoten Islands, and the west coast of Ireland. In addition illegal fishing everywhere, and not least off the British coast, has proliferated. Indeed there are new problems to be faced, and new solutions needed, together with new internal legislation, and new agreements and understanding between the salmon fishing countries. Without such agreements it can hardly be seen how the salmon as a species, let alone salmon fishing as a sport, can survive.

Two other aspects of present day fishing are perhaps of particular interest, one is the present scarcity of the big fish of three or more sea-winters, and the other the newly established artificial rearing of salmon up to the adult stage. With regard to the first of these, some few years ago I asked my great friend Colonel J. P. Moreton, now alas no longer with us, what he reckoned was the main contrast between fishing in these modern days and when he first started in the early 1920s. He replied without hestitation: 'The present absence of the big fish.' J.P.M. in his day caught at least six fish in Britain of 40 lb or more, so he knew well what he was talking about. Whatever may be the reason, whether it be Greenland fishing or now the Faroes, over-netting in our coastal waters, over-fishing by rod, U.D.N., or a natural change in the life-cycle of the salmon (or a combination of all of these), it is now apparent to us all that a 30 lb salmon has become a comparative rarity in almost all our waters. Our former 'big fish' rivers, such as the Wye, Tay, Awe, Tweed, Cork Blackwater, Hampshire Avon, and Dorset Frome, now only yield a very modest return of such fish compared to their erstwhile performance of forty and more years ago. It is all from the angler's point of view very sad. One can only hope that time will supply the remedy.

As to the artificial rearing up to the adult stage of salmon destined solely for the fish market, this is a new development, the ultimate repercussions of which are at the moment unpredictable. Perhaps not enough attention has as yet been focused on this break-through in the history of fish farming; but when it is reliably forecast that within five years of this present date (1982) the production of farmed adult salmon in Britain and Norway alone will outnumber the net and rod catch of naturally bred fish by something approaching eight to one, profound repercussions as regards angling, even if at the moment they are indefinable, are bound to occur. And for that matter, if Britain and Norway alone can produce such a vast return of artificially reared fish, why not Canada, Iceland, the Faroes, the U.S.A., France, and Spain also, amongst other countries? The possible implications are endless.

Indeed in the future there will be many new problems, and a need for much new legislation if salmon fishing is to be preserved as a sport. Perhaps it is unwise to attempt to look too far ahead, sufficient unto the day is the evil thereof. Who for instance in the 1930s could have accurately visualized nylon nets, the Greenland and Faroes fishing, deep freeze (which has exercised such a traumatic effect on the market value of fish caught in remote areas), and the emergence of high speed inter-continental air travel? All these factors give rise to present day problems of one sort or another. No doubt as these are solved others, equally unforeseen at present, will arise; but have we not enough on our plate already for the time being, without attempting to delve too far into the future?

In the meantime the 1982 fishing season is once more approaching, and its long clear call back to the river is becoming ever more urgent. I therefore take my leave, wishing my readers the best of sport and happy fulfilment of anticipation wherever in the future they may chance to cast their line.

ENVOI

'Now fair fa' him where'er he be,
O' th' Angling Guild a Brither free,
May he ne'er want his barley-bree,
    And saumon, a great store o'em.
We'll toast him bravely, four times four,
Toast him bravely, toast him bravely;
We'll toast him bravely, four times four,
    Wi' hip, hip, hip, hoororum;
We'll toast him bravely, four times four,
And wish him blessings many a score,
While every Angler cries encore,
    To the tune o' "Tullochgorum".'

(Songs of the Edinburgh Angling Club, 1878.)

'I wish you all a quick eye, a light hand,
a tight line, and plenty of elbow room.'
                 (Sir Herbert Maxwell.)

Index